M000190958

Explaining the crisis ● Chris Harman

Chris Harman

Explaining the crisis

a Marxist re-appraisal

BOOKMARKS

EXPLAINING THE CRISIS
by Chris Harman

Second printing January 1987
First published March 1984
Bookmarks, 265 Seven Sisters Road, London N4 2DE, England.
Bookmarks, PO Box 16085, Chicago, Illinois 60616, USA.
Bookmarks, GPO Box 1473N, Melbourne 3001, Australia.

ISBN 0 906224 11 X

Printed by A Wheaton and Company, Exeter, England
Typesetting by Kate Macpherson, Clevedon, Avon
Design by Roger Huddle

AUSTRALIA: **International Socialists**, GPO Box 1473N, Melbourne 3001.
BELGIUM: **Socialisme International**, 9 rue Marexhe, 4400 Herstal, Liege.
BRITAIN: **Socialist Workers Party**, PO Box 82, London E3.
CANADA: **International Socialists**, PO Box 339, Station E, Toronto, Ontario.
DENMARK: **Internationale Socialister**, Morten Borupsgade 18, kld, 8000 Arhus C.
FRANCE: **Socialisme International** (correspondence to Yves Coleman, BP 407, Paris
    Cedex 05).
IRELAND: **Socialist Workers Movement**, PO Box 1648, Dublin 8.
NORWAY: **Internasjonale Sosialister**, Postboks 5370, Majorstua, 0304 Oslo 3.
UNITED STATES: **International Socialist Organization**, PO Box 16085, Chicago,
    Illinois 60616.
WEST GERMANY: **Sozialistische Arbeiter Gruppe**, Wolfgangstrasse 81, D–6000
    Frankfurt 1.

Contents

Introduction ★ 9
Marx's Theory of Crisis and its critics ★ 14
The crisis last time ★ 50
State capitalism, the arms economy, and the crisis today ★ 75
Appendices: Other theories of crisis ★ 122
Notes ★ 155
Glossary ★ 175
Index ★ 179

This book is published with the aid of the **Bookmarks Publishing Co-operative**. Many socialists have a few savings put aside, probably in a bank or savings bank. While it's there, this money is being loaned by the bank to some business or other to further the aims of capitalism. We believe that it is better loaned to a socialist venture to further the aims of socialism. That's how the Bookmarks Publishing Co-operative works. In return for a loan, repayable at a month's notice, members receive free copies of books published, plus other advantages. There are about 100 members, as far apart as Hackney and Australia.
Like to know more? Write to Bookmarks Publishing Co-operative, 265 Seven Sisters Road, Finsbury Park, London N4 2DE, Britain.

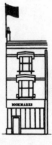

Foreword

This book could not have been produced without advice, help and inspiration from many people. Thanks are due to Roger Cox for first suggesting that explaining stagnation and inflation was a priority for Marxists; to Tony Cliff, Mike Kidron and Nigel Harris for beginning to elaborate many of the ideas I have taken up; and to Pete Binns, Alex Callinicos, Miguel Garcia, and Pete Green for comments and advice on various stages of the argument.

CHRIS HARMAN

Chris Harman is a leading member of the *Socialist Workers Party* and editor of the party's weekly paper, **Socialist Worker**. His previous books include **Bureaucracy and Revolution in Eastern Europe** (1974), **How Marxism Works** (1979), **The Lost Revolution: Germany 1918–23** (1982), and **Class Struggles in Eastern Europe 1945–83** (1983).

Introduction

IT IS NOW more than a decade since the world economy entered a new phase of economic crisis. In late 1973 the Western economies were hit by what was then described as the worst recession since World War Two. In virtually all Western countries unemployment doubled, permanently. For this recession was hardly over before another began, in 1979, and unemployment doubled again.

By the early 1980s the crisis was in many ways more serious than in the 1970s. In the most advanced Western economies the first recession had produced a fall in output. It had ravaged the poorest parts of the Third World. But many countries had continued to expand, barely affected by the general slowdown. Three sectors escaped in particular: the oil-producing states, the economies known as the 'Newly Industrialising Countries', such as Brazil, and the Eastern Bloc.

The second recession hit all these particularly hard. Among the oil-producing states, Mexico and Venezuela were pushed near to bankruptcy, while in 1982 even Saudi Arabia experienced its first balance-of-payments deficit in ten years. The international banking system held its collective breath when the government of Brazil found it was unable to pay the interests on its debts . . . and the plan to solve this, negotiated with the International Monetary Fund (IMF), meant a commitment to cut real wages by 30 per cent. Throughout Eastern Europe growth rates were now the lowest since World War Two, with output falling by 20 per cent in Poland and growing economic problems in Hungary, Czechoslovakia, Rumania and Russia.

At the time of writing (November 1983) there is still little sign anywhere of prolonged recovery from this second recession. The only possible exception is the United States, but any recovery there has served to deepen the problems of the rest of the capitalist world rather than ease them. For US recovery, such as it is, has been based on an upsurge in military spending, paid for by increased government borrowing. The US budget deficit has grown from 2 per cent in 1981 to 3½ per cent in 1982, while the estimated deficit for 1983 is 6½ per cent. The US balance of trade has remained at a deficit of about 30 billion dollars.

The effect of this heavy demand for funds by the US government has been to keep international interest rates very high. So a by-product of the US recovery is that Third World governments have to pay high interest rates on their debts, so deepening recession in their own countries. Likewise another by-product has been a level of interest rates in Europe which discourages new investment and precludes economic recovery there too.

So whereas in the 1950s it was taken for granted that economic boom in North America produced boom elsewhere in the world, today it has the opposite effect, increasing the instability and recession of the world economy.

The crisis in economics

Not so long ago established economic wisdom taught that instability and crisis were things of the past. The doctrine of Keynesianism,* which dominated in the universities, the government ministries and the financial columns of the press, insisted that the crises capitalism had known before World War Two were no longer necessary. They could be avoided by controlled government intervention in the economy.

In 1970 Paul Samuelson — Nobel prize winner, adviser to US presidents and author of the world's best-selling economic textbook — told a conference of economists that crises were a thing of the past: 'The National Bureau of Economic Research has worked itself out of one of its first jobs, namely business cycles,' he said.

When, only three years later, an old-style economic crisis did break out, Keynesians such as Samuelson were at a loss. They found that their theory no longer did any of the things they had claimed. As one Keynesian, Francis Cripps of the Cambridge Economic Policy Review, put it, they suddenly realised that: 'Nobody really under-

---

*In general, Marxist and economic terms will be defined only briefly in the text. Readers who are not familiar with them will find longer definitions in the Glossary. See page 175

stands how the modern economy works. Nobody really knows why we had so much growth in the post-war world . . . how the various mechanisms slotted together.'[1]

Overnight, life-long Keynesians dropped their former ideas and endorsed the 'monetarist' theories propagated by Milton Friedman and the Chicago School of economists. These held that the attempt by governments to control economic behaviour had been misconceived. The world economy could behave correctly, they argued, only if the market mechanism was allowed free play, with government 'interference' reduced to a minimum. All governments could do, they insisted, was to avoid any action which increased the supply of money more quickly than the output of the economy, and take such action as was necessary to break down 'unnatural monopolies' by trade unions or nationalised industries.

Monetarism rapidly took over from Keynesianism in the universities and in the ministries. Keynesians who did not drop their old beliefs were pushed to the margins of the economic establishment. Even social democratic governments, such as that in Britain headed by James Callaghan between 1976 and 1979, put more faith in Friedman than Keynes.

As Callaghan told the Labour Party Conference in September 1976: 'We used to think you could just spend your way out recession by cutting taxes and boosting government borrowing. I tell you in all candour that that option no longer exists; and in as far as it ever did exist, it worked by injecting inflation into the economy. And each time that has happened, the average level of unemployment has risen.'

But the rush towards monetarism by academics, economic journalists and Labour ministers did not mean that monetarism was able to come to terms with the crisis any more than Keynesianism. Monetarism was, after all, little more than a regurgitation of the 'neo-classical' school which had dominated bourgeois economics until the 1930s. It has been unable to explain the unprecedented severity of the slump then. It was just as incapable of explaining the crisis of the 1970s and 1980s.

The followers of Friedman began by taking for granted that which they were supposed to explain. There was, they argued, a rising 'natural rate' of unemployment. Attempts by governments to undercut this 'natural rate' were bound to fail in the long term. Such attempts would merely ensure that rising unemployment was accompanied by rising inflation, they said.

Instead governments must maintain strict control over the money supply and hold down unemployment benefits. Eventually this would reduce the 'natural state' of unemployment as workers found they could make a living only if they were prepared to work for lower wages.

That the monetarists could not explain why the 'natural rate' of unemployment should be higher in the 1970s than it was twenty years earlier did not worry academic economists or government ministries over much in the mid-1970s. Governments as diverse as those of Callaghan and Thatcher in Britain and General Pinochet in Chile held down their expenditure, deflated their economies and took all the measures which were supposed to hold down the rise in the money supply.

These measures produced no economic recovery. Indeed, often they did not even control the money supply in its widest sense (what economists call 'M3'). In Thatcher's Britain and, in a more extreme form, Pinochet's Chile, monetarism merely served to destroy much of local industry and exacerbate the general crisis.

Economists who had abandoned Keynesianism for monetarism in the mid-1970s could be seen deserting monetarism in its turn in the early 1980s. **Financial Times** columnist Samuel Brittan, who had done most to popularise monetarist ideas in Britain, was by 1982 criticising many monetarist policies and calling himself a 'new-style Keynesian'. In the United States, Reagan's economic advisers, faced with the failure of monetarist policies to end a severe slump, quietly abandoned one of monetarism's central principles — the balanced budget.

Both the major schools of bourgeois economics have failed when it comes to the test of the crisis. Their failure has led to a proliferation of other attempts to explain things — in terms of rising wages, rising spending on social welfare, 'long waves' of economic activity, structural changes in the world economy or the effects of monopolisation. Each has found support both among those who favour capitalism and among its radical critics. But none succeeds in explaining the transition from 25 years of boom to ten years of crisis.[2]

The Marxist analysis

It might be thought that the onset of crisis and the failure of existing theories to explain it might lead people to look again at the ideas of the political economist who was most insistent that crises were inevitable under capitalism — Karl Marx. But establishment economists have rarely done so. Marx's ideas, however diluted by some people, imply a challenge to existing society — something that economists are usually anxious to avoid.

But those who do look at Marx all too often reject central parts of his theory of crisis. There is a reason for this. The present phase of economic crisis cannot be explained without some explanation of the long, crisis-free years of capitalist expansion which preceded it. Most 'orthodox' Marxist economists have failed to explain these boom years, so they did not sound particularly convincing when they pointed out that the crisis of 1973 proved that Marx was right.

Yet there *were* Marxist economists who developed Marx's ideas to account for the boom years of the 1940s, 1950s and 1960s. Marxists such as T N Vance, Tony Cliff and Michael Kidron have laid out a framework which, when filled in, enables us to understand the new period of crisis in ways not open to the rival schools of bourgeois economists.

The aim of this book is to elaborate this understanding of the crisis. It starts by presenting Marx's own analysis of capitalist crisis. I then look at the great slump of the 1920s and 1930s in the light of Marx's ideas and in the light of developments within the major capitalist economies. The final chapter then builds on the ideas of Vance, Cliff and Kidron in an attempt to explain both the long boom that followed World War Two and the crisis of the past ten years.

An additional chapter could have been written describing the detailed effects of the present crisis and the inadequacies of government attempts around the world to cope with it. But this has been rendered unnecessary by the publication of an excellent book by Nigel Harris, **Of Bread and Guns**,[3] which does precisely that.

The chapters of this book first appeared as a series of articles in the journal **International Socialism**.[4] I have rewritten parts in an effort to make my ideas clearer, and I have altered the order. But with one or two minor exceptions I have not changed the basic argument.

Finally, an apology. On occasions readers new to the ideas of Marxist economics may find what I have to say a little difficult to follow. I have felt that it was necessary to deal with the many objections to the Marxist account of capitalist crisis, and this sometimes involves technical discussions. As far as possible I have put these into footnotes. Where this has not been possible, I hope that readers will bear with me.

CHRIS HARMAN

Chapter 1: Marx's theory of crisis and its critics

THE PICTURE MARX presented a hundred years and more ago showed capitalism as a system built on contradictions. He portrayed the owners of capital — the bankers and industrialists — on the one hand driven to ever more grandiose plans for expanding the output and scale of industry through massive investments; on the other hand ever more afraid of taking the risks involved. As a result bursts of expansion give way to spells of slump.

At one moment industry is working to full capacity, building new factories, bringing in new machinery, developing human skills — expanding the 'productive apparatus', as Marx calls it; the next moment there is massive stagnation and waste as the factories stand idle, the machinery rusts, and unemployment grows.

Moreover, said Marx, these 'explosions, cataclysms, crisis' . . . 'regularly recurring, lead to their repetition on a higher scale.'[1] He pictures for us a system marked by ever deeper slumps, interspersed with ever shorter periods of boom, a system unable to cope with the amount of wealth that it has the potential to produce.

> The greater the social wealth, the functioning of capital, the extent and energy of its growth . . . the greater is the industrial reserve army [unemployment] . . . the greater is official pauperism. *This is the absolute general law of capitalist accumulation.* (Marx's emphasis)[2]

The more the capitalist system developed, Marx insisted, the more unemployment and poverty would grow.[3] It is this, he contends, that damns the capitalist 'mode of production' — the capitalist way of organising society in order to produce wealth — to historic doom in the same way that 'the guild system, serfdom and slavery' were doomed before it.[4]

Just as societies based on these ways of producing wealth had entered into irreversible decline after a period in which they flourished, so Marx said that capitalism too would enter into such decline. Indeed, when he began work on the first draft of **Capital** (usually known as the **Grundrisse**) in 1857, he believed that this phase of irreversible decline had already started. And nearly 30 years later, when Engels wrote the preface to the English edition of **Capital: One** in 1886, he felt able to conclude:

> The decennial cycle of stagnation, prosperity, overproduction and crisis, ever-recurrent from 1825 to 1867, seems indeed to have run its course; only to land us in the slough of despond of permanent and chronic depression. The sighed-for period of prosperity will not come; as often as we seem to perceive its heralding symptoms, so often do they again vanish in the air.[5]

Marx was, of course, mistaken in 1857 and so was Engels in 1886. Likewise later thinkers who thought they saw the 'final crisis of capitalism' in the great slump of the 1930s were to discover they were wrong too.

The failure of such prophecies has led to a tendency even among many Marxists to reject the fundamentals of Marx's theoretical analysis of capitalism. Some have openly revised Marx's model of capitalism by rejecting one or other of the 'laws' which he considered fundamental to the system. Others give verbal acceptance to Marx's analysis, but throw in so many riders (in the form of 'countervailing economic factors') that they rob the analysis of its ability to tell us anything about the real world.

Yet we are now once again in a period in which the symptoms of Marx's 'final crisis' seem to be present. All the phenomena which Marx pointed to are referred to daily in the media — rising levels of unemployment on an international scale, seemingly irreversible trends towards economic stagnation, frenetic but short-lived speculative booms followed by ever deeper recessions, long-term declines in profit rates, a general feeling that something has gone wrong with the dynamo of the system. Is this merely another illusion? Or is it indeed the vindication of Marx's analysis?

The contention of this book is that the present deepening crisis can be seen as flowing from Marx's basic model of capitalism. It is therefore wrong to reject the fundamentals of his analysis, as some do. It is also wrong merely to throw all sorts of addenda on to Marx's account and deprive it of any explanatory power.

Instead, the amendments that we must make in order to explain the course of the capitalist system since Marx's time must show how, at certain stages of its development, the system itself produces 'countervailing factors' which counteract the pressures towards decline — and how it ceases to produce these factors at later stages. Only on this basis can we see how capitalism could enjoy long spells of prosperity — particularly in the 1950s and 1960s — yet also enter long periods of stagnation and crisis in the 1880s, the 1930s, and again in the past ten years.

The tendency of the rate of profit to fall

At the very centre of Marx's account of the crisis-prone nature of capitalism stands what he called 'the law of the tendency of the rate of profit to fall' (for the sake of brevity we will call this the 'falling rate of profit'). As capitalism grows, says Marx, so the rate of profit, the rate of return on capital investment, tends to fall, and this is a direct result of the way capitalism develops the forces of production, of the way growth takes place.

Latter-day Marxists often deny that the 'falling rate of profit' is central to Marx's analysis. It has become fashionable of late to argue that there are 'several' theories of crisis to be found in Marx's writings, of which the 'falling rate of profit' is but one.[6] Many Marxists reject it entirely.[7] Others accept it, but in a way that seems to deny it any force, saying that it should be called 'the law of the tendency of the rate of profit to fall and its countervailing tendencies'.[8]

Now it is true that the theory of the 'falling rate of profit' does not stand alone in **Capital**. It is complemented by an account of how other factors in the economy interact to cause periodic crises — the role of credit and money, the disproportion between different sectors of production, the wearing out of 'fixed capital' (buildings and machinery), the low level of consumption of the mass of workers. But it is Marx's belief in the 'falling rate of profit' that enables him to assert that capitalism is doomed by the very forces of production which it itself unleashes.

The other factors causing crisis could come and go. But since profit is the central aim of capitalism, any fall in the rate of profit appears as a threat to the system itself. As Marx put it:

> The rate of self-expansion of capitalism, or the rate of profit, being the goal of capitalist production, its fall . . . appears as a threat to the capitalist production process.[9]

This was why, Marx noted, those economists before him who had observed falling profit rates had viewed them with horror. For it created the 'feeling that the capitalist mode of production meets in the development of the productive forces a barrier which has nothing to do with the production of wealth as such' which 'testifies to the merely historical, transitory character of the capitalist mode of production' and to the way that 'at a certain stage it conflicts with its own further development.'[10] It showed that 'the real barrier of capitalist production was capital itself.'[11]

The claim, then, that there was a 'law' of the falling rate of profit was not just one more element in Marx's account of capitalism. It was central to his contention that capitalism was a doomed system. It tied his analysis of the economic mechanisms of capitalism into his general account of history as a succession of different 'modes of production'. And it showed the impossibility that any tinkering with the system, any self-regulation by capitalists, would be able to ward off crises, since any such self-regulation was bound to break down when the rate of profit fell below a certain point and replaced 'the operating fraternity of the capitalist class'[12] with a bitter mutual struggle for survival.

The law itself

At the centre of Marx's argument is the point that, as capitalism progresses, each worker uses more and more 'means of production' — tools, machinery and so on — in his or her work. In Marx's day, for instance, the development of power looms meant that the weaver who previously worked one loom at home became the minder of up to ten looms in the weaving shed of a large mill. This process has continued to today, when a relatively small number of workers may control a highly-automated production line. The 'means of production', of course, include not only tools and machinery, but everything from office blocks to transport systems as well.

Marx uses two ways of describing the relationship between the workers and the means of production. Each expresses a different facet of that relationship. From the point of view of the workers, or 'living labour', Marx refers to the means of production as 'dead labour', since all — tools, machines, factories and so on — are the product of labour by workers in the past, so can be seen as an accumulation of that labour. From the point of view of the capitalist, he describes these same means of production as 'constant capital' — to the capitalist they represent capital investment. The workers employed to operate the means of production are 'variable capital'.

In the course of the argument we will need to refer to both sets of terms, so it is well to set out here that they refer to the same relationship.

For the capitalist, anyway, spending on the means and materials of production grows much faster than spending on employing workers. So the very process of capital accumulation involves an increase in the ratio between the two, between 'constant capital' and 'variable capital'.

It is a law of capitalist production that its development is attended by a relative decrease in the variable in relation to constant capital and consequently to the total capital set in motion . . . This is just another way of saying that owing to the distinctive methods of production developing in the capitalist system, the same number of labourers, ie. the same quantity of labour power, operate, work up and productively consume in a given time span an ever-increasing quantity of means of labour, machinery and fixed capital of all sorts — and consequently a constant capital of an ever-increasing value. [13]

So the level of investment in means of production must grow much more quickly than investment in workers taken on to work those means of production.

This is an expression of that golden factor sought after by all capitalists: higher productivity, the same number of workers turning out an ever greater number of goods.

The growing extent of the means of production as compared with the labour power incorporated with them is an expression of the growing productiveness of labour. The increase of the latter appears, therefore, in the diminution of the subjective factor of the labour process as compared to the objective factor. [14]

Marx called the ratio of the *physical* extent of the means of production to the amount of labour power employed on them the 'technical composition of capital', and the ratio of the *value* of the means of production to the value of the labour power employed the 'organic composition'. [15] The growth of the technical composition of capital takes place as the same amount of labour power moves larger means of production and more material of production:

This change in the technical composition of capital is reflected again in its value composition, by the increase in the constant constituent of capital at the expense of the variable constituent . . . This law of the progressive increase in the constant capital, in proportion to the variable, is confirmed by every step. [16]

So an ever greater investment in means of production — and therefore in total capital — is needed to employ the same amount of labour power.

The reason this happens is competition — the need of each capitalist to push for greater productivity in order to stay ahead of competitors. But however much competition may compel the individual capitalist to take part in this process, from the point of view of the capitalist class as a whole it is disastrous.

Capitalists measure the success or failure of their undertakings not in terms of the total profit they bring in (what Marx calls the 'mass of profit') but in terms of the profit per unit of investment, the rate of profit. The source of profit is the surplus value created by the exploit-ation of living labour — so the mass of profit depends on the amount of labour power employed, the number of workers.[17] But if the level of investment in labour rises more slowly than the total investment, then the source of profit also rises more slowly than total investment. The profit per unit of investment therefore, the rate of profit, must tend to fall.[18]

The falling rate of profit 100 years after

If, as Marx argued, the rate of profit does tend to fall as the capitalist system develops, then this does help us explain many of the problems that beset the system in crisis. It would, for example, explain why the system could tolerate rising real wages at one stage in its development but find them too much at a later stage: with the lower average rate of profit, any rise in real wages would tend to force the least efficient firms into bankruptcy. Likewise public expenditures: if the rate of profit falls, the necessary taxation becomes a greater burden.

The reason why investment in new parts of the globe have failed to compensate in recent years for the weakness of US capitalism is also made clearer if the rate of profit on those investments is tending to fall. And Keynesian methods of managing the economy, while they may iron out some of the other pressures that bring the pattern of boom and slump, will have no effect on a long-term fall in the rate of profit.

But if we try to relate Marx's claims concerning the falling rate of profit to the known facts about past crises, then three problems arise.

Firstly, some important crises — and particularly that of 1929 and after — have not followed immediately from some fall in average profit rates.

Secondly, if the 'falling rate of profit' is an inexorable law, then it is difficult to see how capitalism has escaped from being in permanent crisis since the 1880s. It is true that Marx talked of 'countervailing tendencies' which would counteract pressures towards crisis, but he hardly believed that these could prolong the rapid expansion of the system by more than a century.

Thirdly, studies indicate that the factor which Marx singled out as causing the rate of profit to fall — the rise in the organic composi-tion of capital — stopped operating in Britain at about the time Marx laid down his pen, and in the US by the 1920s. We will look more closely at the factual evidence later, but it is worth noting here that some calculations seem to indicate a renewed rise in the organic composition in the past 10–15 years.

The important point is that the failure of the organic composition of capital to rise, for a long period, caused some questioning of Marx's arguments — and in the case of some Marxists, wholesale rejection of them. Marx himself listed countervailing tendencies which could, at times, offset the downward path of the rate of profit. Faced with the three problems outlined, many critics of Marx's 'law' have found it easy to argue that these countervailing tendencies in fact cancel out this 'law' altogether.

If Marx's 'law' is to be of any use in explaining the current crisis, it must be able to face up to these objections and to the factual evidence from the years since 1880. *It can do so*. If certain 'countervailing tendencies' are seen to be *built into the structure* of capitalism for a certain period of its development and not just presented as afterthoughts (as Marx himself, unfortunately, tended to present them), then and only then can it be seen how they have failed to operate at other periods.

So let us look at the main arguments against Marx's 'falling rate of profit' and at the countervailing tendencies that have been seen to counteract it at certain times.

The effects of technical progress

It has been argued against Marx that increases in productivity are often brought about by innovations that are in fact 'capital-saving' rather than labour-saving. For example the American radical economist Eric Olin Wright argues:

> For the value of constant capital to rise, there must be a net excess of labour-saving technical innovations over constant capital-saving innovations . . .
> In a competitive struggle, it does not matter whether costs are cut by savings on labour or savings on capital . . .
> In fact several plausible arguments can be made that suggest in advanced capitalist economies there should be a tendency for a relative increase to occur in selective pressures for capital saving over labour-saving technical innovations . . .[19]

Marx himself refers to 'a few cases' in which increased productivity is *not* accompanied by a rising organic composition,[20] without explaining why there should only be a few such cases, and again suggests that one of the 'countervailing tendencies' is that: 'New lines of production are opened up, especially for the production of luxuries . . . These new lines start out predominantly with living labour . . .' But he does not explain why capitalism cannot be continually entering into 'new lines' based upon labour intensive innovations, so permanently countering the tendency of the rate of profit to fall.

It is not possible to defend Marx's main contention that capital accumulation must be capital intensive merely by asserting the fact.[21]

But there exists in Marx's writing the outlines of a watertight explanation that can easily be filled out.

The first part of the explanation flows from the very way in which capital accumulation proceeds. With each round of production new surplus value is produced. The individual capitals which own this surplus value are forced by competition (other things being equal) to plough as much as possible of it into the expansion of production in the next round.

> All methods for raising the social productive power of labour . . . are at the same time methods for the increased production of surplus-value or surplus product, which in its turn is the formative element in accumulation . . . The continual re-transformation of surplus value into capital now appears in the shape of the increasing magnitude of the capital that enters into the process of production. This in turn is the basis of an extended scale of production, of the methods for raising the productive power of labour and of accelerated production of surplus value . . .[22]

Or, as Marx puts it in the **Grundrisse**,[23] 'productively employed capital is always replaced doubly' — it transmits its own value to the commodities produced and it involves the creation by workers of additional surplus value that finds embodiment in those commodities.

In a 'pure capitalist system' (one in which there were only workers and capitalists, all other classes having been destroyed, and in which the capitalists were forced by competition to behave as the pure embodiment of capital by investing all their surplus value), the mass of surplus value would increase with every cycle of production *ad infinitum*. The capitalist class would have ever greater quantities of surplus value at its disposal and would be under competitive pressure to invest this in an ever-larger scale of production.

As Michael Kidron has put it, Marx's argument assumed that '. . . All output flows back into the system as productive consumption. In a closed system like this, allocation would swing progressively in favour of investment.'[24]

That in itself does not automatically mean a rise in the ratio of 'dead labour' to 'living labour'. The investment may be 'capital-saving'. If scientific knowledge is progressing and being applied as new technologies, then some of these technologies may employ less machinery and raw materials per worker than old technologies. To give a relatively recent example, the production of newspapers using phototypesetting and lithopresses is less capital-intensive than the old method using linotype machines and letterpresses.

But that is not the end of the argument. It shows only that at any one time there will be *some* new technologies that are capital-saving. The important point, however, is: what will be the *average* result of new technologies? Will they save capital or increase it?

If we take the argument one stage further, it can in fact be shown that if there is a massive amount of profit-seeking investment in the hands of rival capitalists, then the overall tendency will be for the average investment to increase capital, to be capital-intensive.

Firstly, the most competitive capitalists in each line of business will be those who introduce most innovations. At any given level of scientific and technical knowledge some of these may indeed be capital-saving. But when all these have been employed, there will still be other innovations (or at least capitalists will suspect there are other innovations) to be obtained only by increasing the level of investment in means of production.

Secondly, the fact that some technical progress can take place without any rise in the ratio of capital to labour does not mean that *all* the advantages of technical progress can be gained without such a rise.

The point can be simply illustrated by assuming, for a moment, a state of affairs in which in a given field of production new scientific knowledge is not emerging, and in which all existing techniques possible at a given ratio of capital to labour have been exhausted. In this situation, a capitalist who uses more means of production per worker can expect to get access to improved techniques of production which may have been known about in the past but could not then be used because the ratio of means of production to labour was too small — the capital was not available to develop them. By contrast, a capitalist who does not increase his means of production per worker will be stuck with the existing techniques.

Thirdly, if an individual capitalist can increase the ratio of capital to workers he will be able to invest in innovations that need more capital as well as those that need more labour. If he cannot increase this ratio then he will benefit only from those innovations that need more labour — and he will lose out in competition with those who can.

In the real world, every operating capitalist takes it for granted that the way to gain access to the most advanced technical change is to increase the level of investment in means of production or 'dead labour' (including the 'dead labour' accumulated in the results of past research and development). It is only in the pages of the most esoteric journals of political economy that anyone imagines that the way for the Ford Motor Company to meet competition from General Motors or Toyota is to *cut* the level of physical investment per worker. The capitalist usually recognises that you cannot get the benefits of innovation without paying for it. His firm may by accident stumble upon a particular innovation that requires *less* capital per worker, but the only way he can *guarantee* getting such innovations is to increase his level of investment.

If the capitalist cuts the amount of investment in means of production per worker, he might still stumble upon some innovation unknown to his competitors. But luck such as this is also available to the capitalist who *increases* his investment in means of production per worker, while he can also match the innovations stumbled on by his competitors and obtain technical advances unreachable by those who cannot afford his 'capital-intensity'. Since, in theory at least, there is no limit to the possible increase in the ratio of means of production to workers, there is no theoretical limit to possible innovation based on this method of competition.

For these reasons, other things being equal, we can expect there to be always more innovations calling for increased capital than those calling for less. The average amount of means of production per worker — Marx's 'technical composition of capital' — will rise.

Only one thing could stop the pressure for this rise: if for some reason there was a shortage of profit-seeking investment. In such a case the capitalists would be forced to forego hopes of achieving the innovations possible through greater investment and settle for those they might stumble upon by accident.

Productivity and the cost of means of production

The fact that the physical size of the means and materials of production grows in relation to the labour force does not mean that cost of investment necessarily grows faster than the labour force. For, as Marx himself recognised, the very technical progress that follows from increasing the ratio of dead to living labour tends to cut the amount of labour required to produce each machine, factory or unit of raw material.

Once again, this is a factor referred to by Marx.

> The value of the constant capital does not increase in the same proportion as its material volume . . . The same development which increases the mass of the constant capital in relation to the variable reduces the value of its elements as a result of the increased productivity of labour, and therefore prevents the value of constant capital, although it continually increases, from increasing at the same rate as its material volume . . . [in] isolated cases the mass of the elements of constant capital may even increase, while its value remains the same or falls . . .[25]

In other words, machines grow more powerful and complex. But they themselves are made by using techniques which are ever advancing and reducing the number of person-hours required to make them. So although one machine might be twice as powerful and productive as the machine it replaces, it could cost less. The 'technical composition' of capital would increase, but the 'organic composition', the ratio of the *value* of dead to living labour, would remain the same or might even fall.

Marx notes that this 'is bound up with the depreciation of existing capital which occurs with the development of industry . . .' The fact that a machine can be replaced by one which requires fewer hours of labour to produce (because productivity has advanced), means that the value of the machine to the capitalist falls. A portion of its value has to be written off, at a speed much faster than the physical wearing out of the machine.

This *depreciation* or '*devaluation*' of constant capital has been most picked on as disproving Marx's law — for example by Hodgson, Steedman, Himmelweit, Okoshio and Glyn. These critics argue that technical progress means that goods are always being produced more cheaply than in the past. If a rise in the ratio of dead to living labour in a certain industry increases productivity, then the price of its output will fall compared to the output of other industries. But that in turn will reduce the costs of investment in these industries in the next production cycle. Cheaper investment throughout the economy will cheapen further production, both of the means of production itself and of consumption, and so on.[26] So lower investment costs will *raise* the rate of profit.

At first glance the argument looks convincing. It is, however, false. It rests upon a sequence of logical steps which you cannot take in the real world. Investment in a process of production takes place at one point in time. The cheapening of further investment as a result of improved production techniques occurs at a later point in time. The two things are *not* simultaneous.

The investment a capitalist makes today is no cheaper because, once operating, it makes it possible to make the same invstment more cheaply in future. The rate of profit is a measure of the surplus value accruing to the capitalist compared to the amount he has laid down in investment in the past. It is not a measure of the surplus value he gets compared with the cost of his investment if he were making it afresh. The point has added importance when it is remembered that the real process of capitalist investment takes place in such a way that the same fixed constant capital (machines and buildings) is used for several cycles of production. The fact that the cost of the investment would be less if it took place after the second, third or fourth round of production does not alter the cost before the first round of production.[27]

This argument has been well put by Ben Fine and Lawrence Harris. They claim that in Marx's writings there is a distinction between the concept *organic composition of capital* and *value composition of capital*. The organic composition is the comparison of investment in means of production and labour in terms of 'old values', whereas the value composition is a comparison in terms of the 'current value of means of production and wage goods consumed'. 'Changes in the organic composition are directly proportional to changes in the technical composition, whereas changes in the value composition are not . . .'[28]

For the capitalist it is the 'old' composition, the organic composition, which is the vital thing. For capitalism is based not just on value but upon the *self expansion* of the values embodied in capital. This necessarily implies a comparison of current surplus value with the prior capitalist investment from which it flows. The very notion of 'self-expanding values' is incoherent without it.

This does not necessarily mean that the actual accounting procedures used by a firm calculate the rate of profit by comparing the profit with the original capital. They may instead use the current replacement cost of capital as the denominator in their rate of profit calculations. But in that case, before making the comparison they must deduct from their profits the loss in value of their original capital due to the effect of technical progress in reducing the amount of socially necessary labour needed to replace it. The effect is the same. The devaluation of capital does not serve to halt a decline in the rate of profit, but to accentuate it. It reduces the organic composition of capital only through reducing the overall mass of profits — and with it the rate of profit too.[29]

In any case, there is an argument that calculations based on the original cost of investment better capture what is at stake for capitalists when they make investment decisions. For what they want to be sure of before investing is that they will earn an adequate rate of profit on the investment they are making now, not on what it would cost them to make it some years hence. This is their prime consideration, even though when it comes at some point in the future to estimating the rate of profit then achieved, they may, for reasons of convenience (because of the difficulty in calculating the combined historic cost of investments made at successive points in time) compare their profit, with deductions for depreciation made according to rough and ready procedures, to the replacement cost of their capital.

If, for example, the capitalist has borrowed capital from the bank with which to start production, he will have to pay back the original value of that capital, not the amount he would have borrowed some time later to invest in the same means of production, when they may have become cheaper. If those means of production are depreciating quickly, that therefore increases his problems. His fixed capital declines in value more quickly in the second and subsequent rounds of production than in the first. The same portion of means of production is used up in the production process, but it is worth less. So the value of constant capital which is passed over into the value of the commodities produced is also less. The value of the capitalist's output falls — and he has greater difficulty in paying back what he owes to the bank. The fall in the value of capital due to increased productivity therefore eats into surplus value.

This is exactly what is happening in sections of the printing industry at the moment. In a year's time a typesetting machine may cost only half as much as it does now. New technology is making it cheaper. But this does not make life easier for the printing firm. Quite the opposite. To survive, the firm must recoup what it spent on the machine before it faces competition in 18 months time from rivals who will get the machine at half the present price. In other words, the speed of technological change is forcing the firm to try to recover the cost of its investment far more rapidly than in the past.

So increased productivity does accelerate the rate at which constant capital depreciates. But far from easing the problems of the average capitalist, this makes them worse. For it means that unless capitalists can increase the rate of exploitation, they have to use a growing amount of surplus value to pay for that depreciation.

In any case, the cheapening of the cost of new physical means of production cannot be the crucial factor when it comes to the pressures for the organic composition of capital to rise. Our argument earlier as to why the organic composition must rise had to do *not* just with the growth in the physical stock of means and materials of production; it had to do above all with the continual growth of the mass of surplus *value* seeking an outlet for investment. We argued that at any point in time, the more of this surplus value an individual capitalist can get hold of and invest in means of production, the more productivity-increasing innovations he will be able to introduce compared to his competitors. It is the investment of greater amounts of surplus *value* in means of production that concerns him, not just the expansion of the amount of physical means of production at his disposal.

A capitalist may be able to buy today a machine which is twice as productive as one he paid the same price for a year ago. But that is no help to him if a rival is using greater accumulated surplus value to buy a machine four times as productive. The individual capitalist can stay in business only if he spends as much as possible of his surplus value on new means of production. If the means of production become cheaper, that only results in his having to buy more of them in order to achieve competitive success.

So if there is more surplus value available for investment that there was previously then the organic composition of capital will tend to rise, other things being equal. It makes no difference if the physical means and materials of production are cheaper — that just causes more of them to be employed.

There is only one condition under which there will not be this pressure for the value of constant capital to expand — if technical change is devaluing the old means of production so fast that the value of output does not even cover the cost of the original investment. Then the capitalist is making a loss; there is no surplus value; and the rate of profit is negative.[30]

But in that case the condition for the organic composition of capital to fall would be *negative* accumulation, a *negative* rate of profit, and therefore a complete breakdown of the system![31]

Increased exploitation and the rate of profit

Marx lists as one of his 'countervailing tendencies' the ability of capital to increase the rate of exploitation of each worker, even as the organic composition of capital rises.[32] So there are fewer workers per unit of investment; but each worker is contributing more surplus value.

Increased exploitation can mean increasing the length of the working day, increasing the physical intensity of labour, or cutting real wages. But it does not have to involve any of these things.

The technical advance associated with more means of production per worker has the effect of raising the productivity of the worker. In a single hour or day he or she produces more than he/she did previously for the same exertion of labour. So the amount of labour he/she has to exert to produce goods equivalent to his/her own consumption falls. And the amount of the working day's labour which the capitalist can take as surplus value rises.

For example, technical advance may mean that the workforce of a certain country can produce twice as many goods of all sorts as they could ten years earlier. The country's capitalists can then increase their profits, even if living standards remain the same — for the goods required to maintain living standards can be produced with half the previous number of hours of labour; the other half can go into producing more goods for sale abroad, and therefore more profits.

The ratio of surplus labour to necessary labour can grow as the means of production advance — even if there is no fall in real wages. As Marx wrote:

> The tendency of the rate of profit to fall is bound up with a tendency for the rate of labour exploitation to rise . . . Both the rise in the rate of surplus value and the fall in the rate of profit are but specific forms through which growing productivity is expressed under capitalism.[33]

This has led to criticisms of the very notion of a 'law' of the falling rate of profit to which the rise in the rate of exploitation is merely a countervailing factor. For instance, Sweezy argues:

> It seems hardly wise to treat an integral part of the process of rising productivity separately and as an offsetting factor; a better procedure is to recognise from the outset that rising productivity tends to bring with it a higher rate of surplus value . . . If both the organic composition of capital and the rate of surplus value are assumed variable, as we think they should be, then the direction in which the rate of profit will change becomes indeterminate . . .[34]

Marx himself does deal with this argument. His contention is that however much the rate of exploitation rises, it is not possible for the total surplus labour (and hence surplus value) extracted from each worker to rise above the length of the working day.

Take the example of a firm which employs a static workforce of 30,000. Even if it worked them as long as was physically possible each day (say, 16 hours) and paid them no wages, its daily profit could not exceed the value embodied in $30,000 \times 16$ hours labour. There is a limit beyond which profit cannot grow.

But there is no such limit on the degree to which investment can grow. So a point will be reached where profits stop growing, even though competition forces the level of investment to continue rising. The ratio of profits to investment — the rate of profit — *will* tend to fall.

Marx's argument on this point has been reformulated in more precise mathematical terms since his day and is now generally accepted even by critics who reject other parts of his argument.[35]

The profitability of the individual capital and of the system as a whole

In recent years it has been argued, against Marx, that changes in technique alone *cannot* produce a fall in the rate of profit. For, it is said, capitalists will only introduce a new technique if it raises their profits. But if it raises the profit of one capitalist, then it must raise the average profit of the whole capitalist class. So, for instance, Steedman states: 'The forces of competition will lead to that selection of production methods industry by industry which generates the highest possible uniform rate of profit through the economy . . .'[36] The same point has been made by Andrew Glyn,[37] by John Harrison,[38] and has been elaborated mathematically by Okishio[39] and Himmelweit.[40]

They conclude that capitalists will only adopt capital intensive techniques that seem to reduce their rate of profit if that rate is already being squeezed by a rise in real wages. Wages, not the organic composition of capital, hit the rate of profit.

Marx's own writings provide a simple answer to any such argument. It is that the first capitalist to invest in a new technology gets a competitive advantage over his fellow capitalists which enables him to gain a surplus profit, but that this surplus will not last once the new techniques are generalised.

What the capitalist gets in money terms when he sells his goods depends upon the average amount of socially necessary labour contained in them. If he introduces a new, more productive, technique, but no other capitalists do, he is producing goods worth the same amount of socially necessary labour as before, but with less expenditure on real concrete labour power. His profits rise.[41] But once all capitalists have introduced these techniques, the value of the goods falls until it corresponds to the average amount of labour needed to produce them under the new techniques. The additional profit disappears — and if more means of production are used to get access to the new techniques, the rate of profit falls.

For example, let us take a firm producing under the average conditions for its industry. It has a constant capital of 50 units, variable capital of 50 units, and the surplus value produced is also 50 units. It turns out 150 units of output in a single production period. Its rate of profit, therefore, is the surplus value divided by the total capital (50/100) or 50 per cent. We will call this Stage One:

STAGE ONE:	Constant capital	Variable capital	Surplus value	Output (units)	Output price	Rate of profit
	50	50	50	150	150	50%

Now assume that the firm is marginal compared to the whole industry — in other words its output is so small that a change in its costs of production will hardly affect the average for the industry as a whole. It introduces a capital-intensive technique which enables it to produce the same amount of goods with the same constant capital, but half the workforce. Because costs throughout the industry remain the same, the price the firm gets for its output remains unchanged, even though its input costs have fallen. Its rate of profit will rise:

STAGE TWO:	Constant capital	Variable capital	Surplus value	Output (units)	Output price	Rate of profit
	50	25	75	150	150	100%

The surplus value gained by the firm at this stage includes not only surplus value produced directly inside the firm. It includes *excess* surplus value accruing to the firm from the economy as a whole because its production costs are less than the average. So its total surplus value and its rate of profit both rise. It is profitable to introduce the new technique.

But precisely because the new technique is more profitable than the old, other firms will adopt it. It will cease to be 'marginal' and average production costs throughout the industry will begin to fall. With falling costs, firms will begin to reduce their prices in order to grab a larger share of the available market, and average prices will fall towards the new average social costs of production.

Eventually a point will be reached where the new technique prevails throughout the industry — Stage Three. The firm now finds:

STAGE THREE:	Constant capital	Variable capital	Surplus value	Output (units)	Output price	Rate of profit
	50	25	25	150	100	33%

The new techniques have now *cut* the rate of profit for the industry as a whole.

The paradox involved in this process is that for each individual firm the initial effect of introducing the new technique will have been to raise the rate of profit — *and this was true even for the very last firm to change to the new technology*. Before changing over, it will have been producing its goods at the old, higher costs of production, but receiving only the new, lower price for them. Its rate of profit will have fallen to nothing. By introducing the new technique it will raise the rate of profit to the new industry average of 33 per cent.[42]

Crises and the devaluation of capital

We have shown that the cheapening of the means and materials of production due to technical progress could not counter the pressures that force down the rate of profit on the total capital.

However Marx did not simply view the capitalist system as made up of total capital (or, as it is usually called, 'capital-in-general'). Total capital is composed of individual competing capitals. These individual capitals are afflicted by periodic crises of the system (in part brought about by the long term decline in the rate of profit) which drive some of them out of business, with their means of production either passing out of use or being bought up by other capitals.

In this lies part of the secret of capitalism's historic ability to overcome the effects of the 'law' of the falling rate of profit.

The crisis means that huge chunks of capital lose their value — machines rust, goods are unsold or only sold at greatly reduced prices, large amounts of credit have to be written off. If this process were distributed evenly over all the capitals, it is difficult to see how they would ever recover from the crisis. But in fact, because some capitals go out of business, those that remain are able to avoid having to pay for the devalued capital. Not only do they succeed in passing the cost of the crisis on to those that go under, they also often succeed in enhancing the value of their own capital by buying up means and materials of production on the cheap, in other words at less than their current value in terms of labour time.

The surviving capitals get the benefits of past investment made by other capitals, but do not need to worry about covering the original cost of that investment with their profits. They only have to worry about covering its present value (reduced because of technical progress): indeed, with luck they can get control of the investment at less than its present value. The old owners could not gain any benefit from the way in which technical progress was continually decreasing the value of their investment because devaluation was for them a depreciation change against profit; the new owners gain nothing but benefit, for the old owners have borne the cost of depreciation in going bankrupt and they, the new owners, reap all the further profits to be made.

The critics of Marx's law see the cheapening of the means of production as a smoothly operating mechanism that enables capitalism to expand without facing a falling profit rate. But, in fact, this mechanism can work only in so far as *crises* enable some capitals to benefit at the expense of others. To offset the 'law' the cheapening of the means of production has to find expression in enforced depreciation as whole capitals are destroyed.[43] As Marx put it:

> The periodical depreciation of existing capital — one of the means immanent in capitalist production to check the fall of the rate of profit and hasten accumulation of capital value through the formation of new capital — disturbs the given conditions under which the process of circulation and reproduction takes place, and is therefore accompanied by sudden stoppages and crises in the production process.[44]

Crises are in part provoked by the tendency of the rate of profit to fall, but in turn counteract that tendency:

> Crises are always but momentary and forcible solutions of the existing contradictions. They are violent eruptions which for a time restore the disturbed equilibrium.[45]

What is more, the crisis can reduce or stop the pressure for the organic composition of capital to rise.

The destruction of value during a crisis includes destruction of some of the total surplus value. This does not prevent further accumulation, because even if the capitalist class as a whole has less total surplus value at its disposal, this is shared between a smaller number of capitals. Each individual capitalist sees a rise in the amount of profit he can expect in relation to the cost of his investment — a rise in his rate of profit — even though the surplus value accruing to the capitalist class as a whole may have fallen.

The crisis has one final effect of great importance. It reduces the total amount of surplus value in the system as a whole. In doing so, it reduces total funds available for investment. Each individual capitalist knows that his rivals have more difficulty than previously in finding the wherewithal for new, enlarged investments. So there is less pressure for the capitalist to expand his own investment in order to stay in business.

There will be a reduction in the pressure for capital-intensive forms of investment. So a by-product of the crisis is a slowing-down of the rise in the organic composition of capital.

Under such circumstances a modest rise in the rate of exploitation may be sufficient to offset the downward tendency of the rate of profit. And, in the immediate aftermath of a great crisis, with high levels of unemployment, workers will often accept such an increase in the rate of exploitation.

Rationalisation through crisis and the aging of the system

Once periodic crises are taken into account, there is no difficulty in explaining at least some of the failure of the organic composition of capital to rise as fast as Marx's model would seem to suggest it should. Indeed, it can be argued that provided the crises are deep enough, there is no reason at all why there should be a long-term tendency for the organic composition to rise through cycle after cycle, or for the rate of profit to fall. But if that is so, why should crises become ever more serious? Why need the system ever exhaust its ability to expand the forces of production?

The logical conclusion of this line of argument is to see crises as simply a way — a painful but effective way — for the system to rationalise itself, necessary hiccups in its endless movement. The economic turmoil of the last decade then becomes no more than a process of rationalisation and restructuring, a necessary process of transition to a new period of growth.[46]

But this is to overlook the impact on rationalisation-through-crisis of another key feature of the dynamic of capitalism as shown by Marx. Marx's account of capitalism is not of a system that simply undergoes the same motions, year after year, decade after decade, continually reproducing itself in an essentially unchanged form according to fixed and immutable economic laws.

There is, it is true, recognition of the abstract, apparently timeless, laws which govern the motions of any society that has become subject to the dictates of capital: the peculiar features of commodity production which subordinate producers to the unplanned interaction of their products; the uncontrollable drive to the self-expansion of value which follows once labourers become separated from the means of production and labour power itself becomes a commodity; the resultant tendencies for the rate of profit to decline on the one hand and for there to be repeated economic crises on the other; the way in which crises can restore the conditions for further self-expansion of capital.

But even such a minimal outline of the abstract cyclical motions of capitalism implies something else: that the system undergoes continual self-transformation as the abstract laws of capitalist production change the relationships of the different units of capital to each other and to the working class. The rising organic composition of capital is itself one aspect of these changes. Another is the tendency towards increasing *concentration* of capital (the units of production getting ever larger) and *centralisation* of capital (the units getting fewer in number). Crises, at the same time as overcoming the problems associated with the tendency of the rate of profit to fall, push forward the level of concentration and centralisation of capital.

About the concentration and centralisation of capital over the last century, there should be no argument. Successive waves of bankruptcies, takeovers, mergers and nationalisations have reduced the number of major firms and increased the proportion of capital under their control. So, for instance, in Britain in 1910 the top 100 firms produced 16 per cent of total output; by 1970 they produced 50 per cent. In the US in 1950 the top 200 firms controlled 49 per cent of assets. By 1967 they controlled 58.8 per cent. Of course, in such economies new businesses do come into being. But so too do others disappear — more often than not in larger numbers.

The same tendency has operated on a world scale. Before the First World War new national capitalisms, such as Germany and the US, were still able to emerge as viable competitors with British capitalism, which had dominated until then. But as the present century has passed, it has become increasingly difficult for further new capitalisms to gain a similar position in the world. New areas of industrial expansion have usually been offshoots of the existing world leaders — as Hong Kong is to Britain or Taiwan to the US.

The exceptions to this have been where competitive capitals within a country have been more or less completely replaced by state capitals — in Russia, Eastern Europe and a number of third world countries. But even in these cases the pattern of the last two decades has been one of increasing integration into — and subordination to — the operations of the giant corporations of the West.[47]

Concentration and centralisation have important effects on the way in which the basic laws of motion of capitalism find expression. The larger the units of capital and the more a few of them dominate the system, the more difficult it becomes for a cyclical crisis to open up a new period of expansion. While there were a large number of relatively small firms, some could go bust without damaging others. But with a few very large firms, the destruction of any of them can do immense damage to the operations of others.

Each giant closely interacts with the others — through supplying components or raw materials, through provision of finance, through acting as a market for output. The futures of the great steel corporations cannot be separated from those of the giant shipbuilding and auto firms; the oil, chemical, plastics and artificial fibre manufacturers increasingly form a single complex of interests; the stability of whole national economies continues to depend upon the well-being of a handful of banks, which in turn become dependent upon particular giant enterprises or states to whom they have lent immense sums. If any one of these giants goes down, it threatens to bring about the progressive collapse of the others that are dependent on it. Hence the fear in 1981, 1982 and 1983 that the indebtedness of countries such as Poland, Mexico and Brazil would wreck the world's banking system. This, in turn, would have caused devastation to the industrial capitals of other countries. Instead of crisis allowing the efficient to expand at the expense of the inefficient, it can inflict untold, random damage on efficient and inefficient alike.

Under such circumstances, the cyclical motions of the system do not operate automatically to counter the rising organic composition of capital and the falling rate of profit. When crises come, they depreciate the capital of the survivors as well as those driven to the wall, forcing profit rates still further down instead of rapidly restoring them. And fearing the threat of such an eventuality, the giant firms inside each country tend to draw together to prop each other up, hoping at best to postpone crisis indefinitely, at worst to use the power of the state to impose its consequences on the capitals of other countries.

But the effect of this can only be to prevent crises acting as the main countervailing influence to the long-term tendency of the rate of profit to fall.[48]

The more the concentration and centralisation of capital takes place, the less should we expect the system to be able to evade the consequences of Marx's law. If in its youth the countervailing tendency due to crisis could operate as powerfully as the law itself for long periods of time, in its old age the reverse should be the case. Declining profit rates should drag the system down into a slough of permanent stagnation, of short spurts of half-hearted expansion interspersed with long cyclical rises which resolve nothing.

Imperialism and war

The picture of capitalism we have used so far in order to explain Marx's law and the countervailing factors has been an abstract one. In it there are only capitalists and workers. The capitalists are forced by competition to accumulate all their surplus value. The only form of competition between them is through trying to undercut each others' selling price on the market. The state and the use of force against the capitalists of other countries hardly exists in this model of the system.

The real history of capitalism is rather more complicated than this. Capitalism grew up in a pre-capitalist environment, in which there were not only capitalists and workers but pre-capitalist exploiting and exploited classes, lords and serfs; even under aging capitalism other social classes continue to exist between the two great classes. Capitalists have always used some surplus value for things besides accumulation — for goods for their own consumption and that of social groups dependent on them, for waging wars against pre-capitalist ruling classes, for the enslavement of colonies and for wars against one another. Competition has never been *just* price competition — it has always involved as well at least some expenditure on advertising, bribery, and the use of force to prise open markets.

What is more, the role of the state was central in aiding infant capitalism's entry into the world, was crucial in enabling it to dispose of its pre-capitalist rivals as it entered adulthood, and is inextricably linked with all its operations in its dotage.

The move from the abstract outline of the main components of the system to the concrete circumstances in which they operate necessarily affects the way in which Marx's law works out.

One such effect was included by Marx in his list of 'countervailing factors'. Each capitalist economy operated within a world economy, and 'foreign trade', he argued, could offset the tendency of the rate of profit to fall. He pointed to two ways in which this could occur: firstly through access to cheaper raw materials, thus reducing production costs, and secondly through allowing investment in areas where the wages were lower and the rate of profit higher.[49]

Fifty years after Marx, Lenin, following the English liberal economist Hobson, suggested another important effect: capital could be exported to colonies and semi-colonies which could not find a profitable outlet for investment at home. Lenin himself did not explore explicitly the way this related to Marx's law. But it is not difficult to do so. In the period 1880 to 1913 something like 15 per cent of the British national product went into overseas investment.

If there had not been this overseas outlet for funds seeking investment, then each individual firm in Britain would have lived in fear that its rivals would use those funds to get a competitive edge through a vast expansion of the means of production at home. This fear would compel each firm to engage in just such an expansion. The increased availability of funds for investment at home would therefore have increased the organic composition of capital, and so would have led to a considerable fall in the rate of profit.

As it was, a large portion of the surplus value in the hands of British capitalists passed out of the British sector of the world economy, and so did not raise the organic composition of capital within it. [50]

But in itself this could not be more than a transitory mechanism for offsetting the fall in the rate of profit. It assumed somewhere 'outside' the capitalist economy for the surplus. This 'outside' existed when capitalism was still restricted to the Western edge of the Eurasian land mass and to part of North America, with pre-capitalist forms of exploitation dominating even in those parts of the rest of the world which were integrated into the capitalist world market. But once imperialism had done its work, and capitalist forms of exploitation dominated more or less everywhere, the 'outside' no longer existed. [51]

In a world of multinational corporations, surplus value which flows away from one area, reducing the upward pressure on the organic composition of capital, merely serves to increase the upward pressure elsewhere. The average *world* rate of profit falls. The world system is driven to stagnation just as the national economy was in Marx's time.

We can begin to understand why in Britain — the most important imperialist power of capitalism's early adulthood — the organic composition fell in the 1880s, 1890s and early 1900s, but then started rising again. The impact of empire was beginning to be exhausted.

But the search for empire brought into operation another factor — one which was, crucially, to *increase* in importance with the weakening ability of empire to offset the falling rate of profit. Capitalism was increasingly an *international* system. Not just in that capitalists were selling goods abroad, but they were now organising production on a scale that cut across national frontiers. By the time of the First World War the largest firms in the advanced capitalist countries depended upon raw materials in one part of the world, production facilities in another, and markets elsewhere.

Today this trend is even more marked. The seven major oil companies control half the world's oil output; the giant car firms are all racing towards their own version of the 'world car' made of components manufactured in dozens of different countries; while in the computer and aerospace industries firms have to operate internationally in order to stay in business at all.

Yet the only mechanisms that exist with the power to ensure that the rest of society satisfies the needs of the giant firms remain the national states. Each firm — however wide-ranging its international operations — depends upon a national state to protect its operations against any threat of force (whether from other firms or from exploited classes). Indeed, the process of internationalisation of production has taken place step by step with the process (referred to earlier) of monopolisation of each national economy by fewer and fewer giant corporations ever more closely intertwined with the state.

Observation of these two simultaneous, yet apparently contradictory processes — increased reliance on the national state and increased internationalisation — led Lenin and Bukharin to write their classic works on imperialism sixty and more years ago.[52] Their argument was that the contradiction could be resolved only by war. In the modern world, they insisted, 'economic' competition between 'state capitalist trusts' was more and more supplemented and even replaced by military competition. The great powers were continually partitioning and repartitioning the world as each resorted to violence to protect and reinforce its vital economic interests at the expense of the other. War became as normal a capitalist mechanism as price-cutting, boom and slump.

But war has a consequence of immense importance for the basic trend of the system, for Marx's 'law'.[53] Vast amounts of capital are physically destroyed (bombed factories, unharvested crops and so on) and even vaster amounts devalued (as trade patterns are disrupted, goods unsold, credits cancelled). But, typically, the costs of this are borne unevenly — being shifted on to the losers by the winners. War, like crises, enables the mass of surplus value available for new investment in means of production to be reduced, without necessarily reducing the rate of profit for the surviving capitals.

The scale of destruction of values can be massive. Shane Mage, for instance, has estimated the combined effect of the crisis of the 1930s and the Second World War on the US economy: 'Between 1930 and 1945 the capital stock of the US fell from 145 billion dollars to 120 billion dollars, a net disinvestment of some 20 per cent . . .'[54] A fifth of the existing accumulated surplus value and the additional surplus value produced over 15 years were wiped out.

The history of the twentieth century suggests that at the point when slumps became a very expensive and very painful way for capitalism to offset the tendency of the organic composition of capital to rise, imperialist expansion and war took over.

But war also has its problems. As the forces of production grow, so too do the forces of destruction. Weaponry develops which threatens to destroy the capital of all those involved in military conflict, not just some to the benefit of others. Just as restructuring and 'rational-isation' of the world system through slump becomes a very difficult and very painful — even if necessary — process, so does the 'restructuring and rationalisation' through war. Just as you would expect aging capitalism to be permanently on the edge of slump, without gaining its benefits for the system, so you would expect it to be permanently on the edge of war, without *its* rather dubious benefits either.

Unproductive consumption and the rate of profit

In the **Grundrisse** Marx makes, in passing, one remark that points to something of enormous significance for the general theory which he based upon the 'falling rate of profit'.

> There are moments in the developed movement of capital which delay this movement other than by crises such as, eg. the constant devaluation of part of the existing capital: *the transformation of a great part of capital into fixed capital which does not serve as agency of direct production; unproductive waste of a great portion of capital* etc. (productively employed capital is always replaced doubly, in that the posing of a productive capital presupposes a countervalue). The unproductive consumption of capital replaces it on one side, annihilates it on the other . . . [55] (My emphasis)

Marx is saying that if for some reason capitalists divert some of the surplus value available for investment into some other use, then the pressure is reduced, there is less new capital available for capitals seeking innovations that will cut their costs, and the trend towards capital-intensive investment will be reduced.

The same point was made much more explicitly in the 1960s by Mike Kidron[56] — apparently without knowing that Marx had spelt the argument out (the **Grundrisse** was not published in English until 1973). He pointed out that Marx's argument about the falling rate of profit

> rested on two assumptions, both realistic: all output flows back into the system as productive inputs through either workers' or capitalists' productive consumption — ideally there are no leakages in the system and no choice other than to allocate total output between what would now be called investment and working class consumption; secondly in a closed system like this the allocation would swing progressively in favour of investment.[57]

If the first assumption, that all outputs flow back into the system, was dropped — in other words, if some of these outputs are lost to the production cycle — then there would be no need for investment to grow more rapidly than the labour employed. The law of the falling rate of profit would not operate. 'Leaks' of surplus value from the closed cycle of production/investment/production would offset the tendency of the rate of profit to fall. As Kidron put it in a later work:

> In Marx the model assumes a closed system in which all output flows back as inputs in the form of investment goods or wage goods. There are no leaks. Yet in principle a leak could insulate the compulsion to grow from its most important consequences . . . In such a case there would be no decline in the average rate of profit, no reason to expect increasingly severe slumps and so on.[58]

The argument is impeccable, and Kidron goes on to suggest the form these leaks have taken:

> Capitalism has never formed a closed system in practice. Wars and slumps have destroyed immense quantities of output, incorporating huge accumulations of value, and prevented the production of more. Capital exports have diverted and frozen other accumulations for long stretches of time. A lot has, since World War II, filtered out in the production of arms. Each of these leaks has acted to slow the rise of the overall organic composition and the fall in the rate of profit.[59]

Kidron points out that there has always been one way in which capitalists use surplus value which prevents it being used to expand the means of production: when they use it on luxury goods for their own consumption. He suggests that spending by the state on arms — which has expanded enormously this century — should be regarded in the same way.

This argument was bitterly attacked by some 'orthodox' Marxists. It was, for instance, denounced by Ernest Mandel as being 'under the obvious influence of "fashionable" (ie. bourgeois) economics', as resting on 'a truly remarkable confusion between use values and exchange values'.[60]

But insults aside, there is an attempt at an argument against Kidron. All goods that are produced, says Mandel, have the same status (providing they can be sold and the surplus value embodied in them realised). Kidron's mistakes lie in that:

> He is patently confusing the *process of production* and the process of reproduction. When the capital invested in the various branches of production has been valorised and the commodities in its possession have been sold at their price of production, the surplus value from this capital has been realised, irrespective of whether or not the commodities sold enter into the process of reproduction.

In a footnote Mandel goes on to criticise me for an article I wrote defending Kidron's account:

Harman claims that the drain of capital into Department III takes capital away from Departments I and II which would have increased the organic composition if it had been invested there. He is quite right. But he forgets that the investment of this capital in Department III likewise raises the organic composition of capital there. How it can stop the rate of profit falling remains a mystery. [62]

Perhaps if Mandel had read the **Grundrisse** (let alone Mike Kidron or myself) a little more closely, he might have had the key to the 'mystery'.

What he (following many students of Marx in this century) refers to as 'Department III' is the section of the economy which produces goods for consumption by the capitalists and their hangers-on. These are goods used neither for the means of production nor to be exchanged (via money) with workers for their labour power.

Such goods, by definition, do not enter into 'productive consumption'. Goods which form part of the means of production pass on their value to new goods as they are consumed in the production process. Goods which form part of the real wage of workers pass on their value as the workers who consume them create value and surplus value. Goods which are consumed in one way or another by the capitalists end their life without passing their value on to anything else.

The value which is contained in these goods has come into existence through past labour — on this even Mandel is agreed. But it soon passes out of existence without contributing to further capital accumulation — in this respect Mandel is wrong, for it differs radically from the value contained in 'wage goods' and means of production. [63]

OK, it might be said, but can't Mandel be right on another point? Kidron implies that production of arms takes place with a higher organic composition of capital than average. Won't this immediately lower the rate of profit throughout the economy as a whole, regardless of any effect it might have in reducing the future organic composition of capital?

Kidron himself relied upon the technical formula devised by the (non-Marxist) Polish economist of the turn of the century, von Bortkiewicz, for working out prices from labour values (the so-called 'solution to the transformation problem'). This showed that the rate of profit was not affected by the organic composition in parts of the economy producing luxury goods for the consumption of the capitalist class itself.

This use of von Bortkiewicz has been attacked on the grounds that he was not a Marxist [64] and that his equations rest on assumptions at variance with Marx's whole approach. [65] There are problems with von Bortkiewicz's method. [66] But recently both Anwar Shaikh and

Miguel Angel Garcia have produced derivations of prices from labour values, *using Marx's own method* systematically applied.[67] It is easy to see how you can draw the 'von Bortkiewicz' conclusion from them.

According to Marx, if one part of the economy has a higher organic composition of capital than another, then it would, other things being equal, have a lower rate of profit. But this would lead firms to threaten to move away from this area of production, reducing the supply of goods until prices rose and pushed profit rates up to the average level of the economy. Effectively, by a rise in its prices and a relative fall in the prices of goods it gets from the rest of the economy, enough surplus value would be transferred from other areas of production to raise its rate of profit to the average.

As a result prices diverge from labour values. Let us see how this works out for different sectors of production: for Department I, those industries producing the means of production themselves; Department II, where goods are produced for the consumption of the workers; and Department III, which produces everything else — including luxury goods for the non-productive rich, and armaments.

Department I

A rise in the organic composition of capital in Department I, the sector which produces the means of production, means that the investment per worker increases. Investment grows faster than the source of surplus value, so there is downward pressure on the rate of profit in this part of the economy.

The fall in the rate of profit in one Department reduces the average rate of profit for the economy as a whole. But not all firms are affected by this immediately: at first, firms in Department I find they are getting a rate of profit lower than the average, while those elsewhere are getting higher. It is therefore more profitable to invest in Departments II and III.

Capital begins to flow out of Department I, reducing output there. Because demand for the goods produced by Department I now exceeds supply, their prices begin to rise, increasing profits for those firms still in Department I. Correspondingly, the increased capital invested in the other Departments raises output, increases competition, and brings prices down, reducing profits.

The result of this process is that the profits in all Departments eventually stabilise at the new average rate of profit, now lower than previously. The rise in prices in Department I will balance the fall in the rest of the economy, since the amount of value being produced remains the same.

But the process doesn't stop there. A second stage follows.

When the next round of production takes place, the cost of means of production is higher as a result of the price rises in Department I.

This raises overall production costs.

But those price rises were balanced by price reductions in Departments II and III. Goods from Department II — that is, food, clothing, heating, housing, everything that is needed to maintain the workers — have fallen in price. The same standard of living can be maintained on slightly lower wages — and firms can take advantage of this by reducing the level of real wages, which reduces production costs.

This fall in the cost of labour partly compensates for the rise in the cost of means of production, but only *partly* — because the fall in prices in Department III, luxury goods and armaments, does *not* feed back into the production process and so is lost.

So the overall result is that production costs increase slightly and the rate of profit falls a little more.

Department II

An increase in the organic composition of capital in Department II, the sector producing goods for workers' consumption, has an effect similar to that in Department I. The rate of profit in Department II falls; capital begins to flow out; and changes in output and prices follow which bring the whole economy on to a new, lower average rate of profit.

In stage two it is now the cost of *labour* which has risen, now partly compensated for by a fall in the cost of the means of production — but again only partly, because again the fall in the price of luxury goods and armaments from Department III does not come back into the production process.

So the average rate of profit falls, and then falls a little more.

Department III

Department III is the sector of the economy producing goods which are neither means of production themselves, nor goods for the consumption of workers who take part in the production process. They include luxury goods for the non-productive rich, and armaments.

At the first stage, a rise in the organic composition of capital here has the same effect as it does in Departments I and II. The rate of profit tends to fall; capital begins to move out; output falls and the prices of luxury goods and arms rise — followed by the other changes in output and prices which bring the whole economy on to the new, lower average rate of profit.

But things are very different at stage two. The prices of luxuries and armaments are now higher, of course, but none of these feed back into the production process at the next round of production — so there is no further increase in production costs to push down the rate of profit yet further.

In fact, because the prices of means of production from Department I and consumer goods from Department II *have both fallen*, overall production costs will be reduced. The result will be to *raise* the rate of profit in the next round of production.

So, whereas a rise in the organic composition in Department I or II causes the rate of profit to fall and fall again, a similar rise in Department III causes it to fall . . . *and then rise again!*[68]

So investment in the output of goods for 'unproductive consumption' has two peculiar features. Firstly, any investment in this sector, by destroying surplus value, reduces the pressure throughout the system for the organic composition to rise. Secondly, it also reduces the *effect* of any such rise on the rate of profit.

These two effects clearly have immense implications for the dynamic of the capitalist system, in so far as it is determined by the rate of profit.

Aging capitalism, unproductive expenditures and new dimensions of competition

> As capitalist production, accumulation and wealth become developed, the capitalist ceases to be the mere incarnation of capital. The progress of capitalist production not only creates a world of delights; it lays open, in speculation and the credit system, a thousand sources of individual enrichment. When a certain stage of development has been reached, a conventional degree of prodigality, which is also an exhibition of wealth and consequently a source of credit, becomes a business necessity . . . Luxury enters into the expenses of representation.[69]

Thus Marx suggests in passing in **Capital** that capitalism, which initially flourished through the destruction of preceding societies with their vast superstructure of unproductive classes, becomes sluggish as it becomes old and thereby creates its own non-productive superstructure.

In his discussion of commercial capital and commercial profit, he argues that with the expansion of the system, industrial capital has to surrender an increasing amount of surplus value to finance the unproductive buying and selling of its output.

> It is clear that as the scale of production is extended, commercial operations required constantly for the recirculation of industrial capital . . . multiply accordingly . . . the more developed the scale of production, the greater . . . the commercial operations of industrial capital.[70]

Successful capitalist competition is no longer (if it ever was) just a matter of accumulating more rapidly than one's rivals. It increasingly involves spending surplus value on ways of manipulating the market, advertising goods, creating a 'product image', bribing buyers in firms and state agencies. 'Non-productive' expenditures become increasingly significant for each individual capital. They are the price to be paid for adding a whole new dimension to the competitive struggle.

These expenditures are 'non-productive' because, although they nearly always involve the hiring of labour power, this does not produce surplus value. It merely enables the hirer to gain control of surplus value that would otherwise have gone to another capital. That is why Marx refers to them as part of neither variable capital nor constant capital, but as something else, 'the expenses of production'. Yet he also hints that the individual capitalist may regard them as 'productive' in certain circumstances — he has to invest in them if he is to get his appropriate share of the total surplus value already created.

> To industrial capital the costs of circulation appear as unproductive expenses, and so they are. To the merchant they appear as a source of profit, proportional given the general rate of profit, to their size. The outlay to be made on these circulation costs is therefore productive investment for mercantile capital . . . And the commercial labour which it buys is likewise immediately productive for it.[71]

Such areas of 'unproductive' expenditure have grown massively since Marx's time, with the spread of advertising and such like. The development of finance capital has meant the growth of a vast range of activities not concerned with the production of wealth, but rather with the sharing out of surplus value among members of the capitalist class, all at great expense. The stock exchange is the prime example.

Other sorts of expenditures which are unproductive for the individual capital, but essential for its continuance, have grown as well. The elimination of pre-capitalist forms of exploitation more or less everywhere means that the expenses of the state have to be borne by the surplus created in capitalist production. Some of these state expenses are not only unproductive in the sense that they do not add to the creation of surplus value; they do not aid the ability of some capitals to get more surplus value out of the common stock held by the capitalist class as a whole in the course of competition either. They are necessary simply in order to maintain the structures of exploitation — such as spending on the police, on the education system where it acts to maintain the current ideology, on priests in state-financed churches, on social security payments aimed at preventing the permanently unemployed from rioting.

But others do aid the individual capitals to engage productive labour themselves — such as expenditure on the health and education of workers, on keeping unemployed workers on the labour market, on reassuring employed workers that they will be able to survive when they are too old to work. These are what some modern Marxist writers refer to as 'reproductive' expenditures, others as 'indirectly productive' and still others as 'necessary non-productive'. The best way to see them is as 'non-productive' for the individual capital competing within the closed national market, since although it has to pay for them, they give it no advantage over its rivals who likewise benefit from them. To it they are more or less the same as having to pay more for labour power. But for the aggregate of capitalists (or the 'state capitalist trust') operating within one state in their competition with capitalists from other states they are in a sense 'productive': for they ensure that the workers are capable of producing as much as the workers employed by their 'foreign' rivals. [72]

Finally, there are the military expenditures of the state. We have referred already to the contentions of the classic theorists of imperialism that the monopolisation of capital leads to its growing together with the state, and to war and the preparation for war becoming one — if not the main — means by which nationally-based capitals try to drive each other to the wall. As the twentieth century has proceeded, military expenditures have come to consume massive amounts of surplus value, until some estimates suggest that they consume as much as the productive investments of individual capitals. [73]

Like expenditures on the police, military expenditures do not increase either the output of the individual capitalist or the 'aggregate' capitalist. But like expenditures on advertising they enable one bloc of capital — the 'aggregate' national capital, the 'state capitalist trust' — to encroach on the surplus value in the hands of other capitalists.

Addressing the Fourth Congress of the Communist International in 1922, Nicolai Bukharin suggested that

> Competition between various industrialists whose methods consisted in lowering the price of commodities . . . is almost the only form of competition mentioned by Marx. But in the epoch of imperialist competition we find many other forms of competition wherein the method of reducing prices is of no significance. The main groups of the bourgeoisie are now of the nature of trustified groups within the framework of the state . . . It is quite conceivable that such a form of enterprise should resort chiefly to violent forms of competition . . . Thus arise the new forms of competition which lead to military attack by the state. [74]

The argument can be rephrased. In Marx's model of capitalism there is only one dimension of competition, that based upon competition for markets through the accumulation of productive investments aimed at reducing costs and so also selling prices. But as capitalism gets older new dimensions of competition supplement and even on occasions replace this. [75]

Any assessment of capitalism in the twentieth century has to look at how these new dimensions of competition, and the various expenditures of surplus value which accompany them, affect the basic dynamic of the system and the 'law of the falling rate of profit'.

Different dimensions of competition and the falling rate of profit

With some of the new forms of competition there is not a great deal to discuss. Marx himself, for instance, dealt very well with the effects of expenditure on the selling of goods (what he referred to as 'merchants' capital). Such expenditure does not increase the total amount of surplus value. But the productive capitalists are forced by competitive pressures either to engage in such expenditure themselves or to pay part of their surplus value over to other capitalists to do the job for them, in proportion to the amount of investment undertaken by those capitalists. Such spending therefore serves to reduce the average rate of profit.[76]

At the same time, in so far as these expenditures divert funds from productive investment, they will serve to reduce the general pressure for the capitalist class as a whole to increase the organic composition of capital, and will reduce long-term pressures on the rate of profit.

The real problem arises when we come to the question of the effect of arms expenditure. This cannot simply reduce the rate of profit — if only because the period in which peace-time expenditures on arms reached an all-time high (1949 onwards) was a period in which capitalism no longer seemed condemned by the 'falling rate of profit' to stagnation and crises.[77] Hence attempts to treat arms as a form of 'luxury' expenditure by the ruling class.[78]

If arms *are* 'luxury' expenditure, then expenditure on them both offsets the pressures for the organic composition of capital to rise progressively *and*, through the process outlined above, may not in the long term cause the average rate of profit to fall. Of course, capitalists have to use some of their surplus value to pay for them. But since the state represents the sum of the capitalists operating from its territory, this is merely a question of how capitalists expend the surplus value they already possess, and cannot alter the fact that they possess it, or the ratio of the total surplus value to the total investment — the rate of profit.

Such an account has the advantage of providing some sort of explanation of why capitalism was able to expand after 1945 for nearly 30 years without running into the crises that seemed endemic until then.

What exactly happened in this period will be looked at in detail in chapter three. But before we can understand changes in the rate of profit and dynamic of the system under aging capitalism, we must look at ways in which different dimensions of competition, with different implications for the organic composition and the rate of profit, reinforce or contradict one another.

Each form of competition has the same goal: the preservation and expansion of the individual capital (or aggregate national capital) through gaining control of surplus value which would otherwise accrue to rival capitals. But this does not mean that all are equally effective at each stage in the development of the global system. At any particular point, from the point of view of the particular capital (or national capital), one form of competition is likely to be seen as most effective and therefore as most important, and other forms as a diversion from success in this.

The case Marx considered was one in which relatively small-scale capitalist enterprises were expanding within what was still a pre-dominantly pre-capitalist world and were doing so very successfully on the basis of 'pure' economic competition through the price mechanism. Under such circumstances, expenditures on the state were necessarily seen as a diversion of the individual capital's surplus value from areas of investment which would produce its self-expansion.

It is easy to suggest cases in which things would operate quite differently: situations in which military expenditure would seem to provide the individual capitals of a particular country with better opportunities for expansion than expenditure oriented to price competition, or even situations in which investment oriented to price competition would seem like a diversion from the major means of preserving and augmenting individual capitals' military expenditures.

There is the situation where the rate of profit is so low that individual enterprises are unwilling to embark of new investments. Without new investments there is massive excess capacity in whole sectors of industry, goods are being dumped at below their value, there is massive 'overproduction'. Even attempts by the state to mobilise the mass of surplus value for investment seems unlikely to be able to produce goods at a low enough cost to break into new markets.

Under such circumstances, military expenditures can seem like a way of directing otherwise idle surplus value into channels that can be used to expand the share of the home market available to 'national capitalists', by forcibly closing it to outsiders through protectionist methods, and can then go on to forcibly prise open foreign markets at present protected by foreign states.

The fact that such arms spending does not actually create any fresh value at all need not worry them: it provides them with access to surplus value created via the use of means of production belonging to foreign capitalists. It expands national capital more than civilian investment would, even if it does not expand capital in general. Under this set of circumstances, although arms expenditure is motivated by other considerations than the luxury consumption of the capitalist class and its hangers on, it has the same effect on the rate of profit. It neither cuts it in the short term, since it is simply a matter of how capitalists freely decide to use their already existing surplus value. Nor does it necessarily cut it in the long term, since even if it involves a high organic composition of capital, the 'von Bortkiewicz effect' may prevent this reducing the average rate of profit. And in addition it reduces the long-term pressure for the organic composition to rise.

Then there is the situation in which arms expenditure seems the *only* effective dimension of competition, as in the all-out wars of 1914–18 and 1939–45. In such circumstances capitalists no longer have a choice. They have to spend money on arms if they are to survive. They hope that this will, through victory, enable them to gain access to new sources of surplus value and thus to expand their capitals. But they have to undertake it even if these hopes are meagre, since the alternative is the loss of their existing sources of surplus value to foreign capitalists. Arms spending is now as much a cost of continuing in production as is expenditure on the police.

At such a point, the rate of profit for the individual capitalist must fall, unless the rate of exploitation of the workforce can be forced up enormously. Arms as a cost of maintaining production have cut right into surplus value in the hands of the capitalist class here. But it is no longer the rate of profit of the individual capitalist which matters. Total war, by definition, means that considerations of price competition become completely subordinate to considerations of military survival. If capitalist relations still prevail, it is because the efforts or the rival capitals to outshoot each other mean that each has to reduce the price of labour to the minimum in order to invest the surplus in producing more arms. Investment decisions become military, state, decisions, over-riding the decisions of particular owners of capital.[79]

The effects of the tendency of the rate of profit to decline now express themseves at the level of state decision-making, in terms of reducing the ability of the state both to engage in military activity it needs in order to survive, let alone win, *and* to expand (or even simply reproduce) the existing level of non-military production.

Finally, there is the situation under aging capitalism where the trend is towards an interaction of military and economic competition. At such a stage, the dimensions of price competition and military competition must come into contradiction. Success in both depends upon past levels of accumulation. But one involves further raising those levels through reproductive expenditures. The other involves, instead, non-reproductive expenditure, which it is hoped, will lead to the grabbing of surplus value produced elsewhere in the system. A certain level of military expenditure therefore cuts one's ability to engage in price competition. Yet today war itself has become so expensive and dangerous that it is not easy to use military power in order to protect a national capitalism from the effects of such price competition — especially in export markets.

Over time, the heavy arms spenders can be expected to grow economically more slowly than the non-so-heavy arms spenders. This is, of course, what has happened over the past two decades, with the US growing more slowly than Japan and West Germany (and now, with the USSR tending to grow more slowly than the US). This can be put another way: those with most 'leaks' offsetting the tendency of organic competition to rise, grow more slowly than those with fewer leaks. The world-wide organic composition of capital will rise under such circumstances, until increases in the rate of exploitation can no longer prevent a fall in the rate of profit.

Conclusion

So far we have attempted to deal, at an abstract level, with the dynamics of the system as depicted by Marx, and the factors (including those pointed out by Marx himself) which could offset the basic dynamic at various points in the development of the system.

It has been argued that as the system gets older, the individual units of capital become a bigger and bigger proportion of the total system, making it more difficult for these offsetting factors to work — whether you are referring to crises, colonial expansion, or unproductive expenditure on war preparations. If this is true, we should expect Marx's prediction of a hundred years ago concerning the long-term trends in the system to begin to be realised.

We now need to go beyond such abstract, general considerations to look at the actual trends of capitalism in the twentieth century and its development today. That will be the aim of the next two chapters.

Chapter 2: The crisis last time

AS CAPITALISM AGES, it finds it more and more difficult to overcome the pressures leading to stagnation and deep crises. Its efforts to do so involve measures that are in themselves increasingly devastating to the system and those who live in it.

To recap, the basic contradiction in the system is the way in which the scale of investment tends to rise much more quickly than the source of profit (labour power), so producing a decline in the rate of profit. The main factors that could offset this tendency are three fold: the destruction of certain capitals to the benefit of others through periodic crises; the flow of investment away from old areas of capitalist development into new ones through imperialism; the employment of a growing proportion of the investable surplus value in ways which aid particular sections of capital in their competition with other sectors but do not contribute to productive accumulation – such as marketing costs and arms.

Each of these factors could operate for a certain period of capitalist development. But as the system came to fill the whole globe, as the units grew ever larger and ever more interdependent, as the scale of production required to remain 'viable' (whether in economic or military terms) grew ever more immense, each factor became less useful to the system and more destructive in its side effects. The period in which economic expansion had been rapid gave way to one of immense crises – the crisis years of the 1870s and 1880s, the crisis years between the wars, and now the crisis years that started in the early 1970s.

To see how this happened, we need to look at each phase of capitalist development in turn.

The first phase: classical capitalism

Capitalism in its classical phase is that described by Marx. Units of production (firms) were usually small compared with the market. Periodic crises drove certain firms to the wall, allowing others to resume their expansion in an unhindered fashion. If the long-term rate of profit tended to fall, the fall was not on such a scale as to deter firms from joining in a vigorous surge of investment after each crisis. This was the period in which industrial capitalism expanded out with great speed from its initial bases in Britain and Belgium to the beginnings of industrialisation in the USA, Germany, Scandinavia and France, and with the opening up to capitalist trade of almost all of the rest of the world.

But with the so-called 'Great Depression' of the 1870s and 1880s this initial rapid expansion slowed down. The US and Germany were hit by severe depression which lasted several years in 1873. Revival came at the end of the 1870s, but only to be followed by further crises in the US in 1884.

By 1889, the steel magnate Andrew Carnegie could express the feelings of many industrialists:

> Manufacturers . . . see savings of many years . . . becoming less and less, with no hope of a change in the situation. It is in a soil thus prepared that anything promising of relief is gladly welcomed. The manufacturers are in the position of patients that have tried in vain every doctor of the regular school for years, and are now liable to become the victim of any quack that appears . . .[1]

Yet for the 1870s and 1880s as a whole, the American and German economies still enjoyed considerable growth. These were the decades of the first sustained industrialisation of Germany, and in the US 'production in spite of cyclical fluctuations, mounted steadily, from $3,336 million in 1869 to $9,372 million in 1889 . . .'[2]

It was Britain – which in the 1870s still produced between 40 and 50 per cent of the world output of key goods such as iron and steel, coal and textiles – that suffered most. The initial slump was not as severe as in Germany and the US. But recovery was not as sustained either and for two decades the pattern was one of stagnation interspersed with relatively short periods of boom.

The climate of the times has been well described by historian Eric Hobsbawm: 'Both new and old industrial economies ran into problems of markets and profit margins . . . As the titanic profits of the industrial pioneers declined, businessmen searched anxiously for a way out.'[3]

This was to be found in the transition from classical capitalism to monopoly capitalism and imperialism.

Monopolies and imperialism

The way out of the depression went, initially, by two separate routes.

In the US and Germany there were further waves of bankruptcies and mergers, leading to a massive restructuring of industry under the control of relatively large concerns. 'The formation of trusts, cartels, syndicates and so on ... characterised Germany and the USA in the 1880s,' wrote Hobsbawm.[4] This was the period in the US when the 'robber barons' such as Rockefeller, Carnegie and Morgan bought up rival concerns on the cheap and established their dominating position:

> By 1897 there were 82 industrial combinations with a capitalisation of more than $1000 million, in the three years 1898-1900 eleven great combinations were formed with a capitalisation of $1,140 million, and the greatest combination of all, the United States Steel Corporation, appeared in 1901 with a capitalisation of $1,400 million.[5]

This restructuring of capital allowed a certain amount of writing off of old capital and a deployment of resources into production using technologies that could not be adopted in countries (such as Britain) where the restructuring did not take place. It allowed the new giant firms to protect their profits by monopoly pricing at the expense of weaker competitors. So expansion could continue at quite a fast speed through the twenty-year 'depression' and afterwards, even though the organic composition of capital continued to rise rapidly – by 100 per cent between 1880 and 1912 according to one calculation, by 25 per cent between 1900 and 1918 according to another.[6] As Gillman notes: 'The organic composition of capital displays a fairly persistent tendency to rise' in this period, although 'it was a fairly slow rise compared to Marx's hypothetical example.'[7] All the same the economy could grow at a rapid pace, with output doubling between 1890 and 1907.[8]

But there was another path out of the crisis years of the 1870s and 1880s. This was that followed by British capitalism. Rationalisation through mergers and bankruptcies was avoided by using Britain's imperial might to provide safe markets and outlets for investment in the Empire, dominions, and other areas under British influence (such as parts of South America).

> Britain was disinclined to take the path of systematic economic concentration ... She was too deeply committed to the technology and business organisation of the first phase of industrialisation. This left one major way out ... The economic (and increasingly political) conquest of hitherto unexploited areas of the world. In other words, imperialism ...[9]

Capital flowed overseas from Britain at an increasing speed: 'the total investment in foreign and colonial stock, which was £95 million in 1883, rose to £393 million in 1889.'[10] The outflow rose to about 8 per cent of the gross national product and absorbed about 50 per cent of savings.[11]

The pressure on individual capitalists to engage in 'capital-intensive' innovations at home was reduced, and the development of the system could take place with a minimum of restructuring through bankruptcies and mergers. In fact the capital-output ratio actually *fell* from the 1880s onwards. It rose from 2.02 in 1855-64, to 2.11 in 1865-76, to 2.16 in 1875-83. From then it fell to 2.08 in 1884-90 and to 1.82 in 1891-1901. At the same time, the near doubling in the rate of bankruptcies that marked the 1870s gave way to a fall. In 1884-88 they numbered 8,662, falling to 7,521 in 1889-93, to 6,417 in 1894-98, to 6,017 in 1899-1903, and to 5,965 in 1904-09.[12]

The two paths out of the crisis years of 'classical capitalism' could not diverge indefinitely. They were bound to remerge, producing what Marxist writers of the early part of the century called 'monopoly capitalism', 'finance capitalism' or 'imperialism'.

The continued rise in the organic composition of capital in the US and Germany meant that profit rates were eventually bound to come under pressure. Employers could attempt to compensate for this, as they did in Germany, by halting the rise in real wages that had been experienced in the 1890s, and by turning to new techniques based on increased productivity – the first use of mass production techniques. But they were also bound to be attracted by the English solution – to using the forces of the national state to carve out areas of economic and political privilege for themselves overseas. Hence from the 1890s onwards there were the first attempts by Germany and the US to develop formal empires and informal spheres of influence. Among the results were the German colonies in Tanganyika and South West Africa, the drive towards German hegemony over parts of central and eastern Europe, the alliance with the decaying Turkish empire and the American war with Spain. But such an outward expansion could only come into collision with the established empires and spheres of influence of Britain and France, putting into question the mechanism by which British capitalism had emerged from the crisis years. In the end, only all-out war could resolve the question as to who was to dominate where.

While the great concentrations of capital in the US and Germany moved towards imperialism in Britain's footsteps, British capitalism began, belatedly, along the road of restructuring and concentration of capital. The first decade of the twentieth century saw a number of significant mergers, especially in banking, where five banks came to dominate the field, and the adoption of new techniques in certain industries. But this could not stop renewed pressure on the rate of profit via the organic composition of capital, as the capacity of the Empire to absorb investable funds became exhausted – the inflow of interest and dividend from the overseas investments came to exceed the outflow of new investments. The capital-output ratio began to rise once again, according to one calculation from 1.92 in 1891-1902 to 2.19 in 1908-13.[13]

The First World War was thus the product of the previous forty years, of the transformation of classical capitalism into a monopoly capitalism that more and more depended on imperialist expansion to overcome its internal contradictions. But the war also served to accentuate these trends. In all the major powers the concentration of industry now proceeded at a much accelerated pace, supervised by the state, which stepped in to organise the major industries directly while the war lasted. New technologies which might have taken two decades to come into effect were pushed through in two years. New patterns of work – based upon mass production and the 'dilution' of old skills – were rammed through with great speed. And, as the war cut off many of the trade links that had been established over the previous half century, a boost was given to capitalist development in many agrarian countries – such as the dominions, India, China and Spain).

Yet in terms of the dynamics of the system the war had opposite effects in Europe and the US. In Europe it served to destroy considerable quantities of value – as surplus value which would otherwise have been accumulated was turned into arms and as war damaged and destroyed industrial plant. Some calculations suggest that the combined industrial production of the powers involved in the war was 30 per cent less in 1919 than in 1914[14]. In Britain it has been estimated that the war cut the capital-output ratio (and therefore the organic composition of capital) from 2.19 in 1908-13 to 2.02 in 1922-30[15].

In the US, on the other hand, the war gave a boost to industrial production and the organic composition tended to rise. One calculation has manufacturing industry's organic composition rising from 3.2 in 1912 to 4.3 in 1919 and 5.6 in 1921.[16] Another has that of all 'productive' industry rising from 3.18 in 1910 to 3.65 in 1920 and 3.95 in 1925[17].

After the war it was increasingly what happened in the US that mattered from the point of view of the *world* system. The war served to move the centre of gravity of the system across the Atlantic, as America's share in the total world production shot upwards. Thus in the 1920s a large, relatively prolonged (seven-year) expansion of the American economy provided the means by which the German economy could overcome the effects of the war. The old pattern of European investment in America had now given way to a new pattern of US investment in Europe. Through the Dawes and Young plans the US financed the expansion of German industry.

At first the new dependence of Europe on America seemed wholly beneficial. Despite a sharp recession in 1921, until 1929 US industrial production rose in what seemed at the time a near miraculous boom, until it was double the 1914 figure. A whole host of new industries grew up – radio, rayon, chemicals, aviation, refrigeration – the wave of car production that had begun in 1915 really took off, and there was substantial re-equipment of industry on the basis of electrification. The average level of profits rose, so that in 1929 profits were 22.9 per cent higher than in 1923.[18]

The boom in the US found its echo in Europe. In Germany industrial production rose 40 per cent above the 1922 level. And in France it doubled. Only in Britain, with its declining older industries not yet supplanted by new ones, did the economy remain more or less permanently depressed, with production not reaching the 1919 figure until 1929.

No wonder that by 1927 or 1928 economists abounded who declared that capitalism had overcome its previous tendency towards crisis. So, for example, Alvin H. Hansen could write in 1927 that the 'childhood diseases' of capitalism's youth were 'being mitigated' and the 'character of the business cycle was changing', while in Germany Werner Sombart insisted that since 1875 'there has been a clear tendency in European economic life for antagonistic tendencies to balance each other, to grow less and finally to disappear.'[19]

Yet all these hopes came tumbling down in 1929. The period of monopoly capitalism ended, as had the period of 'classical' capitalism, in prolonged economic crisis. But this period of crisis was much more devastating than its predecessor. While the 'great depression' of the late 1870s and 1880s witnessed a considerable overall growth of output and a massive expansion of foreign trade (it trebled from 1869 to 1892),[20] the slump from 1929 onwards saw considerable falls in both. World industrial production dropped by a third, American production by 46.2 per cent, French production by 29.4 per cent. Only British production fell by a smaller amount, but it was starting from an already depressed figure. Never before had there been a slump that had been so deep, or lasted so long. Three years after the slump had begun in the US and Germany, there was no sign of any upward movement at all. And the slump hit all the industrial countries at once, not only driving their industries to the wall, but also destroying demand for the output of the agricultural countries, knocking the bottom out of the prices they received and driving their populations to dire misery.

The crisis of the 1930s

Among Marxists the most popular explanations of the crisis of the 1930s have been the 'underconsumptionist' sort of theories of Baran and Sweezy, Gillman, Sternberg.[21] These start from the fact that in the US economy of the 1920s there was a sharp divergence between a high growth of output and a limited growth of wages and consumption. Gross industrial production grew by about a third between 1922 and the beginning of 1929, but real wages by a mere 6.1 per cent and total consumption by only 18 per cent. Between 1927 and 1929 total manufactured output rose nearly 14 per cent, but consumption only about 5½ per cent.[22]

It was easy to draw the conclusion that the crisis was to be explained in terms of a famous quotation from Marx:

> The ultimate reason for all real crises always remains the poverty and restricted consumption of the masses as opposed to the drive of capitalist production to develop the productive forces of society as though the absolute consuming power of society constituted their only limit.[23]

But Marx differs from such 'underconsumptionists' by filling in an important gap in the argument. They cannot really explain why for long periods of time capitalism is able to sustain booms and avoid crises. Marx is able to do so because he insists that the demand for goods depends upon production. Of course, what workers can buy with their wages is always less than the total product – otherwise there would be no profits. But providing capitalists continue to accumulate this should not matter: their investment in expanded means of production can ensure that there is a demand for that portion of output not going to workers' consumption.

It is only if new accumulation fails to use the portion of the social product left after providing for workers' consumption that crises of overproduction can occur.

This explains the crucial importance of the long-term tendencies of the rate of profit. If the motive force for new investment gets weaker, then overproduction becomes a real possibility. But when looking at any particular crisis, it is not sufficient to say simply 'falling rate of profit, onset of crisis', because all sorts of intermediary factors can be involved.

The rate of profit had been falling in the US until the early 1920s, (according to the calculations of Mage and Gillman) but no real decline is shown after that; it tended, if anything, to rise. Gillman has it falling from 69 per cent in 1880 to 50 per cent in 1900 to 29 per cent in 1919 and 1923, but then rising again to 32 per cent in 1927. Mage's figures are different, but the trend is the same. He has it at 10.84 per cent in 1900, and 12.97 per cent in 1903. Thereafter it falls to 12.03

per cent in 1911 and to 6.48 per cent in 1919. But then it rises again to 7.19 per cent in 1923 and 7.96 per cent in 1928.[24]

What does seem to be the case, however, is that the rising organic composition of capital had already diminished the rate of profit sufficiently, *before* 1919, to produce a decline in the rate of productive accumulation. According to Steindl, the rate of accumulation in the period 1879-99 was 5 per cent a year; it fell to less than 3 per cent a year in the 1920s.[25]

According to Gillman,[26] capital formation fell from between 13 and 14 per cent in the 1890s and 1900s to 10.2 per cent in 1919-28. Baran and Sweezy claim that this 'stagnationary' tendency found reflection in the fact that the pre-war crises after 1907 were more severe than those before.[27]

By the 1920s the rate of profit was no longer high enough to sustain a level of productive accumulation that would absorb all the surplus value in the US economy. This opened up a gap between the total social production and total social productive consumption (wages plus productive accumulation) which meant overproduction – unless it was filled by something else. The reaction of individual employers to the relatively low rate of profit – increased exploitation of the workforce while keeping wage increases to a minimum – could only increase this gap. The organic composition of capital was already so high that an increase in the total profit did not markedly increase the ratio of total profit to means and materials of production. The rate of profit could not rise enough to provide outlets for the growing mass of funds seeking investment.

The blind self-expansion of capital led to an ever-greater accumulation of constant capital compared with living labour. This expressed itself in one way in the long-term decline in the rate of profit; in another in the creation of productive potential that could only be anything like fully utilised if the low consumption of the masses was supplemented by ever larger new accumulations of capital. 'Overproduction' and the low rate of profit were two sides of the same coin.

The low level of accumulation in the 1920s did not, however, lead to a slump before 1929 because the gap between total productive consumption and the total social product was filled by the *nonproductive* forms of consumption.

In part this was simply a case of luxury consumption by the ruling and middle classes. According to a pioneer Marxist analyst of the period, Lewis Corey, 'the bourgeoisie' (in which he includes the non-farm petty bourgeoisie) were responsible for 42.9 per cent of consumption.[28] For him 'the equilibrium of capitalist production came to depend more and more on artificially stimulating the "wants" of small groups of people with excess purchasing power.'[29]

This luxury consumption was supplemented by a typical product of aging capitalism – the tendency of each capital to spend more and more in ways which did not add to the total surplus value, but which did attract to itself a greater share of the already created surplus value. According to Corey distribution costs of US industry grew from 30 per cent of consumer prices in 1870 to 59 per cent in 1930.[30] Advertising revenue alone amounted to $2000 million in 1929[31] – only 25 per cent less than total expenditure on plant and equipment in manufacturing industries. Gillman argues that 'non-productive expenses' (advertising, marketing costs and so on) grew from half the total surplus value in 1919 to two thirds by the end of the 1920s.[32]

Finally, the very search for profitable investment outlets for vast accumulations of funds itself created a temporary means of absorbing excess surplus value. A succession of speculative booms pushed stock market and real estate prices to dizzy heights. These in themselves did not absorb surplus value (they merely transferred investible funds from one set of hands to another) but they did involve a great deal of unproductive expenditure as a by-product (new buildings, salaries to unproductive personnel, conspicuous consumption) and led to a certain amount of resources going into 'productive' enterprises that could not have been thought of as profitable if a speculative climate had not existed.

> Superabundant capital became more and more aggressive and adventurous in its search for investment and profit, overflowing into risky enterprises and speculation. Speculation seized upon technical changes and new industries which were introduced regardless of the requirements of industry as a whole . . .[33]

All these factors had one thing in common. Although they served temporarily to speed up the tempo of economic activity and to ensure that a demand existed for virtually everything that the productive parts of the economy produced, they all depended, in the last resort, upon the productive economy. The moment it experienced any serious setback, they would all fall – and the profitability of the productive sector would be further hurt as the demand for its products fell, cutting prices until they were below costs. The speculative frenzy could give an added boost to the boom, could even sustain it for longer than otherwise – but once the boom began to wilt, the collapse of the speculative frenzy could drag the rest of the economy even further down.

In reality, the underlying productive economy was weak. As we have seen, the rate of accumulation was low throughout the 1920s. In no year did the number of workers in manufacturing exceed the 1919 figure. Excess productive capacity was available throughout the period: even in the 'boom' year of 1928 there was 18 per cent unused industrial capacity.[34] It has been claimed that by 1928 'most American industries were capable of producing from 25 per cent to 75 per cent more goods than the market could absorb.'[35]

Marx, in volume three of **Capital**, discusses the exact ways in which a boom suddenly begins to turn into a slump. He suggests three mechanisms, which can work together or separately.

The first is the way in which, as the boom eats into unemployment, wage rates are forced up and the rate of exploitation is reduced, until the least profitable firms are forced out of business, pulling other firms down with them. But although wages did rise a little in 1927-9, this did not seem to have been a real precipitating factor, given the much greater rise of total production.[36]

The second is the disproportion that can arise out of the blind competitive accumulation of different sections of the economy, so leading to 'partial' overproduction as some industries produce goods for which there is no demand. This certainly was the developing pattern in the US at the beginning of 1929. The speculative frenzy led to the undertaking of more investments than in any year since 1920,[37] despite the large overcapacity that already existed. Some industries were bound to find that they could not sell all the goods they had produced and so could not get the funds needed to cover these investments. However, this in itself could not explain why this partial overcapacity and overproduction in certain industries should lead to a *general* slump.

This depended on the third element in Marx's explanation – the role of credit and interest. Capital investment is not a continual process for the industrial capitalist. It involves the buying or building of large material objects (factories and equipment) which embody large amounts of value. When these are put to work they pass their value on to products (which also embody the labour of the workers). But this passing on of the value of the plant and equipment does not occur all at once. It can take the capitalist many years to cover his capital costs and to get the sums of value necessary to undertake the similarly large investments needed to replace worn out plant and equipment. And so production undergoes a cycle in which large sums are paid out in one go and then small sums collected back over a long period of time.

While the capitalist is recuperating his costs in dribs and drabs he cannot immediately invest them himself. Under modern capitalism what he tends to do is to lend them to other capitalists – either via the stock exchange or more likely via the banks. And when he wants to make large investments, he does not necessarily wait until he has accumulated enough capital personally to do so, but he borrows – again from the stock exchange or via the banks. Financial institutions

serve as mediators between industrial capitalists[38] who are accumulating surplus value for future investment, and industrial capitalists
who are wanting to invest without waiting. Those who lend are
promised by those who borrow part of the surplus value to be created
as the investment is put to use.

This interest has to be deducted from the surplus value they make
– and so reduces the final amount of profit they have in their hands.
But one important discovery made by Marx was that the rate of
interest they paid was not determined by the same factors that determined the rate of profit they could make. In fact, at important points
in the industrial cycle, it would move in the opposite direction.

For what determines the rate of interest is the conflicting pressures
of supply and demand for loans. The supply of loanable capital to the
banks will be highest when the rate of profit in industry is highest –
when expansion is proceeding, but before wages have risen and before
any serious disproportions have arisen in the economy. The moment
the rate of profit in parts of the economy begins to fall – for instance,
because of partial overproduction – then the supply of loanable capital
will begin to fall. By contrast, it is precisely at this point that the
demand for loans will rise. Capitalists, in laying down large-scale
investments, use up much of the loanable capital, and when they find
they cannot sell sufficient goods to pay off the interest on these debts
they go to the banks for still more loans. The banks can respond by
granting these loans, and reducing the supply of credit still more, or
by pushing the firms to bankruptcy, thus destroying the market for
the goods of suppliers to those firms and raising *their* demand for
loans. In either case, just as a partial crisis of overproduction reduces
the supply of loanable capital, it raises the demand for it. This forces
up interest rates throughout the economy and *generalises the crisis*.[39]

The bankers do not cause the crisis, nor do the breakdowns in the
flow of credits, nor do high interest rates. High interest rates and
breakdowns in the flow of credits are, rather, a product of industrial
crisis. That is why it is useless in any crisis to moan, as do many
good-intentioned bourgeois economists (or bad-intentioned fascists)
about the role of the banks or the level of interest rates. The bankers
with their interest rates are merely one symptom of the general
irrationality of the capitalist mode of production.

Although the beginning of the slump of the thirties is usually
identified with the Wall Street Crash of 29 October 1929[40], the crisis
really began before that, in industry. In the US, Kindelberger rightly
notes, 'business was in trouble before the crash'.[41] Auto production
had fallen from 622,000 in March to 416,000 in September.[42] The
output of machinery began to fall from June onwards, until by the end
of the year new orders for machine tools and foundry equipment were

down 50 per cent with 10 per cent unemployment in the machine industry as a whole. Iron and steel output followed autos and machinery downwards from August, falling a total of 42 per cent in four months; construction too fell 52 per cent by the end of the year.[43] By September and October, industrial production as a whole was falling at an annual rate of 20 per cent.[44]

In Europe too the slump began before the Crash. Conditions were worst in Germany. Already at the beginning of the year one of the factors fuelling the stock exchange boom in the US was that American funds that had been invested short-term in Germany returned to the US as German investment opportunities became limited. 'Many German industries were reaching a saturation point in the rationalisation programme which followed in the wake of the world war and were approaching the end of the job of capital rebuilding . . . Forces were working to produce a sharp decline in the volume of American investments abroad . . .'[45] 'By the summer of 1929 the existence of depression was unmistakable'[46] as unemployment reached 1.9 million and the spectacular failure of the Frankfurt Insurance Company began a series of bankruptcies. The Belgian economy started declining from March onwards, and had fallen 7 per cent by the end of the year, while in Britain the turning point came in July. Only in France was production still rising at the time of the Crash.

But if the Wall Street Crash was a result of the industrial crisis, it reacted back on it to make it worse. Faced with declining sales, industrialists were already beginning to borrow from rather than lend to the banks. Those who had engaged in the speculative boom (including both industrialists and banks) now tried to borrow more in order to cover their losses after the crash. Those who could not borrow went bust, creating further losses for those who had been relying on them to repay debts. It suddenly became very difficult for businesses to balance their books and the slump spread from one sector of the economy to another. What happened in America also rebounded back on a Europe that had been floating upwards on the basis of US loans. Hard-hit American institutions recalled their short-term loans from Germany, creating difficulties for German industrialists who had been relying on them to finance their own industrial overcapacity. They reacted by borrowing funds from London, which in turn raised interest rates there and put increased pressure on British industrialists.

Once the decline started there seemed no end to it. Industrial decline produced the stock market crash and pressure on the banks, which in turn deepened industrial decline and put more pressure on the banks. Hundreds of locally based banks went bust in the US, and some of the giant banks of Europe collapsed spectacularly. Governments tried to ease the pressure on the banks by cutting their own expenditure. But that only further exacerbated the disproportion between productive capacity and consumer demand, further worsening the crisis in industry. The non-productive expenditure that helped to fuel the boom was cut right back as companies tried to conserve their funds, and the slump grew deeper.

The automatic market mechanisms which had always in the past been capable, at the end of the day, of lifting the economy out of crisis no longer seemed to be working. Three years after the crisis started, industrial production in the US, Germany, Britain and France was still declining. Unemployment worldwide had leapt from about 10 million in 1929 to 40 million in 1932:[47] in the US at one point nearly a third of the workforce was on the dole; in Germany there were six million unemployed by January 1933; in Britain the figure briefly rose above 20 per cent. World trade fell catastrophically to a third of its 1929 figure.

The aging of the system was taking its toll. It was no good any longer merely waiting for some capitals to collapse, so allowing others to expand at their expense. Such was the size of individual industrial or financial capitals that the collapse of any one dragged others down with it. Hence the characteristic pattern of the slump. The downturn in industry provoked the downturn in the stock exchange. The downturn in the stock exchange provoked further downturn in industry and the first bank closures. These in turn pulled still more of industry down. Then still more banks followed. As one avalanche followed another, it seemed that no-one was safe. The different parts of the system were so large and so closely intertwined that one capital could not devour another without threatening to destroy a source of its own livelihood.

This did not mean that there was no chance of a limited revival on such a basis. But it did mean that it could only occur after really massive destruction. So, for instance, there was the beginnings of some pickup in British industry in mid-1932. But this was after 12 years, rather than just three years, of high levels of unemployment in the old-established industries such as coal, iron and steel, shipbuilding; and the pickup very much left these industries aside since the new growth was in light engineering and motors.

The 1930s – from monopoly capitalism towards state capitalism.

Until 1932 ruling classes practically everywhere expected the crisis to resolve itself as had the crises before the First World War and the crisis of 1921. The only thing governments had to worry about was balancing their budgets, cutting back on civil servants', teachers', and even armed forces' pay and on dole handouts in order to do so. Only if this balance could be achieved, could there be any attempts to mop up a little of the unemployment with public works schemes.

Overall, there was what we would call today 'Thatcherism'. This was the basic approach of Hoover in the US, MacDonald in Britain, Brüning, von Papen and Schleicher in Germany. But by the end of 1932 this policy was clearly not working – especially in the US and Germany. On the one hand immense damage was being done to capital itself, as it tried to operate profitably at a little more than half its previous production levels. On the other, social forces were being created that could easily turn the whole of society over. Some sort of new approach was needed.

The shift that eventually took place was from a monopoly capitalism in which the state kept in the background, responding to the needs of the giant firms by providing a limited range of services that ensured the reproduction of the labour force (such as education, health and employment insurance), social discipline (law and order) and the satisfaction of imperialist ambitions (defence), to one in which the state intervened to ensure the international competitiveness of the different components of the national capitalism, consciously re-structuring industry, shifting surplus value from one sector of the economy to another, endeavouring to even out cyclical fluctuations.

The shift had been foreshadowed during the First World War. Once it became clear that what was involved was not a five-month campaign on the pattern of the Franco-Prussian War, but a life and death struggle between rival imperialisms, in the major combattant countries the state was given draconian powers to force individual capitals to subordinate their production to the military effort – it rationed supplies of raw material and foodstuffs, ordered factories to produce certain goods, itself organised munitions production, the coal industry and the railways, if necessary confiscating firms which would not cooperate, and took powers virtually to conscript labour.

It was the experience of these years that led Lenin and Bukharin to write of 'state monopoly capitalism'[48] of 'state capitalist trusts'[49] or simply 'state capitalism'.[50]

Yet once the war was over, there was a marked withdrawal of the state from its central role in Western Europe. In Britain, for instance, the state gave up its control of the railways and coalfields. The centrally directed war economy gave way to a market economy in which increasingly monopolistic industrial and financial concerns were free to do as they wished. The same trend was to be seen in Germany, even if there the state retained a greater direct stake in production (owning the railways, the aluminium monopoly, power production, and some coal mines). And in the US the state played virtually no productive role at all.

The 'state monopoly capitalism' of the war was a temporary

phenomenon, abandoned once the major sections of industry and finance believed that they could maintain their international position without subordinating themselves to a centralised military-bureaucratic direction. They still preferred to maintain their individual identities and their freedom to associate with capitals from other countries without state restrictions.

But the inability of monopoly capitalism to recover from the slump on its own accord began to build up pressure for at least a *partial* return to state-organised monopoly capitalism. At the lowest point in the slump, at the end of 1932, Roosevelt won the presidency in the US, and a series of meetings with the heads of big business and the army led to Hitler being given power in Germany.

In the US the increased supervision of private capital by the state was relatively limited. Hoover had already tried to use state funds to shore up businesses and banks and had undertaken small scale public works schemes to mop up a little of the unemployment. Roosevelt's 'New Deal' extended these measures just as a limited revival was taking place in the economy in any case. The Federal Reserve system guaranteed the funds of the remaining banks to prevent further collapse. Government money was used to buy up and destroy farm crops in order to raise prices. A civil construction corps provided work camps for 2,300,000 young unemployed men. The National Recovery Act provided for a limited form of self-regulation for industry through encouraging the formation of cartels, which could control prices and production levels, while it also made it a little easier for unions to raise wages (and so consumer demand). There was a limited experiment in direct state production through the Tenessee River Authority. At the same time, the government withdrew the US from the gold standard, so that the value of the dollar and the level of funds in the US no longer depended purely on the free flow of the market but upon conscious government intervention designed to aid US exports.[51]

The New Deal was a recognition that capitalism in its monopoly stage could no longer solve its problems without systematic state intervention. To that extent it marked a watershed between two phases in the development of the system. But the precise degree of state capitalist control was limited. The state tried to boost the private sector but made no real efforts to impose its own control. Even 'fiscal means to expand employment remained limited since the Democratic Administration under Roosevelt remained committed to balanced budgets . . .'[52]

Such timidity could have only a limited impact on the crisis. All the efforts of the New Deal could not push the upturn that began in the spring of 1933 beyond a certain point. In fact: 'The upturn . . . was neither widespread nor rapid'.[53] Industrial production rose from 59 per cent of the 1924-5 figure in March 1933 to 100 per cent in July, only to slide back to 71 per cent over the next year. There was a fall of 1,700,000 in the number of unemployed – but that still left 12 million jobless.

It was not until 1937 – eight years after the start of the crisis – that production reached the 1929 figure. But with a 10 per cent larger workforce and 15 per cent higher productivity, this left a 14.3 per cent unemployment figure. Yet this 'miniboom' soon gave way to a slide back into slump.

After August 1937 there was 'the steepest economic decline since the history of the US' which 'lost half the ground gained by many indexes since 1932'.[54] By December 1937 only 26 per cent of steel capacity was in use and textile output was a mere 60 per cent of the March figure. For industry as a whole unused capacity was 40 per cent in 1938[55] and unemployment was up to 19 per cent. Unemployment continued to be above 14 per cent right until 1940.

The 1920s showed that the forms of non-productive expenditure associated with *non*-state monopoly capital (marketing expenditures, advertising, speculative ventures, luxury consumption) could postpone crisis but not stop its eventual impact being greater than previously. The 1930s showed that 'pump priming' by governments could not give a new lease of life to the system either. A more profound change was needed.

The first great Western power to undergo this change was Germany. For the first couple of years economic policy under Hitler was very similar to the New Deal. Public works – especially those with a possible military function, such as the building of *autobahns* and the extension of the railway system – were undertaken on a scale not possible for the weak governments of 1930-33. Subsidies were provided for housing repairs, industry was given tax exemptions and cheap loans, firms were forced to form cartels to protect prices and profits of large enterprises, wages were fixed by law at the slump level. An economy which was already showing the first signs of recovery was given a boost by these measures, and industrial production rose from 53.8 per cent of the 1929 figure to 79.8 per cent in 1934.

However, these measures did not eliminate the pressures that had produced the crisis. Unemployment remained three times the 1929 figure and prices began to rise as the cost of paying for the public works created inflationary pressures. The Nazi regime reacted by moving further towards state-regulated monopoly capitalism: it used its dictatorial political powers to impose regimentation on the economy. The major capitalist groups remained intact. But from now on they were subordinated – as in 1914-18 – to the needs of an arms drive which they themselves wholeheartedly supported. The mild reflationary measures of 1933 gave way to the 'preparedness economy' – the arms economy – of 1935 onwards.

The state took control of the savings bank and imposed strict supervision on the commercial banks in order to ensure that their deposits were used to finance its new arms drive. Industrial concerns were compelled by law to deposit all profits above a certain level with the state for the same purpose: if big business was able to evade this by clever book-keeping, small and medium business could not. Under the four years plan of 1936 Goering was made 'economic dictator'. His aim was to push through an investment programme, of six to eight billion marks 'whether it was profitable or not, using every method – financial investments, subsidies, tax exemptions, guarantees of prices, orders and profits'[56]. The great majority of large scale industry willingly went along with these measures. But industrialists who disagreed with them soon learnt who was in control. The head of one of the biggest concerns, Thyssen, had his property confiscated by Goering and was forced to flee the country, despite the fact that he had financed the Nazis before they took power.

The effect of these measures was to pull the economy right out of the slump and to keep it booming while the British, French and American economies slumped again in 1937. By 1936, German economic output had reached the 1929 figure, and by 1939 it had climbed another 30 per cent.[57] The number of employed workers rose from 12.9 million to 20.8 million in 1939, while unemployment fell from six million down to 70,000 in May 1939. Most of the new production went into arms and industries that provided military preparedness, heavy industry. Private consumption rose by only $1.2 billion 1932-7, while the total national product rose $10.7 billion[58].

'The main line of policy adopted by the government was simple: to channel the increase of production primarily into those industries that were important for the realisation of military goals . . .' 'The index of production of producer goods industries' rose from 45 per cent above 1928 in 1932 'to 136 per cent by 1938'. 'The index of the consumer goods industries rose from 78 per cent to 107 per cent in the same period'. Thus, producer good output grew 200 per cent, consumer good output 38 per cent.[59]

Armaments and the expansion of heavy industry drove the whole economy forward, providing the markets and outlets for investment that had been so lacking in 1929-32. The economic expansion itself paid for a large percentage of the cost of fuelling the boom, in contrast with the rather lame efforts of the New Deal in the US. 'While one half of the United States' government expenditures were deficit financed in the years 1932-36, the pre-war period produced a deficit of only one fifth or one fourth of the government receipts in Germany . . .'[60] And again, in contrast to the New Deal, the Nazi policy was not obstructed by big business: 'The generals established an association with big business, in the process of which private concerns adopted economic rearmament as the preferred economic goal that was fully in their own interests.'[61]

However, there was one major problem with any such policy. Germany was not a self-contained economic unit. The forces of production internationally had long since developed to the point where they cut across national boundaries. Economic expansion inside Germany depended upon imports – especially of raw materials – which could not be financed by exports because of the stagnation of the rest of the world economy.

This problem made itself felt within a year of the Nazis taking power. A surplus of exports over imports of 1000 million marks in 1932 turned into a deficit of 316 million marks in the first six months of 1934. As Germany's gold and foreign currency holdings fell dramatically, the regime imposed very tight controls over foreign trade. Specific permits had to be obtained before businesses could import goods, and these permits were only available for 'essential items', with military requirements having top priority. The result was 'the economic insulation of Germany' as 'price connections with other countries were severed or greatly modified'.[62] At the same time, the government unilaterally cancelled interest repayments on Germany's foreign debts.

All these measures constituted a powerful drive towards 'autarchy' (economic self-sufficiency) within the German economy. But they could not go as far as to break the country's dependence on other parts of the world. As the armaments boom took off, there was a growing need for certain strategic imports. While food imports could easily be cut, the demand for raw materials grew incessantly. At first this demand could be met by using the economic power of the now massively centralised German economy to brow-beat small foreign suppliers. They were effectively told they could not sell goods to Germany or recover past trade debts unless they were prepared to pay over the odds for German exports. In this way, for instance, the economies of the Balkans came increasingly under the thumb of the German economy.[63]

But such expedients could provide only an interim, stopgap relief. Attempts to apply similar pressures on Latin American states so as to get from them raw materials previously supplied from North America failed, and there were 'temporary interruptions in trade that lasted until the debt at any given time was reduced . . .'[64] The only way to overcome such instability in raw material sources was to expand the boundaries of the German Reich so as to incorporate neighbouring economies, and to subordinate *their* industries to the German military drive. Beyond a certain point, expansion out of the slump on the basis of a state-controlled arms economy was not possible without imperialist war.

Germany was the most significant capitalism of the period to follow the path of state-controlled monopoly capitalism leading to war. It was not the first. If in the US, Britain and France state control was limited by the power of particular competing capitalist groups, this was not the case in certain late-developing capitalist countries. Here no substantial industrial development could have been successful in the first place in the face of foreign competition but for the intervention of the state bureaucracy. Japan was the typical example. The state had set out to promote the development of capitalism with the Meiji Restoration of 1868, and the state bureaucracy and the handful of large scale capitalist concerns had worked closely together ever since. So Japan *entered* the world economic crisis as a *state* monopoly capitalism. The crisis cut industrial production by much less than in the other major capitalist states, by about 10 per cent in the first two years. And then, in 1931, a turn was made to military expansion. Japanese troops moved into Manchuria, used the conquered areas as an adjunct to an increasingly militarised Japanese economy, and both economies underwent sustained industrial expansion on the basis of integrated four-year plans.[65] Japan emerged from the slump two years before the rest of the world. By 1934 industrial production was 28.7 per cent above the 1929 figure and by 1938 73 per cent.[66]

Yet even in Japan state capitalism did not develop to its maximum possible extent out of the crisis of 1929. That privilege was to be reserved for, of all places, the former workers' state of Russia.

The degeneration of the Russian revolution in the 1920s has been amply documented elsewhere.[67] It suffices here to note that by 1928 a relatively small nationalised industrial sector of the economy, run by an increasingly self-conscious bureaucracy, coexisted with a large private agricultural sector. The controllers of the industrial sector, however, had a monopoly of armed force through their control of the state. Faced with increased belligerency from the Western powers – especially Britain – in the late 1920s they reversed their previous policies and decided on a massive expansion of the industrial sector through five-year plans at the expense both of agriculture and of workers' living standards.

The initial goals in this respect were, however, relatively modest. There was no intention either of developing Russian industry in isolation from the rest of the world or of destroying the private agricultural sector. The aim instead was to tax the peasants so as to use an agricultural surplus to buy producer goods from Germany and the

US. But just as the plan began to be implemented, the crisis of 1929 forced agricultural prices right down. To pay for imported producer goods, the share of the agricultural product that had to be exported had to rise – from 0.14 per cent in 1928 to 7.33 per cent in 1931. On top of this, there was an increase of 15 per cent in the share of the harvest going to the industrial centres. Such amounts of food could be obtained from the countryside only by the most draconian of measures – seizing the land from the peasants and handing it over to 'collectives' that were under tight bureaucratic control. As peasants' and workers' living standards were slashed, a tight totalitarian dictatorship was needed to contain discontent and ensure the fulfilment of economic goals.

On this basis the country could experience massive industrial-isation. The official claim was that gross industrial production rose from 18,300 million roubles in 1927-8 to 95,000 million in 1937 (all at fixed 1926-7 prices),[68] overtaking the figures for Britain and France. While in 1929 Russia accounted for 4 per cent of world industrial production, by 1939 it accounted for 12 per cent.[69]

But, as in Germany, the industrial expansion was above all an expansion of means of production and of armaments, not of consump-tion. Goods for consumption had made up 67.2 per cent of output in 1927-8; by 1940 the figure had fallen to 39 per cent according to official figures – which almost certainly understate the change.[70] 'Between 1928 and 1936, while the productivity of labour more than trebled, real wages were actually cut by more than 50 per cent.'[71]

As the inheritor of the huge Czarist empire in Asia, the bureaucracy of the USSR was not driven, as were Japan and Germany, to rapid territorial expansion in pursuit of control over raw materials and regions that could be industrialised. But in 1939, the USSR divided Eastern Europe with Germany (Hitler got Western Poland; Stalin got Eastern Poland, Lithuania, Estonia and Latvia), showing that it was as prepared as any other imperialist power to use military expansion to gain new sources of surplus value.

The examples of what military state capitalism – whether in its 'partial' form in Germany and Japan or its full form in the USSR – could achieve in escaping from slump had a powerful affect on the rest of the world. 'Planning' came to be seen as the only real alternative to repeated crises and was adopted in one form or another in many of the weaker capitalisms: there were powerful state sectors in the small countries of Eastern Europe, in fascist Italy, in those Latin American states with 'populist' governments. Even in Britain there was a certain trend towards state intervention under the Tory governments of the 1930s. The political turmoil which affected other countries could be avoided since the world-wide slump cut the cost of food and raw material imports. This allowed rising living standards for both the middle class and employed workers, which in turn created a market for certain new, consumer-oriented industries (such as light engineering and the car industry). Neverthless, sections of the ruling class looked with increasing favour on the ideas of the Cambridge economist and millionaire, John Maynard Keynes, and younger Tories such as Harold MacMillan preached a semi-state capitalist 'middle way'. The Conservative governments moved slowly towards increased state regulation with the imposition of import controls, the forming of cartels in iron and steel and coal industries, the creation of state monopolies in electricity production, air transport and broadcasting, and the provision of investment grants to industry.

From slump to war

There were, we have seen, important differences in the ways in which the different national capitalisms responded to the crisis of the 1930s – just as there had been different responses to the crisis years of the 1870s and 1880s. At one extreme there was Roosevelt's America, at the other Stalin's Russia, with Britain, the Latin American states, Italy, Germany, Japan, scattered along an axis of increasing state intervention in between. And it was only in those countries which moved furthest in the direction of *state* capitalism that boom was resumed.

Yet in all of them the state did take on a much greater role than previously – even if it was only by stepping in to separate national prices from world prices through controls on currency flows and imports. Protectionism had existed before in many countries – but in the 1930s it increased everywhere with a vengeance. The law of value in international trade was increasingly mediated by state controls which decisively influenced price calculations and the flow of commodities. World trade, which had quadrupled between 1891 and 1925,[72] fell until in 1932 it was no higher than in 1905. The widespread tendency – in Germany, in Japan, even in Britain – was towards 'autarchy', towards individual capitalist powers attempting to produce as many goods as they could inside the boundaries of their own state power.

But it was impossible to be completely self-contained in a world in which virtually every production operation depended upon components and materials from scores of countries. The autarchy could not be an autarchy of individual nations – it had to be the autarchy of 'blocs', each dominated by a particular national capitalism. This was no great problem for the US, Britain or France, each of which was able to mould a currency bloc based upon its formal or informal empire: the dollar area, the sterling area, the gold bloc dominated by France.

These existing empires could be held together at a minimal cost (none of these countries spent more than about one per cent of its national income on 'defence' until 1938). But it was an immense problem for Japan, with its small empire at the start of the crisis (Taiwan and Korea) and for Germany with no empire at all. They could expand economically from the crisis only if they took military measures to extend their state boundaries – to establish empires and spheres of influence of their own. But this was bound, eventually, to lead to a clash with the existing imperial powers.

Once the path of military expansion had been decided upon, it fed upon itself. To challenge the existing empires required the maximum military-industrial potential. Every successful imperialist adventure increased this – for example, the Japanese take over of Manchuria, the German annexation of Austria and then Czechoslovakia. But at the same time it increased the hostility of the existing empires, leading to the need for a greater arms potential and further military adventures. The breaking points were, of course, the German seizure of Western Poland and the Japanese onslaught on Pearl Harbour.

Yet neither Germany nor Japan could avoid such adventures. Armaments expenditure had been able to pull the economy into a boom, despite the low initial rate of profit. The freezing of wages meant that the boom could very much finance itself up to a certain point. But there were bound to be limits on this. The profits on which the allegiance of big business to the armaments programme was based could only be sustained if new sources of surplus value were obtained, if the arms could be used for annexing adjacent countries, confiscating much of their accumulated surplus value and using their workforces as cheap labour. The arms economies of the 1930s inevitably led to the war of 1939-45.

State capitalism and the economics of total war

Total wars are rarely planned. They begin as military moves designed to gain or to defend particular, limited targets. It is the power of the military opposition to frustrate these aims that leads to an escalation of the struggle, involving ever larger forces and an ever greater expenditure of resources.

Once the war is under way, however, all the existing interests of the ruling classes on either side are put into question. The only way to preserve what has been gained by one means or another in the past is to step up the level of military effort – often regardless of cost. What matters is no longer a simple economic calculation as to whether a particular increase in arms expenditure will produce a corresponding increase in the surplus value in the hands of the ruling class. For, if the increased expenditure is *not* undertaken, both the surplus value accumulated in the past and that which may be accumulated in the future are put at risk. The stakes have to be raised merely in order to defend what has been staked before. That is why, once war has begun, it becomes virtually impossible to distinguish the offensive from the defensive. So what begin as limited, 'rational' moves take on an irrational existence of their own, as military expenditures on one side force military expenditures on the other in an ever-rising spiral that knows no limit beyond the complete physical exhaustion of the one or the other side.

The whole process is not qualitatively different from what happens in 'pure' economic market competition under classical capitalism. One side must accumulate as rapidly as possible because the other may accumulate too. The only difference is that in market competition it is accumulation of productive forces that matters; in war it is the accumulation of the destructive forces, which in their turn depend upon the level of the productive forces.

Total war is the ultimate horrific expression of the world of alienated labour, in which human beings become dominated by the products of their own past activity.

Yet a certain distinction can be made between the dynamics of the military state capitalisms before the outbreak of World War Two and afterwards. Until that point their arms expenditures were, in a certain sense, 'productive' – they could gain new sources of surplus value for the national capitalism at the expense of other national capitalisms. Given that most of the resources that had gone into arms were re-sources which would have remained unemployed if the transition to a state capitalist arms economy had not been made, this was a great advantage to the German or Japanese capitalisms. The ratio of total surplus value at their disposal to total past accumulations of surplus value (the national rate of profit) was raised a little – particularly since military expenditure also provided an excuse for holding down living standards and raising the rate of exploitation.

But once all-out war had begun, things could be rather different. Both sides were converted into military state capitalisms in which all that mattered was the growth of the national military potential, even if this did not necessarily lead to an increase in the surplus value available to the national capitalist class. Any reserves of surplus value had to be ploughed straight into the war effort, regardless of all considerations of profitability. The existence of a *mass* of surplus value, rather than of any particular *rate* of profit, was the factor determining whether new industrial and military investments were embarked upon. Indeed, things could go so far as to lead to what Bukharin in 1921 had called 'negative expanded reproduction'[73] – to a state of affairs in which not only all new surplus value went into military spending but in which the depreciation funds for replacing the existing stock of accumulated surplus value were run down. This happened to the European powers in both world wars.

For the sake of convenience, certain areas of the warring economies continued to be run as if they were operating under market competition in pursuit of an average rate of profit. But they were marginal areas, with their activities closely circumscribed by the priority given to war production. Again, individual firms engaged in the war production continued to be paid profits on the services they supplied to the state – but these profits were little more than conventional accounting devices, dependent upon the political decision-making of the state and no longer determining the pattern of accumulation within the economy. If the system remained capitalist, it was not because of these things but because the dynamic of the system remained competitive accumulation between different capitals – in this case between the rival military state capitalisms.

From the point of view of the workers, many of the effects were the same as those of market competition: every success in accumulating military hardware in one state capitalism forced efforts to accumulate similar levels of military hardware in the other state capitalism. Just as the efforts of rival car producers to outsell each other bring the concrete forms of labour in different car plants into an unplanned inter-relationship with each other, transforming them into different amounts of a homogenous abstract labour, so do the efforts of rival tank-producing states to outshoot one another.

But this means too that the rate of profit within the state capitalism *as a whole* does exercise a determining impact on events: if the ratio of total national surplus value to total investment in the military-industrial machine falls, this weakens the ability of the national state capitalism to sustain itself in warfare with its rivals. The decline in the rate of profit cannot lead to economic slump, since the war machine will go on growing as long as there is any remaining mass of surplus value to be used up, however small. But it can contribute to miltary defeat.[74]

This logic of total war worked itself out during the course of World War Two. At the time of Dunkirk Germany was by far the largest arms producer in the world. But its arms economy coexisted with a still thriving civilian economy, complete with living standards that were rising, however slowly. This continued to be the case right through to the beginning of the German invasion of Russia in 1941. But then the pressures of total war forced military production ever upwards, until it was three times the 1940-41 level – something which could only be achieved by cutting non-military production right back and forcing down the living standards of workers and soldiers.

In Britain rearmament did not start until 1938, and not until well into 1940 was it given effective priority over the rest of the economy. Unemployment and spare capacity at the beginning of the war enabled a considerable expansion of the war machine without taking resources from elsewhere. But soon, as in Germany, the civilian economy was reduced to a mere adjunct of the centrally planned war economy.

The most interesting case in many ways, however, is the US. When the European war broke out in 1938, 17.2 per cent of the US labour force was still unemployed and 28 per cent of industrial capacity was not being used. Once the US had entered the war in 1941: 'The state not only controlled the armaments sector of the national economy – which represented about half the total production of goods. The state decided what consumer goods should be produced and what consumer goods should not be produced . . .'[75]

The federal government spent huge sums building new weapons factories which it then handed over to private industry to run for it. In 1941 its capital expenditures were 50 per cent higher than the country's entire manufacturing investment in 1939 – and this on top of private capital investment of the same order. In 1943 the state was responsible for 90 per cent of all investment.[76]

The effect of this vast expenditure on non-productive output was not, however, to depress the civilian economy. As the unemployment and excess capacity of the 1930s was put to use, there was a record output of goods. 'As pre-war business went, 1940 was a record year, with a national production of $97 billion . . . Yet 1940 was a year of substantial under-employment of manpower and industrial facilities . . . By the end of 1943 the gross product had increased to between $185 billion and $190 billion. On top of the $90 billion war programme, consumer expenditure in 1943 – even when measured in 1940 prices – exceeded those of earlier years, rationing, war priorities and war saving notwithstanding.'[77]

The nine million unemployed became less than one million three years later. And the employed labour force grew enormously to 62.9 million: 17.3 million on war output, 55.1 million on civilian output and 10.5 million in the armed forces.[78]

The war economy could achieve what eight years of the New Deal could not – full employment of the productive capacity of the largest of the aging capitalisms. As even Kenneth Galbraith has noted: 'The Great Depression of the 30s never came to an end. It merely disappeared in the great mobilisation of the 40s'.[79]

The stage was set for a new phase of expansion of the system on the basis of state capitalism and arms production, just as it was after the 1880s on the basis of monopolisation and imperialism. The new phase, like the one before, was for a time to bear spectacular economic fruits, but in the end to fall foul once again of all the ailments of the aging monster.

Chapter 3: State capitalism, the arms economy and the crisis today

THE GREATEST SUSTAINED boom in its history. That was the experience of the world capitalist system from the 1940s to the early 1970s. Country after country experienced enormous economic growth. The American gross national product grew until it was three times as great in 1970 as it had been in 1940; German industrial output grew five-fold from the (depressed) level of 1949; French output four-fold. Even the miserable, long declining British economy was producing about twice as much at the end of the long boom as at the beginning.

The new era of growth was not confined to the existing industrialised countries. Japan, still thought of as a third world type country in the 1940s, resumed its pre-war industrial growth; until, with a thirteen-fold increase in its industrial output, it was the second largest western economy after the US. Russia's economy likewise grew, until its industrial output was about seven times as high in the mid 1970s as in the mid 1940s.

Elsewhere the dream of full industrialisation was often not fulfilled. For every success story there were half a dozen failures. India and China built huge centres of industry, but the mass of the population in each case continued to live in rural impoverishment. In Latin America urbanisation often took place more rapidly than industrialisation, creating massive shanty towns of more or less permanently unemployed subproletarians. 'Modernisation' too often meant no more than the creation of an urban elite with western tastes, while the conditions of life for most people remained as appalling as before.

Yet on a world scale, the transformation brought about by the great boom was as great as anything achieved in the previous history of the system. When Marx wrote the **Communist Manifesto**, the factory was characteristic only of some parts of Britain and Belgium. Elsewhere in the world it was hardly known. When Lenin wrote **Imperialism** it was characteristic of western and central Germany, the north east of the US, some of the cities of eastern and central Europe, of Milan and Turin in Italy, of parts of Catalonia. Yet in Italy, Spain, Austria, Poland, Russia, France, and Japan the majority of the population still lived off the land, and even in the industrial giants of US and Germany, a third of the people did. By the end of the great boom of the 1950s and 1960s, however, there were industrial centres right across the globe, the rural population had shrunk to small minorities in the advanced countries, and even in Spain, Italy or the Irish republic to less than one third of the total.

Humanity was producing wealth on a scale that had only been dreamed of previously. And the amount grew year after year, decade after decade. If the growing wealth was still very unevenly distributed, if it was accompanied by pockets of enduring poverty in the advanced countries and by vast static pools of misery in the 'third world', people could, nevertheless, believe that changes in the policies of governments would soon put an end to that.

It became the orthodoxy on both the right and the left to proclaim that the contradictions in the system perceived by Marx had been overcome.

Within bourgeois economics, Keynesianism – the contention that governments could ensure sustained economic growth and full employment at no greater cost than a slow rate of inflation – reigned supreme. The doctrine won many converts from those who had been adamant in the 1930s that the system was finished. In Britain, John Strachey, who before the war had probably done more than anyone else to popularise Marxist economic doctrines, explained in 1956 in his **Contemporary Capitalism** that Marx had been wrong, that trade union pressure and intervention from enlightened governments could prevent crises indefinitely.

On the left there remained many who wanted to maintain a more traditional Marxist perspective. But in the great majority of cases they did so either by denying the reality of the boom, or by at least half-accepting the Keynesian contention that governments could ward off crisis.

For the veteran German-American revolutionary philosopher, Herbert Marcuse, the system had become 'one dimensional', absorbing all the elements of protest from the workers of the advanced countries.[1] For the radical sociologist, C Wright Mills,[2] it was only nostalgia which led the left to look to the working class; real hope had to lie with intellectuals and students. For the American economists Baran and Sweezy[3], the bulk of the working class in the advanced countries worked in a privileged monopoly sector, and the central contradiction of the system no longer lay in the class struggle in these countries, but rather in the conflicts between imperialism and the peoples of the third world. For the Belgian economist Ernest Mandel, early attempts to deny the possibility of prolonged boom gave way to a notion of 'neo-capitalism' from which tendencies to crisis seemed to have all but disappeared.[4]

Then, in the early 1970s, the great boom came to an end. A short recession, which for the first time since the Second World War hit nearly all the major countries at once, gave an inkling in 1970-71 of what was to come. It was followed by a very sharp, coordinated world boom in 1972-3 – and this in turn gave way to a recession the like of which had not been seen in 35 years. As both unemployment rates and inflation rates soared throughout the world, the Keynesian orthodoxy no longer fitted. Suddenly, Keynesian economists found themselves being upstaged in the universities, in business circles and in the quality press by people who mouthed 'monetarist' theories – little more than a rehashing of the views Keynesianism had itself replaced a generation before.

For Marxists the problem should have been less acute. Yet it was not all that easy merely to accept that Marx's theory of crisis had always been correct, when everyone knew it had not explained the real world for 30 years, even if it suddenly did now. Within Marxism debates raged between 'fundamentalists' who insisted that the present crisis could be understood as the crisis Marx had described, but had no explanation of the boom, and 'revisionists' who insisted some account had to be given of the great boom.

There had been, however, a minority current within Marxism, right from the inception of the great boom, that had both explained that boom and argued that there were long-term pressures at work which would end it after 20 or 25 years. This current was born out of the writings of an American Marxist economist who wrote under the names WT Oakes and TN Vance in the mid 1940s and early 1950s.

Oakes/Vance's first article was written towards the end of the Second World War, in 1944. In it, he argued that in Germany since the advent of Hitler and in the US since the inception of the war, a 'new era' of capitalist development had opened up, that of the 'Permanent War Economy'. Previously the single aim of capitalist production had been the production of commodities for the market. But now, 'government expenditures for war become a legitimate and significant end-purpose of economic activity'.[5]

The basic laws of capitalism as analysed by Marx – 'the increasing organic composition of capital and the falling rate of profit' – found expression in new ways in this 'new era'. The result was a *temporary* stabilisation of the system: 'It is not my belief that the Permanent War Economy will provide a lasting solution for capitalism. But it can work for the period under consideration'.[6]

Oakes/Vance further developed this analysis in a series of articles in the semi-Trotskyist magazine **New International** in 1951,[7] and the analysis was further deepened by Tony Cliff writing in 1957[8] and by Mike Kidron in 1961 and 1968.[9]

There were important differences in the three formulations of the analysis.[10] But on one crucial point all three, writing at the height of the great boom, concurred: the boom arose from modifications to the system that occur in the period of state capitalism and military competition, but within it contradictions persisted that at a later stage would lead to a new period of crises and intensified class struggle.

The two previous chapters of this book have been based on the theoretical insights of these writers. I have tried to draw them together in a coherent framework and link them with Marx's analysis of the dynamics of capitalism and with the accounts of imperialism provided by Lenin and Bukharin. Now we are in a position, using this framework, to look at the transition from the great boom to a new period of crisis.

Arms, profits and the great boom

The experience of the First World War and the period 1933-45 was that, *provided* the competing groups within any country allowed it, the capitalist state could intervene to ensure that production proceeded on an upward course – even if the rate of profit declined. For the state could collect into its hands the mass of surplus value and direct it into investment, regardless of estimates of profitability. All the resources of the national capitalism could then be directed to meeting external competitive challenges – whether of the market or the military kind.

The extent to which the state intervened in practice after the Second World War varied enormously. In the US and Britain direct state controls over much of the economy were dismantled, in West Germany the ideology of the 'economic miracle ' of the 1950s was *laissez faire*, while, by contrast, in Italy the state owned much of large scale industry and in Japan and France strong traditions of state intervention prevailed under right wing governments.

But in one important respect post-war capitalism was almost everywhere more 'statified' than anything the system had known before: levels of *military* expenditure were much higher than ever before in peacetime.

Above all this was true in the US – which emerged from the Second World War as by far the largest economy, with half of world industrial production within its borders and a gross national product about twice that of Western Europe and Japan combined.

Until 1939, the US spent very little on arms – less than one per cent of its national product. In the course of the Second World War this figure leapt upwards, until it reached 45 per cent in 1943 and 1944. Even with reconversion to a 'peace economy' and disarmament in the early post war years, war outlays never fell back to the pre-1939 figure. In 1948 they were 4.6 per cent of the national product (and 9.8 per cent if indirect outlays were taken into account). Expenditure on war in peacetime had quadrupled. And the onset of the Cold War soon meant they were soaring up again, to reach 14.4 per cent in 1951 (21.1 per cent if indirect outlays were taken into account).

This expenditure of vast quantities of surplus value on arms had a peculiar effect on American capitalism, as was already clear in the course of the war. The amount of surplus value remaining in the hands of private capital *after* the state had taken its share for arms was actually *higher* than before, the organic composition of capital tended to fall and the rate of profit rose.

Mass profits of US capitalism[11]
Net Profit of listed US manufacturing corporations in billions of US dollars

	Before tax	*After tax*
1938	1.6	1.3
1940	3.7	2.6
1942	7.0	2.6
1944	8.2	3.0
1946	6.0	4.1

The rise in the net profit remaining in capitalist hands after tax is indisputable.

Organic composition of capital

	1939	*1941*	*1944*	*1946*
Vance's calculation[12]	72.2	73.7	68.0	74.8
Gillman's calculation[13]	4.3		2.1	
Mage's calculation[14]	3.5	2.71	2.03	2.63

The three calculations measure different definitions of the organic composition and express them in different ways.[15] But they all show a trend in the same direction – the organic composition falling as arms spending rises with the war, then rising a little as disarmament begins.

Rate of profit (percentages)[16]

	1939	1941	1943	1945	1947
Vance's calculation	25.6	28.1	32.6	33.3	27.7
Mage's calculation	8.12	10.3	11.1	11.1	10.23

Again, the direction of movement is clear – upwards as arms expenditure soared during the war, and then stagnating or falling with disarmament.

The upturn in the level of arms spending during the Korean war (1950-53) was followed by a decline to between two and three times the 1948 level (and six or seven times the 1939 level).

Arms spending as a percentage of GNP[17]

1939	1948	1951	1953	1955	1957	1959	1961	1963	1965	1967	1969
1.5	4.3	13.4	13.6	9.9	10.2	9.7	9.3	8.8	7.6	9.1	9.0

Throughout this period the rate of profit seemed to defy Marx's 'law'. Thus, in an analysis often quoted[18] as proving that the rate of profit fell, Nordhaus gave figures that showed that during the 1950s and early 1960s it stabilised with a narrow range:[19]

	1951-5	1956-60	1961-5	1966-70
Before tax	14.3%	12.2%	14.1%	12.9%
After tax	6.4%	6.2%	8.3%	7.7%

In an analysis critical of Nordhaus's figures, Fieldstein and Summers show, if anything, a small rise for net profits for non-financial corporations, from 11.1 per cent in 1950/9, to 10.9 per cent in 1956/65, to 11.7 per cent in 1960/69.[20]

The picture for Britain in the 1940s, 1950s and early 1960s is not substantially different from that for the US.

The level of arms expenditure was still at a quantitatively higher level than previously in peacetime, accounting for 10 per cent of national output in the early 1950s, from which it slowly slid down to about 6 per cent in the late 1960s.

With so much potentially investable surplus value going on arms, it was not surprising that the level of civilian investment remained fairly low and the organic composition of capital rose only slowly from the low level to which it had been reduced by slump and war. From a high of 2.0 in 1931/8, it fell to 1.61 in 1948/52. From there it rose to 1.68 in 1953/8, 1.78 in 1959/62, and 1.85 in 1963/67.[21] Thus even after 20-odd years of growth it still had not quite reached the level of more than 2.0 which produced the long period of crisis and stagnation of the interwar years.

Again, the rate of profit before tax showed only a very limited tendency to decline in the first part of this period, from just over 16 per cent in the early 1950s to between 13 and 14 per cent in the early 1960s – and *after tax* it was as high in the later period as in the earlier.[22]

What applied to the US and Britain applied also to the other West European powers. French arms expenditure was above 5 per cent for most of the 1950s and West German between 3 and 4.5 per cent. And, as one Marxist analysis of West Germany notes, there was no increase in the organic composition of capital in the 1950s.[23]

Any honest empirical study of the 1940s, 1950s and early 1960s thus has to see that a historically high level of arms expenditure was accompanied by a stabilisation of the system, an offsetting of the tendencies for the organic composition of capital to rise and the rate of profit to fall, and a prolonged period of boom.

Theory and reality

The factual evidence leads back to the theoretical points we looked at in chapter one. There it was argued that the intensified level of military competition could, temporarily, mitigate some of the elements of contradiction internal to each national economy. A high level of arms spending meant that the state took control of a substantial portion of the surplus value which would otherwise have sought profitable investment.

The result was that:

(1) Part of the investible surplus value that might otherwise have stood idle was ploughed back into the process of production. The state ensured this occurred even if the general rate of profit was low.

(2) The goods produced by this state-induced investment neither competed with the consumer good output of the civilian economy (and so did not force down prices and profits rates even more or threaten to bring about overproduction) nor took the form of new means of production that would have raised the ratio of capital to labour throughout the economy (and so again did not reduce the rate of profit). Instead what were turned out were goods destined for self-destruction – for 'non-productive consumption'.

(3) Even when the state-controlled arms sector was capital-intensive (when it had a high organic composition of capital) this did not necessarily serve to reduce further the average rate of profit for non-state capitals because of the 'von Bortkiewicz effect'[24]

Of course, the large arms sector represented a massive waste of resources that could otherwise have gone into expanding productive investment. Yet for a long time this did not seem to matter. The burden was shared more or less equally between the great corporations that dominated the US economy, so that the ability of each to expand productive investment was held back by roughly the same amount as the others. And while the result was that short-term economic growth never reached the frenetic pace it had in the 'boom' part of the economic cycle previously, it did not suffer anything like the stoppages it had endured in the slump parts of the cycle.[25]

Comparing the post-war and the pre-war economy was like comparing the hare and the tortoise of Aesop's fable. The pre-war economy bounded forward at great speed – and then stopped short, out of breath. The post-war economy, 'burdened' by the waste of huge arms expenditure, moved forward more slowly, but did not stop short in the same abrupt way. Its rate of profit was not forced down, and so it could continue going forward, year after year, decade after decade. Its *long-term* growth rate was greater than anything the system had ever known before: the world system grew 'twice as fast between 1950 and 1965 as between 1913 and 1950, and nearly half as fast again as during the generation before that'[26]

As Vance put it at the beginning of the great boom: 'enormous production and enormous waste go hand in hand'.[27]

One indication of the success of the capitalist economy from the late 1940s through to the early 1960s was that the remedy the Keynesians had preached as a solution to the crisis of the 1930s – deficit budgeting – was not actually needed. If the government spending – especially arms spending – was at a high level, this was compensated for by a high rate of growth.

For Britain, an examination of government finances concluded in 1968: 'Throughout the post-war period, the government, so far from injecting demand into the system, has persistently had a large current account surplus . . . Fiscal policy as such appears to have been deflationary in the post-war period . . .'[28]

This only began to change with the Maudling boom of the early 1960s and the Barber boom of the early 1970s (both under Tory governments). Keynesianism may have been the ideology of the post war period – but for a long time it was an ideology divorced from practice.

As Megan Desai has noted:[29] 'In the USA Keynesian policies were slow to be officially adopted . . . They finally triumphed with the Kennedy-Johnson tax cut of 1964'. That was after the Great Boom had already lasted 15 years (25 years if you exclude the short-lived and shallow recession of the late 1940s).

The logic of arms-based economic expansion has escaped many Marxist economists. It is absurd, they argue, to see a deduction by the state from the total surplus value as somehow overcoming the tendency for surplus value to grow more slowly than total investment costs, as overcoming the fall in the rate of profit. Rather than admit to that 'absurdity' they have denied the reality of what happened in the quarter of a century after the Second World War.

What they fail to understand is that this 'absurdity' is just part of the greater absurdity of the capitalist system as a whole, of its contradictory nature.[30] They do not see that engaging in military competition can be just as much a 'legitimate' capitalist goal as engaging in economic competition for markets – indeed, *has* to be in the epoch of imperialist conflict between state capitals. Such Marxists were not the first to fail to see how absurdities can be logical for capitalism. One of the greatest followers of Marx, Rosa Luxemburg, could not understand how capitalism could continually expand the value embodied in means of production without producing more goods for consumption. Similarly, these Marxists could not understand how capitalism could possibly benefit from continually expanding the means of destruction. Like Rosa Luxemburg, they were so bemused by the irrationality of what capitalists were doing as to try to deny that this was how the system worked.

The 'irrational' logic which underlay the western arms economies had its parallel in the eastern state capitals. There too arms spending had a contradictory effect – on the one hand, slowing down the short-term rates of growth; on the other, creating conditions which prevented entanglement in catastrophic crises.

The central drive of the rulers of these countries was to 'catch up and overtake' the advanced capitalist countries of the west. All the internal resources of the territory controlled by the state capital had to be directed to this single goal. The individual production units were too small and too technically backward to relate directly to the rest of the world through market competition without the risk of being forced into subordination to western capitals. Only autarchy – cutting normal market ties between the territory and the rest of the world – could fend off that risk. But autarchy had to be defended by armed might, lest western capitals take direct military measures to 'open up' the territory of the state capital to their penetration.

The state capital could not stop itself being forced into direct market competition with the economically more advanced western capitals except by engaging in military competition with them.

Had it opted for economic competition, then the growth of its economy would have come to depend directly upon the ups and downs of the world economy, on world booms and slumps. The drive for international market competitiveness would have meant an immediate raising of the ratio of means of production to workers to the world average, thus exerting a downward pressure on the rate of profit for each internal production unit. As the rate of profit fell in this way, those controlling investment decisions would have postponed them, waiting for some upturn in the world economy to create a more favourable investment environment. The pattern of boom and slump would have appeared inside the national economy.

Massive arms spending deflected many of these pressures – although it did not stop there being cycles of investment and economic growth in the eastern states, sometimes as marked as those of the western economies during the Great Boom.[31]

During the 1940s and 1950s the eastern states were able to sustain very high growth rates, by investing any mass of surplus value that existed, regardless of its ratio to past investment (the rate of profit). They could do so *only* because arms spending provided the Russian rulers with a means of insulating their sphere of influence from external market pressures. The dimension of military competition enabled them for a long period to play down the significance of the dimension of market competition.

At the same time, their vast expenditure on arms reduced *worldwide investment* in productive industry, and with it the worldwide tendency for the organic composition to rise and the rate of profit to fall. Because of Russia's vast expenditure on arms, its industry could never reach the point of being able to undercut western industry in market competition – and of therefore destroying the profitability of western industry. And, by the same token, it stopped itself running into a situation where it suffered the effects of a worldwide crisis of overproduction.

In general, state capitalism, east *and* west, was not conceivable without the arms economy. Without their arms spending the rival state capitals would have had to relate to each other solely through market competition – and would therefore have reproduced all the elements of crisis of the interwar years. Indeed, even with their arms spending they were unable to stop the element of market competition between state capitals growing more important – and leading to the eventual re-emergence of crisis.

Arms, the state and imperialism

The basis for the Great Boom was the state capitalist arms economy. Yet the whole project of state capitalism was built on a contradiction – as Bukharin pointed out in his writings during and soon after the First World War.

The very thing that produced the merger between the state and capital – the enormous growth in the scale of production and therefore of the units of capital – also produced pressure on the units in which production was organised to break through the constraints of national frontiers. To try to keep state production confined within those frontiers was to ensure that it was carried on inefficiently and that the national economy became increasingly plagued by disproportions betwen its different component parts.

It was these factors, as we saw in the previous chapter, that led the pre-Second World War state capitalisms of Germany and Japan to stretch their boundaries by repartitioning the world in their own favour, until world war was the inevitable result. They lost the war and were dismembered (Germany was permanently divided in two, Japan lost its Taiwanese, Korean and Manchurian possessions and did not achieve a level of economic output higher than that in the 1930s until 1953). But that was not the end of pressures to 'partition and repartition the world'. These now emanated from the state capitalisms that had defeated Germany and Japan in the war.

The US and Russia emerged from the war as the two most powerful state capitalisms, both in economic and military terms. Both had become relatively autarchic during the 1930s, as foreign trade dropped to a very small proportion of total product and as ideologies had predominated within the ruling class that belittled the importance of links with the rest of the world (isolationism in the US, 'socialism in one country' in Russia). Both had ben forced into a new awareness of the rest of the world by the attempts of Germany and Japan to repartition it. Both now hastened to absorb the subject peoples of the defeated empires into their own 'spheres of influence'.

This was first done by mutual agreement at the international conferences of 1943-5 (Tehran, Yalta and Potsdam). Apparent harmony reigned at these, with each allowing the other to suppress anti-Nazi resistance movements whose ideological colouration it did not like (thus, the British and Americans were allowed to crush the Communist-led resistance movement in Greece, the Russians the non-Communist Home Army in Poland). But the harmony was, in fact, but a sentimentalisation of cynical real-politik – it reflected the crude calculation by each that it was not strong enough to deny the other what it wanted.

Such harmony was bound to break down within a couple of years. Each power was bound to fear that the other would use the strength it had gained from expanding its sphere of influence so as to expand it even more.

Much ink has been spilt by apologists for both sides (and for none) in arguments as to who started the Cold War. But the whole argument is misplaced. Once American and Russian state capitalisms had expanded into the lands of the former German and Japanese empires they were bound to clash with each other. The dividing line between their 'blocs' was based upon a calculation of the existing balance of forces between them. Each was bound to fear that the other would somehow succeed in shifting that balance of forces and then push for a further repartition of the world. The only way to resist that was to apply continual pressure against it, engaging in border wars (for example in Korea) if necessary and preparing for the possibility of world war by a relentless accumulation of military hardware.

There was not, however, a *pure* symmetry between the two dominant powers. Russia emerged from the war the most powerful military force in Europe, but was much weaker economically and certainly did not have the strength to engage in military struggle far beyond the boundaries of its own bloc. Its imperialism therefore consisted in the main of a subjection of the peoples of eastern Europe; engaging in a crude pillage of the area in the years 1945-8, and then forcing through an industrialisation at the expense of workers and peasants so as to increase the military-industrial capacity of the bloc as a whole.[32]

In the years 1949-61 it tried to subordinate the newly independent state capitalism of China to its own imperialist needs, but only succeeded, at the end of the day, in provoking China into breaking from its bloc.[33]

In the 1960s it extended its involvement beyond its own bloc, developing interests in India, Egypt (although it was later to lose these), Syria, Iraq, Somalia (again only for a period), Ethiopia, Angola – and, of course, Cuba. But its overall presence outside eastern Europe and northern Asia remained a pale shadow of that of the US.

By contrast, as the most powerful *economic* power, the Americans had less need of a formal empire than the Russians. In the early post-war period their economic strength was sufficient to draw within their sphere of influence the ruling classes of most smaller countries unless a direct Russian military presence prevented that.

Thus they easily drew the individual west European state capitalisms into their orbit, picked up most of the pieces of their disintegrating empires (displacing the British in the Middle East, the French in Indochina, the Belgians in central Africa) and were also able at a later stage to pull back countries that had been temporarily allied with the Russians (Egypt, Somalia, especially China). Provided the US could effectively maintain the world's existing ruling classes in power, it could expect to continue to dominate everything outside Russia's immediate control. Its imperialism was indirect,[34] with exploitation usually being based upon agreements 'freely' entered into between US companies and companies and rulers elsewhere, its political power safeguarded by bases from which troops would fly to prop up local ruling classes rather than by armies of occupation.

The lack of symmetry explains how the argument as to who was the 'aggressor' could take place. The compact Russian bloc could be presented as 'defensive', the extensive US presence as 'free', depending on one's preference. Yet such arguments concealed the underlying similarity between the two camps.

Both were imperialist, in the sense that in both the needs of competitive accumulation forced the ruling class to exercise military influence outside its own national boundaries. Yet in neither case was the imperialism simply a carbon copy of the imperialism of the 1890s, which could be justified in terms of crude profit and loss calculations, with the expenses of empire being small compared with the much greater increase in profit that it brought in.

In the new period of imperialism, the cost of empire could be much greater than any direct material benefit to the ruling class.

Thus at no stage in the 1940s or 1950s did total US overseas investment (let alone the much smaller *return* on that investment) exceed US spending on arms. Even in the period of 'disarmament' prior to the outbreak of the Korean War: 'Military expenditure totalled something like $15 billion a year. Thus it was not only 25 times as high as the sum of private capital export, but it was also many times greater than the sum of foreign aid. Marshall Aid did not total more than $5 billion in any one year'.[35]

Thirty years later US overseas investment had grown many times over. The total was now about $500 billion ($200 billion of direct investment plus bank loans worth perhaps $300 billion). On top of this there were something like $300 billion of foreign assets controlled by US multinationals.[36] But total expenditure on 'defence' had also risen, to around $200 billion – less now than total overseas investment, but still substantially more than the profits that could possibly accrue from that investment.

What is more, the *direction* of the overseas investment had also changed. It was no longer predominantly investment by strong, established capitalist powers in countries, not yet fully capitalist, which could provide 'super-profits'. Instead, it was in fully developed capitalist countries – whose ruling classes invested, in turn, in the US.[37]

By the late 1970s only a quarter of the overseas investment of the advanced western countries was in the 'third world' – the rest was in other advanced countries. Each advanced capitalism 'gained' a certain amount of profits from investment in other advanced countries but simultaneously 'lost' a certain amount through their investments in it. The resulting net return could hardly justify by itself the huge expenditure on arms.

The imperialism which necessitated arms spending was not the imperialism of a single empire, in which a few 'finance capitalists' at the centre make huge super profits by holding billions of people down. Rather it was the imperialism of *rival* empires, in which – as Bukharin had described it as early as 1916 – the combined capitalists of the whole of each ruling class have to divert funds from productive investments to military expenditure in order to ensure that they hang on to what they already possess.

In the late 1940s, the calculation in both Washington and Moscow was simple. To relax the level of military spending was to risk losing strategic superiority to the rival imperialism, enabling it to seize territory.

So the Russians lived in fear of an attempted US 'roll back' of eastern Europe, which would have seized these economies from Russia's grasp. Russia would then be left with little choice but to accept terms for the untrammelled entry of US goods into Russian markets – a challenge which Russian state capitalism was too weak to confront. In the same way, the Americans lived in fear of Russia pulling one or other of the western states – in particular West Germany or Japan – into its sphere of influence, enabling it to vastly increase its military-economic potential for challenging US interests everywhere.

As one US spokesman put it at the time of the Korean War:

> Were either of the two critical areas on the borders of the Communist world to be overrun – western Europe or Asia – the rest of the free world would be immensely weakened . . . in the economic and military strength required to resist further aggression . . .

> If western Europe fell, the Soviet Union would gain control of about 300 million people, including the largest pool of skilled manpower in the world. Its steel production would be increased by 55 million tons a year to 94 million, a total almost equal to our own . . . Its coal production would leap to 950 million tons compared to our 550 million. Electric energy in the area of Soviet domination would be increased from 130 to 350 billion KW hours, or almost up to our 400 billion . . .[38]

The logic of the new imperialism was simple: grab, and exploit as much of the world as possible so as to build up the military potential to stop your rival grabbing and exploiting areas to build up its own military potential.

'Classical' capitalism as described by Marx was based upon the logic of exploiting workers in order to accumulate means of production, so defending your ability to exploit more workers. The logic of state capitalist imperialism was exploit workers in order to accumulate means of destruction, so defending your ability to exploit still more workers and accumulate still more means of destruction.

We saw, in examining the Second World War, that this logic could override all other considerations. It meant, under conditions of total war, that individual capitalists were forced to invest, even if their individual rates of profit were low. All that mattered was the survival of the state capitalist ruling class as a whole, and that necessitated the continued investment of all the surplus value in arms production.

This was the state of affairs that continued to prevail in the USSR after 1945. It fitted a state capitalism which was both more backward than the American (in terms of the size and development of the means of production it controlled) and more advanced (in terms of the subordination of the interests of individual members of the ruling class to the needs of the state capital as a whole). Economic backwardness meant more pressure to invest regardless of the immediate rate of profit – although, of course, the rate of profit on the whole national economy remained crucial, since it determined the limits of future possible investment.

In the US the competing capitalist concerns were more strongly placed to resist the all-encompassing embrace of the state, while the external pressures for them to accept it were not so great. The short-term rate of profit remained crucial in determining investment in many non-military sectors of the economy. However, as we have seen, this hardly mattered, since military expenditure managed to create conditions in which profit rates *even after tax* were relatively high and investment could be sustained *without* direct state control.

Post-war state capitalist imperialism was not 'profitable' in the sense that it did not lead to 'super profits' greater than the cost of imperial defence. It was 'profitable' in the sense that it enabled capital to expand for a long period of time without major slumps, avoiding the tendency of the rate of profit to fall.

Finally, this had one very important consequence for the pattern of imperialism in the period of the long boom. It meant a softening of the rivalries between the different west European imperialisms. Twice in a generation these had led to world wars. And it still seemed in the early post war period that a powerful German capitalism could not coexist in Europe alongside British and French capitalisms – hence early attempts to forcibly prevent German industry from recovering from the war.

Yet after 1948 German capitalism could grow to be more economically powerful than ever before *without* military confrontation with France or Britain.

The reason was that, just as the arms spending of US state capitalism guaranteed the profitability of US civilian industry, so it provided an international economic environment in which the different European capitals could invest profitability and find markets without the need to seize new territories. Those European capitalisms that attempted to hang on to old empires (France up until the loss of Algeria in 1962, Britain until economic weakness forced abandonment of its East of Suez foreign policy and entry into the European Economic

Community in the early 1970s) found themselves increasingly less competitive than those which had no empires and based their expansion on an orientation towards the industrialised areas of the globe.

The softening of the rivalries of the various western capitalisms even found its parallel in a softening of the rivalry between the US and the USSR in the last decade of the long boom. With both major powers enjoying 'prosperity' and sustained high growth rates the pressures for each to repartition the world at the expense of the other seemed very low indeed. Neither a 'Communist' takeover of western Europe nor a western 'rollback' of eastern Europe seemed credible. And in the third world, both sides seemed to have grown accustomed to states such as Egypt, India, Iraq or Algeria swinging from one to the other and back again.

After two last major confrontations – over Berlin in 1961 and Cuba in 1962 – 'detente' was the order of the day. The rulers of the US and Russia believed that the world was big enough for them both to achieve their ambitions. While the Great Boom lasted nothing was any longer allowed to disturb that belief – not the US war against Vietnam, not the Russian invasion of Czechoslovakia, not the Middle East War fought out by the great powers' clients in 1973. The US and Russia had larger nuclear stockpiles than ever – but also seemed less likely than ever to use them. Their 'armed truce' did indeed seem an alternative to war.

But detente in reality depended on the boom. And as that boom died, so did the dream of everlasting 'peaceful' coexistence between the great state capitalist imperialisms.

Contradictions: (1) national capitals and international production

The arms economy was a response to the contradiction between the growing statification of production and its growing internationalisation.

Yet increasingly it could not resolve that contradiction. In 1914 or even in 1939 it had been possible for rulers to imagine that a quick *blitzkrieg* attack could force their rivals to accept a repartition of the world at minimal cost. In the age of the atom bomb, it was more difficult even to pose the issue in those terms. The drive towards war remained as powerful as ever – but even the craziest capitalist or bureaucrat could see that an atomic war could destroy vast existing accumulations of capital long before it provided control over new masses of capital. The nuclear balance maintained in fact the main outlines of the partition of the world decided in 1944-5, despite occasional rhetoric from the US about 'rolling back eastern Europe'. It was to be more than 30 years before the great powers began to think again in terms of what they could win through *blitzkrieg* type 'theatre wars'.

But the freezing of the boundaries between blocs did not stop the pressure towards internationalisation of the forces of production. With the relentless upward path of global output during the great boom, this pressure became greater than ever. If national state capitals dared not relieve the pressure by turning cold war into hot war, they had to relieve it in another way – by allowing an increasing number of direct linkages between internal production and world production.

In the interwar years, the trend had been for the state capitalist empires and blocs to try to operate self-contained economies, producing internally as great a proportion as possible of the different sorts of output they needed. World trade slumped, and the internationalisation of production was internationalisation within each bloc.

The more economically backward state capitalisms continued in this direction in the 1940s and 1950s – Russia forced its east European satellites to reorient their trade towards itself; Japan used all sorts of measures to 'ration' foreign imports; emerging industrial capitalisms such as Brazil and Argentina forced national firms to pursue policies based on 'import substitution'; both China and India, each in its own way, consciously copied the Russian experience of five-year plans.

But between the old established industrial powers, a new pattern soon emerged. World trade grew at something like twice the rate of growth of world output, and there was a growing tendency for key areas of output to be dominated by *multinational firms*, coordinating investment, production and sales in many different countries.

The multinationals had advantages that no single national capital could match. They could mobilise *world* forces of production, while individual state capitals could only rely upon a fraction of these world forces. So they tended to dominate in the most technologically advanced areas of industry – in oil and petrochemicals, in computers, in electronics, in autos. Individual state capitals that wanted to continue to produce the most modern forms of output in the most efficient ways increasingly found they could only do so by establishing links with the multinationals – through joint investment projects, licensing agreements and so on. In the 1960s this was increasingly true of states such as Brazil or Argentina, in the 1970s it was increasingly true of Russia and eastern Europe as well.

The growth of trade and the growth of the multinationals led in turn to another form of internationalisation – the massive growth in the late 1960s and the 1970s of vast pools of international finance that had no single national home – Euromoney.

There is an argument between some Marxists as to whether 'statification' or 'multinationalisation' is the predominant feature of capitalist development today.[39] The whole argument is misconceived. One trend implies the other.

The state cannot develop national capital to compete in world terms unless it finds access to productive resources (capital and raw materials) and productive developments (new technology) outside its own borders. It has to deal with the multinationals and to borrow from the international capital market.

For their part, the multinationals continue to depend upon national home bases (even if some – for example Unilever or Shell – have more than one national home base) for the resources states can provide (finance, research and development undertaken in 'defence' establishments and so on) and for the protection of their interests internationally (in trade negotiations, against threats from radical governments and so on).

The multinationals and the individual state capitals are mutually dependent on each other. Yet, at the same time, the activities of the one continually interfere with the activities of the other. The multinational depends upon the national state for defence, yet at the same time engages in international operations that can undermine the domestic industrial-military potential through shifting investments abroad, moving funds across frontiers at great speed, or evading taxes. The national state depends on the multinational for access to the developing world forces of production, yet continually puts obstructions in the way of the free flow of trade and capital (through taxes, through giving preference to national firms when awarding government contracts, through efforts to influence exchange rates) which can only serve to hamper the multinationals' efforts to develop these world forces.

The rise of multinational capital undermines the ability of individual states to impose order on their internal economies: an increasing proportion of 'national' resources are completely outside the control of 'national planning' mechanisms. At the same time the continued existence of the various states, and their enormous military machines, threatens to disrupt the 'international planning' which operates within each multinational company.

Capitalism has always been a system in which 'order' can only emerge through the blind interaction of many competing capitals. In Marx's time the key mechanisms which imposed order were the markets for commodities, labour power and capital, and the crises which served periodically to bring them back in the 'right' proportions to each other. By the late 1930s a different sort of interaction was dominant – that between military state capitals. Yet here too a certain sort of 'order' could emerge. Fear of its rivals forced each state to engage in a 'planned' deployment of its internal resources, and the result was the Great Boom.

But the continuing internationalisation of productive forces undercut the ability of national states to deploy their internal resources in this way. States – regardless of their ideological hue – increasingly required the collaboration of multinational capital. They could obtain it only by delivering an adequate rate of profit to the multinational corporation. So they could not continue along the old state capitalist path in which investment was maximised, regardless of any decline in the profit rate.

In a multinational world, the state capitals could no longer guarantee fast growth rates and full employment. The 'order' that had emerged in the late 1930s and early 1940s became a thing of the past. Yet the states that had given rise to that 'order' continued to exist – and this in turn prevented any return to the rather different order, based on 'pure' market competition and regulation-through-crisis, that had existed in Marx's time.

Contradictions (2): the rise of non-military state capitalisms

So far we have assumed a world in which only *military* state capitalisms exist. This was effectively the world into which the Great Boom was born: economic life internationally was dominated by the industrial nations that had won the Second World War – the US, Russia, Britain, and to a lesser extent France. And these were countries with high levels of arms spending designed to protect empires and spheres of influence.

But in the course of the Great Boom a change occurred. Just as multinational capitals grew up which cut across the boundaries of the state capitals, so too the state capitals began to have to pay attention to market as well as military dimensions of competition. In particular, state capitals emerged which devoted almost all their resources to market penetration of their rivals, and which simply refused to engage in military competition.

This was a necessary outcome of the long period of economic expansion. As the system grew, so too did the scale of expenditure required for any state that wanted to play an independent part in military competition. Eventually, only two or three states could claim to be able to do so (the US, Russia, and to some extent, China). Other states had no choice but to throw their lot in with one or other super-power. And it was a short step from that to deciding they did not need to devote the same proportion of their national output to arms as the superpowers did. The advanced economies began to break into two groups – the high arms spenders and the low arms spenders – with countries like Britain and France occupying an intermediate position.

The result was a double contradiction. The unequal economies of the superpowers had to bear equal burdens (Russia had to match the arms potential of a country, the US, with more than twice its national output, and the relatively backward Chinese economy had to be able to face up to both the US and the USSR). On the other hand, the other advanced countries, with economies more or less equal in size, bore unequal burdens – for example Britain had an arms burden something like six times the level of Japan and 50 per cent higher than West Germany).

The two capitalisms which had lost the Second World War and which, therefore, had been excluded from the first phase of rearmament in the late 1940s found themselves in a position to benefit from the world arms economy sustained by the 'victors' without, however, having to contribute a great portion of their own national output to arms. They could therefore put a higher proportion of output into investment in productive industry, reap corresponding benefits in terms of efficiency and mop up the competition in international markets.

West Germany spent only 3 or 4 per cent of its Gross National Product on arms, and 'The first post-war boom, which began in 1950, had foreign trade to thank for its intensity'.[40] 'At every stage of reduced or stagnating capital accumulation in the history of the Federal Republic, the export surpluses have had a stimulating effect upon production'.[41]

Japan followed a similar path. Arms spending was on an even smaller scale than West Germany's, amounting to less than 1 per cent of national output. This enabled it to put more of its resources into productive accumulation than any other of the western states, while still benefitting from the international market created by the arms economies of the others.

Thus its long boom – with growth rates nearly twice its rivals – began with the demand created by the western forces fighting in Korea in the early 1950s. As one early account of the boom tells, 'boom has been produced entirely by the great expansion of foreign demand.' Between 1952 and 1956, US procurement payments – purchases from Japan by the US military – amounted to $3,331 million, 'equivalent in value to more than a quarter of Japan's commodity imports in the same period'. 'Even though there was a tendency for them to decline in subsequent years, procurement expenditure in 1958-9 was sufficient to pay for 14 per cent of imports'.[42]

After a slight lull, the Japanese economy boomed in the late 1960s as never before. A key contribution to this boom came from 'the rapid increase in exports especially to North America'.[43] On top of this there was a new flood of orders for Japan from the US military – this time in connection with the Vietnam War. In the single year of 1971, this added one billion dollars to Japanese exports.[44]

Low arms spending did not mean a low level of state intervention in the economy. Instead, it tended to mean state intervention to build up *exports*.

Thus in the case of West Germany in the early years of the boom, as one Marxist account tells: 'Far more than in any other capitalist country the bourgeoisie in the Federal Republic made use of the state apparatuses and the monetary and fiscal system to force capital accumulation by means of favourable depreciation rates, credits for reconstruction at favourable rates of interest and finance for investment. All this took place in contradiction to the official neo-liberal economic theory . . .'[45]

In Japan state capitalism advanced further in its influence over civilian industry than almost anywhere else in the western world – despite a low level of direct state ownership. The state and the largest private firms worked together to ensure that that portion of the national income that had gone into arms before 1945 now went into productive investment: 'The motive force for rapid growth was fixed investment in plant and equipment. Private fixed investment grew from 7.8 per cent of GNP in 1946 to 21.9 per cent in 1961'.[46]

In the late 1940s and in the 1950s, for example, imported raw materials were in short supply. The government took charge of their allocation to industries it thought would best contribute to the growth of the economy and the expansion of exports: 'The "tilting" or "priority projects" system was introduced, with the main expansion in key industries such as coal mining, iron and steel . . . Raw materials were allocated to industries by priority'.[47]

A key role was played by the Ministry of International Trade and Industry (MITI), which issued 'guidelines' to industry which they ignored at their peril:

> MITI formulated and implemented the basic strategy for developing heavy industry in the 1960s and knowledge-based industries in the 1970s . . . MITI's goal has been to channel the movement of resources into favoured industries. Domestic and imported financial and technical resources have been allocated preferentially to these industries. Various forms of tax incentives and subsidies have been formulated, enacted and provided by MITI's efforts . . . Additionally, the ministry takes measures to promote rationalisation and reorganisation of industry . . .[48]

Thus in the early 1970s it pushed for greater concentration of industry in order to prevent foreign takeovers. 'Administrative guidelines' allowed it to consolidate 97 shipping companies into six groupings, to merge three different firms into Mitsubishi Heavy Industry, and to achieve the merging of Nissan Motors and Prince Motors, and of Yairata Steel and Fuji Iron and Steel.[49]

In addition to the wide powers of MITI, the Central Bank uses its influence to ensure that the individual commercial banks finance certain investments and not others.[50]

Japanese state capitalism has not suffered the enormous tensions that have at times arisen in a country such as Britain between the demands of the state and the demands of individual capitalist groups – probably because until recently Japanese investment overseas was relatively low and individual capitalist concerns saw their activities as national rather than multinational (although this is now changing). They could identify with the state in following a path of *national* capital accumulation.

> Japanese entrepreneurs are vigorous in investing. They will not confine their fixed investment within the limit of gross profits or internal accumulation, unlike the case of entrepreneurs in other advanced countries. Even if the fixed investment is over and above their gross profits, the enterprise will undertake investment so long as bank finance is available . . .[51]
>
> The primary goal of Japanese corporate management is to maintain a high and rising volume of sales . . . Maximisation of profits is not a corporate goal', although 'maintaining an acceptable level of profits is . . .[52]

In other words, the heads of big business and the state have worked together to ensure the growth of Japanese national capitalism by mobilising the whole mass of surplus value and directing it towards 'strategic' sectors, regardless of considerations of short-term profitability. What other state capitals have done when military considerations have been uppermost, has been done by Japanese state capitalism in the interests of overseas market competition. A vice-minister in MITI has summed up the approach: 'According to Napoleon and Clausewitz the secret of a successful strategy is the concentration of fighting power on the main battlefields; fortunately, Japan has been able to concentrate its scant capital in strategic industries . . .'[53]

The result of this strategy was a more or less continual growth of capital accumulation throughout the 1950s, 1960s and early 1970s – a much faster rate of growth than was possible to those economies bearing the burden of sustaining the world arms economy. Capital growth in Japan 1961-71 was 11.8 per cent per annum, while in West Germany 1950-62 it was 9.5 per cent per annum. These compare with figures for the US 1948-69 of 3.5 per cent per annum.[54] The figures for fixed investment as a proportion of GNP in 1967 are also striking. In Japan it was 32.3 per cent, in France 21.9 per cent, in West Germany 22.8 per cent, and in the UK 18.2 per cent.

In 1952 the per capita income of Japan was less than that of Brazil,

Malaysia or Chile; 40 per cent of the population worked in agriculture; labour productivity in industry was low; the country produced only 1.7 per cent of world exports; it was plagued with balance of payments problems; the maximum predicted rate of economic growth was 5 per cent a year.[55]

By the end of the 1970s the country was the world's third industrial power; its share of world trade was equal to that of the giant US; it had a huge trade surplus:

Percentage share of combined advanced countries' GNP[56]

	1953	1977
US	69	48
Japan	3.6	17.7
W Germany	6.5	13.2
France	8.0	9.7
Italy	3.8	5.0
UK	8.9	6.3

Percentage share of world trade in manufactures[57]

	1961	1978
US	17.9	11.5
Japan	5.0	11.5
EEC (inc. UK)	46.6	44.1

The success of West Germany and Japan might, on the face of it, seem to contradict the Arms Economy thesis. After all, here were the fastest growing economies – one with a smaller than average level of arms spending, the other with a very low level. But in fact the strategy of a civilian-output state capitalism only made sense if it was assumed that other state capitalisms were producing arms. For these could then provide a market for exports. Had they been civilian-output state capitalisms as well, then they would have had comparable levels of investment to the West Germans and Japanese, so that *either* world output would have exceeded demand *or* it would have found its demand in a very rapid accumulation of means of production, a rising organic composition of capital and a downward trend in the rate of profit.

Thus the Japanese experience did not contradict the Permanent Arms Economy thesis as an explanation of *world* growth and stability. But the Japanese economy was a contradictory factor in this growth. Its very success meant that a growing chunk of the world economy was not wasting investable output on arms; its growth reduced the proportion of the world product going to arms.

Nor was that the end of the matter. The very success of the low arms spending economies put pressure on the high arms spenders to switch resources away from arms and towards productive investment. For only then could they begin to meet the challenge they faced in market competition from Japan and West Germany.

This was most clearly the case for Britain, which faced balance of payments crises every time it tried to expand its economy from the late 1940s right through to the mid-1970s. Successive British governments were forced, reluctantly, to abandon notions of imperial grandeur and to reduce the proportion of the national product going on arms (although not the total arms budget). Defence spending fell from 7.7 per cent of gross domestic product in 1955 to 4.9 per cent in 1970.

In the case of the US, the pressure was less obvious at first, since the country enjoyed a balance of trade surplus throughout the 1950s and 1960s. This enabled it both to sustain a high level of arms spending and to invest overseas on a growing scale. Nevertheless, the level of arms spending declined from the very high figures of the Korean War (13.4 per cent in 1951), to between 9 and 10 per cent of national output in the late 1950s, and to between 7 and 9 per cent in the early 1960s.

The depth of the problems faced by the US was shown during the Vietnam War. In a desperate attempt to ward off defeat, Johnson and Nixon pushed the US arms budget up by about a third. The new level was not, however, anything like that of the Korean War – it moved to around the 9 to 10 per cent of GNP of the late 1950s, not the 13 per cent of the early 1950s. But it was too much for a US industry facing vigorous competition for markets. There was an upsurge of inflation at home, Wall Street turned against the war, and then, in 1971 for the first time since the Second World War, US imports exceeded US exports. Nixon was forced into two measures which further undermined the stability of the world economy: he cut US arms spending back to the lowest figure since before the Korean War and he devalued the US dollar, in the process destroying the system of fixed international currency exchange rates that had acted as a framework for the expansion of world trade throughout the post-war period. US arms spending as a proportion of gross national product thus fell from 13.4 per cent in 1951/7, to 10.7 per cent in 1958/68, to 8.5 per cent in 1969/73, to 6.6 per cent in 1974/77.[58] The dynamic of market competition was relentlessly undercutting the dynamic of military competition.

What some people have called the 'crisis of hegemony'[59] of the system in the 1970s was, in fact, the offspring of something else – the inherent instability of a world of state capitalisms engaged in two quite different dimensions of competition with each other.

The difficulties for the US economy have been more than matched by difficulties for the other main arms spender – the USSR.

In the 1930s, 1940s and 1950s the USSR had been able to grow faster than most western economies despite a huge arms budget and a very low level of foreign trade. But in the 1960s it became clear that long term growth rates were falling – from a claimed 11.3 per cent a year in 1950-55 to 6.3 per cent in 1960-65. The very success of past investment was creating difficulties for new investments. Each unit of investment created less additional surplus for the national economy than a decade before[60] – in other words, the rate of profit on the total national investment fell. The resources available to expand the economy and the military machine were thus cut – unless there was an increase in pressure on workers and collective farmers, denying them improvements in living standards promised in order to prevent a growth of discontent. Without pressure on living standards, either the arms burden had to be reduced or the rate of growth of the economy sacrificed (thus reducing the long term arms potential).

The only other alternative was to try to make investment more efficient, by forming new trade-for-technology links with the western multinationals. But this meant allowing these multinationals to have some say in what happened to the output of the Russian economy – in other words negating the centralised bureaucratic direction that had allowed all resources to be used for economic expansion even when the rate of profit was low.

The effect on the world system of these contradictory pressures on its different units, east and west, was for the amount of global output going on arms to fall – from about 7 per cent in 1953 to about 4 per cent in 1965, according to one estimate.[61] By the mid-1970s the world level of arms spending could have been no higher as a proportion of total output than it was in 1948 – the year in which it had been low enough to allow the signs of full blown economic crisis to reappear, briefly.

The new period of crisis

This time crisis was to make more than a fleeting appearance. Throughout the western world there began to proliferate complaints from industrialists and economists that the rate of profit was no longer high enough to sustain investment, growth rates and full employment.

The reasons are not hard to find. There had already been a sharp increase in the level of productive investment per worker in the low-arms spending countries in the 1960s. In Japan, 'capital has grown much more rapidly than the labour force – at more than 9 per cent a year, or more than twice the average rate for the Western industrialised countries . . .'[62]

In West Germany, it has been claimed that a static organic composition of capital in the 1950s gave way to a rising one in the 1960s.[63]

But for these individual countries the rising organic composition of capital did not immediately express itself in falling profit rates – providing they could increase exports. Higher capital investment enabled them to out-compete their rivals in export markets. What would otherwise have been falling domestic rates of profit were boosted by the excess profits on foreign sales – excess profits available because international production costs (and therefore international prices) were influenced by the more inefficient productive methods of their rivals.[64]

One of the paradoxes of capitalism is that although a rising organic composition of capital reduces average profit rates, it raises the profits of the first capitalist to introduce it. For high investment gives the first capitalist access to new productive techniques not available to the others and cuts his costs below the average. The total profit of the entire capitalist class declines because of what he has done – but he gets a bigger share of that total profit. It is only when other capitalists copy him and introduce the new capital-intensive technique that he loses his competitive advantage and his profit falls as well.[65]

So the Japanese and West Germans, by engaging in capital in-tensive forms of investment, cut world profit rates, while raising their own national share of world profits. Their increased competitiveness in export markets forced other capitalisms to pay, with falling rates of profit, for the increased Japanese and German organic compositions of capital. But this, in turn, put pressure on these other capitalists to increase their competitiveness by turning to higher organic com-positions of capital so as to match Japanese and German technology.

The rising organic composition of capital increased competitive-ness between the major economies, and this in turn led to further upward pressure on the organic composition.

So, for example, in the US in 1948, total foreign trade only amounted in value to 12.7 per cent of output and even in 1965 to only 13.7 per cent. Under such circumstances what mattered for the bulk of industry was competitive costs *inside* the country. But by 1979 the ratio had risen to 31.1 per cent[66] – a much larger proportion of industry now had to worry about the international comparisons of its costs. Whole industries suddenly found that the value of their output had to be recalculated on the basis of what it cost to produce it with the more advanced techniques of other countries – and that meant it was not high enough to provide 'adequate' profits.

This seems to explain the well-known stagnation of labour prod-uctivity in the US in the 1970s – the value of the machinery on which labour worked was originally reckoned in terms of how much it cost to produce or replace inside the US, not the lower figure that would have obtained if world comparisons were used.[67]

There was only one way in which US capital could respond to this increased competition – it had to raise its own capital-labour ratios. Some such growth seems to have occurred from 1968 onwards:[68]

Annual growth rate of capital/labour ratio in US[69]

	1957-68	1968-73
manufacturing	1.43	2.24
non-financial corporations	1.32	1.65

In Britain – as might be expected for an economy which spent less than the US on arms right through the period (other things being equal) – the growth of the organic composition of capital starts earlier:

Capital-output ratio[70]

1948-52	1959-62	1968-71	1972-75
1.61	1.78	1.97	2.19

Interestingly enough, according to these figures, by the early 1970s it had begun to reach the level that preceded the long drawn out British crisis of the interwar years. The **Bank of England Quarterly** has also given figures showing a rise in the capital-output ratio of 50 per cent between 1960 and the mid-1970s. 'These changes', it writes, 'mean that the downward trend in the rate of return on capital from 1960 to 1973, and the more dramatic fall since, have been much more marked than the decline of real profits in company value added'[71] (total output after deducting cost of materials).

Samuel Brittan, the **Financial Times** columnist, has noted with bewilderment a similar trend:

> There has been an underlying long term decline in the amount of output per unit of capital in manufacturing . . . This is a fairly general experience in the industrial countries . . . One can construct a fairly plausible story for any one country, but not for the industrial world as a whole.[72]

Such changes in the organic composition were bound to curtail the Great Boom. As investment grew more rapidly than the labour it employed, either the rate of profit had to fall, *or* there had to be a drastic reduction in the proportion of output going to workers (an increase in the rate of exploitation). Unless the 'workers' share' was hammered down, the pressure for firms (and states) to undertake new and ever more massive investments would be accompanied by a fall in the average level of profits to be expected from those investments – so that any cyclical or other increase in the cost of the investment (an increase in the price of energy or raw materials, upward pressure on wages, a sudden upward surge of interest rates) would make the investments unprofitable. Under those circumstances firms would start huge investment projects, then curtail them half way through. But in doing so, they would create precisely the disturbances to the cost calculations of other firms that would destroy their profit possibilities too. A generally low level of investment and a high degree of economic instability would follow.

However, increasing the rate of exploitation of the workforce was not an answer either. It might enable individual capitals to protect their levels of profit.[73] But only by cutting back on the total market for consumer goods, thus making the system ever more dependent upon a high level of investment for its expansion and open to ever greater damage if this was not forthcoming.

This combination of stagnating investment and economic instability was precisely what developed in the 1970s. The oil crisis of 1973 was the straw which broke the camel's back, tipping into crisis a system which was already operating with an increasingly high organic composition of cpital.

But to see the form taken by the crisis that ensued, it is necessary to look first at some of the changes produced in the system by the Great Boom.

Labour power in the Great Boom: the welfare state, the family and immigration

There had been a surplus of labour in almost all countries before the Second World War. In the western states there had been huge levels of unemployment in the 1920s and especially the 1930s. In the USSR, the high levels of unemployment of the 1920s fell with the arms-oriented expansion of heavy industry from 1928-9 onwards – but even then there was sufficient surplus labour for between five and ten million people to be put to work at very low levels of productivity in slave camps.

With the advent of the war economy, unemployment fell to levels experienced by the system before only during brief boom periods. Thus, in the US unemployment fell from 17.1 per cent in 1939 to 1.7 per cent in 1944 and 1.0 per cent in 1945; if it rose to 5.3 per cent with disarmament and the mild recession of 1948-9, it was back down to less than 3 per cent in the early 1950s. In Britain, the figure had been 10.3 per cent in 1938; it fell to about 1 per cent in the course of the war, and hovered between 1½ and 2 per cent in the 1950s. In Germany, the Nazi war economy virtually abolished unemployment in the mid-1930s; there was a high level of unemployment with the economic dislocation of the early post war years; but the figure fell to 4 per cent in 1957 and a mere 1 per cent in 1960.

For two decades and more, what worried the capitalist state was not coping with unemployment, but rather ensuring that employment grew at sufficient speed to keep pace with the ever greater demand for labour power. In the US for instance the number of manual workers grew from 20½ million in 1940 to 27½ million in 1970; the number of clerical and salesworkers from 8½ million to 18½ million.[74] All the advanced countries experienced similar expansions in the working population.

So coping with unemployment was *not* a worry for the main capitalist states for the duration of the long boom. In fact, their problem was quite the opposite – absorbing the previously unemployed into production was not enough, in itself, to feed the long boom's seemingly insatiable appetite for labour power. In the US, for example, the employed workforce rose by 60 per cent between 1940 and 1970. Such expansion demanded completely new supplies of labour power. Whether politicians and government administrators liked it or not, the state had to bear some of the burden of ensuring these. It had to regulate the labour market as never before.

The role of supplying the raw material, labour, for economic or military competition could no longer be left to the 'free' labour market. The state had to supplement – and even partially *supplant* – the wages system with services and subventions provided by itself.

One answer to the shortage of labour power lay in reducing the agricultural workforce still more – whether through state-sponsored amalgamations of small farms as in western Europe or through state-enforced 'collectivisation' as in Russia and eastern Europe. Another lay in encouraging massive emigration of people from the less developed countries to the cities of the advanced countries (from Turkey, eastern and southern Europe to Germany; from Yugoslavia, Portugal, Spain and Algeria to France, from the West Indies and the Indian subcontinent to Britain, from Puerto Rico to the US). A third – again adopted almost everywhere – was the drawing of married women into paid employment.

Yet each of the ways of enlarging the labour force created new problems for capital and state.

Squeezing labour from agriculture could work only if resources were put into agriculture in order to increase its productivity. This could be very expensive. But the alternative was that the provision of food for the growing urban population and raw materials for industry would suffer, creating working class discontent and bottlenecks in accumulation. While there was a low level of industrial development such problems could be relatively minor. But as expansion proceeded, they could become more and more of a drag on further expansion – as we have seen most vividly in recent years in the eastern bloc countries.

Migration from the Third World was a very cheap way of getting labour power. The advanced country had to bear none of the costs of rearing and educating this part of its labour force – effectively, it was getting a subsidy from the immigrant workers' country of origin. The new workforce was usually younger than the 'native' workforce, and demanded less in the way of health care, old age pensions and so on. And its members were usually more prepared to tolerate low wages, harsh working conditions, rigid discipline and so on – in short, to be super-exploited. The pool from which this new labour came was potentially limitless.

Yet there were practical limits. As migrant workers became accustomed to living and working in their new home, they demanded conditions closer to those of established workers: they wanted decent accommodation, education and welfare benefits for their children. The state had either to increase its expenditure on these things – or to see growing social tensions that could lead to either intensified class struggles (to a considerable extent the revolt in France in 1968 was a revolt of such new workers) or to 'racial' explosions. Unable to afford the social expenditure needed to head off such sources of social instability, the state usually reacted by imposing controls on further immigration.

The wholesale entry of married women into the workforce also demanded a certain level of investment by the state. Means had to be found to ensure that it did not lead to neglect of child rearing – or the socialisation of the next generation of workers – or a breakdown in the provision of food, shelter and clothing for the male workforce. Many of these means could be provided, at relatively low cost, with the application of new technology. The refrigerator, washing machine and vacuum cleaner, the replacement of the coal fire by electricity, gas or oil heating, the popularisation of frozen foods, the spread of fast food outlets, even the television set – all had the effect of reducing the amount of effort needed to ensure the reproduction of both present and future labour power.[75] And they usually cost not a penny to the state or capital, being paid for by the family out of the enlarged income it received as the wife took up paid employment. Caring for young children while both their parents worked created greater difficulties, since the provision of nursery facilities could be costly for the state – even if these costs too could often be recouped from the wage of the working wife.

So all the methods of expanding the labour force could work, up to a certain point – but beyond that they tended to imply quite considerable overhead costs. These costs could be borne while the system was expanding rapidly. But they became a burden once the Great Boom collapsed.

There was another solution available to the labour shortage. But it was even more expensive than these. This was to increase state expenditure on the reproduction of the labour force, so as to increase the average level of skill.[76]

In all the advanced countries there was a considerable increase in educational expenditures during the Great Boom – particularly in the upper grades of secondary education and in higher education.[77] As James O'Connor has noted for the US: 'In the late 1950s and 1960s, this emphasis on technical progress . . . stimulated a rapid expansion of low level technical education and the establishment of a vast system of higher education by local and state governments. The state replaced the family as the main socialising agency of the youthful apprentice'. This fitted a situation where '95 per cent of employment growth was in the "upper half" of the labour market (workers with high school diplomas or better)'.[78]

Alongside the growth in 'educational' expenditures there has also been – in most countries – growth in health expenditures. These were necessary if the impact on production of sickness was to be reduced at a time of labour shortage. Hence the trend towards split health services, with one sector very efficient at mending sick or injured workers and getting them back into the workforce, the other concerned with those unlikely to enter productive labour again – the chronically sick, the old and the mentally ill (of course, there is usually a third sector as well: a private sector – or in eastern Europe a privileged part of the state sector – which treats the rich and powerful).

Finally, there was a third area of expansion of state expenditures designed to increase productivity – expenditures designed to provide a feeling of security for employed workers. In this category fell old age pensions (especially those at least partly financed by company schemes) and unemployment benefits. Again O'Connor has correctly noted: 'Although social security contributes to social and political stability by conservatising unemployed and retired workers, the primary purpose is to create a sense of economic security within the ranks of employed workers and thereby raise morale and reinforce discipline'. Hence it was that in many countries in the late 1960s wage-related benefits and redundancy payments were introduced. They were the other side of the 'shake-out' of labour from older industries.

All these measures can be seen as necessary to capital if it was to increase the productivity of the labour force. Yet they are also often seen from another perspective – as concessions made by capital to the political and economic demands of the working class movement. There is no doubt, for instance, that political considerations did play roles in the introduction of the 'welfare state' in Britain at the close of the Second World War: as the future Tory cabinet minister Quintin

Hogg (now Lord Hailsham) put in in 1943, 'If you do not give the people reform they will give you revolution'. Again, the expansion of welfare with the 'great society' programme of President Johnson in the US in the 1960s owed much to the disturbing experience for the ruling class of the ghetto uprisings of 1964-8.

Yet the spread of welfare services was not just a reaction to working class pressure. Countries with a relatively weak and quiescent working class often had a higher level of services by the late 1960s than those with stronger movements. Japan, for instance, was a country with a low level of welfare expenditure in the 1950s and early 1960s (only a third of that in Europe and the US). Yet by 1980 this expenditure had grown sufficiently to help create a very large public sector deficit. As the expansion of the labour force came to depend on the reproduction of urban workers rather than migration from the countryside, the state had to step in.

But the two sorts of explanation for the growth of welfare are not necessarily contradictory. For a long period capital felt that welfare expenditures could satisfy simultaneously two different needs – to buy the acquiescence of the working class, but at the same time to raise productivity so that the cost of doing so was not a burden on accumulation. Just as wages both reproduce labour power *and* are seen by workers as justifying the toil of work, so the 'social wage' element in public expenditure both increased the productivity of labour power and made workers believe society cared for them.

This 'socialisation' of labour costs had some important consequences for the system as a whole. It meant that from the point of view of the national state capitalism labour was no longer 'free' in the traditional sense. In the classical picture of the system, workers, cut off from the means of production, were only able to sustain themselves in so far as they sold their labour power. And capitalists paid only for the labour power, without having to sustain the human being who was the bearer of it: this was capitalism's great advantage over slavery from the point of view of efficient exploitation. For under slavery, the human being was the property of the exploiter and had to be looked after like any other piece of property, whether or not he or she was particularly productive.

In a sense the welfare state introduced into the economics of capitalism an element of the economic calculations relevant to slavery. Under conditions of acute labour shortage, the national capitalist state had to see the national working class as its property, to be tended and cared for as well as exploited if productivity was to match international levels. This was most clearly displayed in the case of the state which built a wall along its border to prevent expensively trained labour fleeing to work elsewhere. But it was visible everywhere, as wages came to constitute only part of the living standard of the worker. This was why the state was repeatedly driven to apply measures designed to force people into the productive workforce – prison sentences for those guilty of 'parasitism' in the USSR, laws against vagrancy and 'abusing' social security in Britain, elaborate schemes to make sure that selling one's labour power was always much more remunerative than living on the welfare state safety net. There was a partial negation of the character of free labour – but only a *partial* negation (as was shown by the way in which those previously outside the labour market – those in the slave camps of Russia, many housewives in the west – were drawn into it).

Yet even this limited 'negation' of the free labour market was a burden that put up the overheads of each national capital. It does not matter a lot exactly how these overheads are categorised (whether as expenditure on 'social capital', as 'indirectly productive expenditures' or as 'non-productive costs of production') they all served to raise the level of expenditure that had to be undertaken by the national state in pursuit of international competitiveness. As such they exerted a downward pressure on the rate of return on the total national investment.[79]

For a long period this did not seem to matter. Other factors were at work protecting the rate of profit. But once the upward dynamic of the boom began to weaken, the costs of welfare became a crucial problem. The two functions – of increasing productivity *and* buying consent – were no longer complementary. Capital had to try to reduce the cost of maintaining and increasing productivity, even if doing so upset its old mechanisms for keeping control over the working class. The trend now was increasingly for welfare benefits to be related to the potential productiveness of the recipients. Those in employment (or thought likely to enter or re-enter it in the near future) were to get one level of treatment; those who had dropped out of it permanently, a much lower level.

The fact that the 'social wage' had become something taken for granted by workers presented problems for governments who tried to follow such a policy. Just as each individual capital has to worry about keeping workers' resistance in check when it plans cuts in wages, so governments have to worry about reducng resistance to a minimum when cutting the 'social wage'. The result is that the creation of 'two welfare states' does not proceed nearly as fast as the most ruthless capitalist economists demand.

Hence even the Thatcher government in Britain has not been able to follow capitalist rationality through to the end in its treatment of the unemployed. That would mean estimating how many of the unemployed needed to be kept as a reserve army for future production needs, providing them with a level of dole sufficient to keep them fit for production (although not so high as to 'destroy their incentive to work') – and writing off the rest of the unemployed, forcing them down into pauperage. Instead, in Britain, the government has felt compelled to keep the value of 'long term' social security payments close to the level of inflation. This has caused the total costs of welfare payments to rise with mass unemployment, leading the public sector deficit to grow, despite all the government's efforts.

Poland's ruling class faced a similar problem in 1980. Its attempts to restrict food subsidies so as to ensure that only the most productive workers (and, of course, the completely unproductive bureaucrats, police chiefs and army officers) were adequately fed provoked resistance from the whole working class.

The fact that the competitive pressures of the world system demanded a 'rationalisation' of the 'social wage' did not at all mean that this could simply be imposed. It is true that the dynamic of the system imposed certain pressures on each of its component ruling classes. But it was the class struggle that determined whether they were able to do as those pressures dictated, or whether they got torn apart in the process.

Capital centralisation and the role of the state

The classic mechanism for the centralisation of capital was the crisis. It bankrupted some capitals and enabled others to buy them up on the cheap. In doing so, it enabled the remaining capitals to raise their rate of profit, and it enabled the system as a whole to write off the costs of the depreciation of constant capital due to technical progress.

But for three decades or more there were no major crises. Bankruptcies occurred, of course, but they were of small firms, of little importance to the system as a whole.

Yet capital continued to be concentrated in fewer and larger units:

US: **percentage of total assets held by:**[80]

	100 biggest firms	*200 biggest firms*
1925	34.5	—
1929	38.2	45.8
1933	42.5	49.5
1939	41.4	58.7
1954	41.9	50.4
1958	46.0	55.2
1962	45.5	55.1
1965	45.9	55.6
1968	48.4	60.4

**UK: Percentage share of largest hundred firms
in net manufacturing output[81]**

1909	1935	1949	1958	1963	1970
16	24	21	32	37	46

This concentration took place, by and large, through mergers and takeover bids which did not, typically, involve the writing-off of the capital of the taken-over firm. In Britain 'between 1966 and 1968 about 80 per cent of deaths [of firms] were due to merger, and between 1948 and 1972 half of all quoted firms were subject to merger activity.'[82]

And so, in the 1950s and 1960s, the destruction of capital through crises played a very small role in offsetting the decline in the rate of profit.

It still meant, however, that at the end of the period the system was made up, even more than it had been in the 1930s, of gigantic, interlinked firms, each very dependent on others for its survival.

Alongside the concentration of capital went an increased dependence on the state. The level of state control tended to increase everywhere as the Great Boom showed the first signs of faltering in the late 1960s and early 1070s. Governments were reluctant to allow inefficient firms to go bankrupt when this would damage other firms – either through debts owed or loss of workers. When, for instance, the US railroad giant, Penn Central, got into trouble in 1970, the US government rushed in to prop it up. When Rolls-Royce in Britain went bust, a right-wing Tory government nationalised it: hence the paradox of a government committed on principle to denationalisation ending with more of industry under its control than when it took office. When a host of dubious banking operations throughout the world collapsed, ranging from smallish 'secondary banks' right through to the off-shore giant IOS, the central banks pressurised the rest of the financial institutions to pick up the pieces. Indeed, one of the significant things about the crisis of the mid-1970s was that, because of state and central bank intervention, there were virtually no major bankruptcies.

Increased concentration of capital and growing state intervention to stave off bankruptcies had an important effect upon the overall performance of the system. The old pressures to *reduce* prices during recessions no longer operated. For firms with a near monopoly position felt able to increase prices so as to protect their profit levels on a reduced level of output.

The radical American economist Howard Sherman has shown the impact of this monopolisation: 'In almost all the recessions and depressions up to the recession of 1948, prices *fell* in every economic contraction. In the recession of 1948 prices in the non-monopoly industries fell by 7.8 per cent. But the prices of monopoly industries fell by much less, by 1.9 per cent. Since that time, the competitive [non-monopoly] prices have still fallen in each recession. But monopoly prices have *risen* in each recession . . .'[83] Thus in the competitive sector prices fell by 1.5 per cent, 0.3 per cent and 3.0 per cent in the recession years of 1953, 1958 and 1969; while the monopoly sector experienced *rises* of 1.9 per cent, 0.5 per cent and 5.9 per cent in the same years.

As a means of actually protecting monopoly profits, the raising of prices became less effective over time. For it could work only while there was a substantial non-monopoly sector whose falling prices cut the costs of the monopolies as their own prices went up. Once most of the economy was dominated by monopolies, the costs of goods bought by the monopolies tended to rise as fast as the goods they sold. All they were doing was chasing their own tails. Only cutting *wages* could restore profitability then. And that was difficult with full employment – usually requiring, in fact, state intervention to police wages by the use of incomes policy.

However futile it was for all capitalists to raise prices at once, this could not stop each feeling compelled to do so. The result was an important new problem for the system. Prices had always risen in capitalist booms – but had then fallen again in slumps. Now they rose in slumps as well as booms. The concentration of capital meant that *inflation* was a permanent feature of ageing capitalism.

Waste

The extreme concentration of capital had one other consequence. It meant, necessarily, an increase in the level of inefficiency and waste.

Capitalist firms had always developed in inefficient and wasteful ways. Production would develop in certain directions and at a certain tempo in response to market needs. The 'relations of production' within the firm – the allocation of resources within the managerial hierarchy, the relations between managers and workers – would be moulded accordingly. But when market needs shifted, there was no automatic adjustment of these internal structures. For a time the firm would go on producing its output in much the same manner, often using outmoded technology – and in a boom would probably be able to get away with doing so. It was only the crisis which forced the adjustment, as more innovative firms threatened to make the less efficient insolvent.

A prolonged period without crises necessarily meant an increase in inefficiency. Monopolisation exacerbated this trend. A firm with a tight hold over a large chunk of the national market could continue to dispose of its output, even if its technology was increasingly out of date. There were numerous examples of this in the 1950s and 1960s. Thus the world's biggest manufacturing corporation, General Motors, was characterised for years by the way it turned out new car models that contained virtually no new technology:

> There hadn't been an important product innovation in the industry since the automatic transmission and power steering in 1949. That was almost a quarter of a century of technical hibernation. In the place of product innovation, the automobile industry went on a two-decade marketing binge which generally offered up the same old product under the guise of something new and useful . . . [84]

The reason for this was that a managerial structure had crystallised in which 'the men in power . . . put personal loyalties from one executive to another and protection of the system above management skills; and put the use of corporate politics in place of sound business leadership . . . There was no forward planning to speak of at GM . . . '[85]

Models were launched which did not sell, and parts were produced which only made a 'profit' because other parts of the corporation or its dealers were forced to buy them. All this was possible for several decades because of the firm's hold over the market. Not until the late 1970s was it forced to come to terms with gross waste and inefficiency that had been already visible 15 or 20 years before.

Inefficiency was not automatically reduced as the boom began to falter. As we have seen, firms could try to protect their profits by upping prices. And if this failed, their sheer size was usually a guarantee that they would not go bust: the state would step in with subsidies first. Instead of the inefficient and wasteful firms being wiped out, the cost of their inefficiency had to be borne through taxation and bank losses, by the efficient.

But waste did not merely arise from a failure to adopt more efficient production methods based on new technology. It also arose from the search for such methods.

Attempts to harness the most advanced technology increasingly required huge levels of capital expenditure. The state was often the only body with the ability to gather together such resources, and so the development of technology was a national effort. Yet the scale of the investment itself had to be determined by the development of the productive forces on a world scale, and so led to a growth of capacity out of all proportion to the national economy in which it was located, twisting its priorities away from balanced development.

Thus the history of the US arms programme is in part a history of very expensive projects undertaken and then abandoned at enormous cost. In the late 1950s and the 1960s 'at least 68 weapons systems, worth $9 billion had to be abandoned as unworkable . . .' The others 'come off the assembly line two years later than promised.'[86] 'Of 13 major aircraft and missile programmes with sophisticated electronic systems built for the airforce and the navy since 1955 at a cost of $40 billion, only four, costing $5 billion, could be relied on to reach a performance level of 75 per cent or above of their specifications.'[87]

The British aerospace industry – both military and civil – has an equally long list of failures, right through from the giant Brabazon airliner of the 1940s to the Blue Streak rocket of the 1960s and the Concorde of the 1970s.

The situation in other industries based upon advanced technology is not substantially different – witness the record of civil nuclear projects that have had to be abandoned because of the cost of safety precautions, or the pathetic attempts of rival governments to get into microchip technology.

Such waste could be borne by the system during the Great Boom. But once the boom faded, there were difficulties in absorbing its cost. Worse, the waste of huge advanced technological white elephants multiplied. Thus for instance British governments of the early and mid-1970s poured vast sums into a technological transformation of the steel industry, aiming to produce 32 million tons a year in plants as advanced as anything else in the world. At least half this investment was wasted, since by the early 1980s global overproduction meant the industry was not able to dispose of more than 12-16 million tons. Instead of acting as a boost for the rest of British-based capital, the investment in steel was just one more drain on its ability to compete internationally. Things were not that different in the US: there were even cases of technological regression as firms mothballed large, expensive, technologically modern plants built in the early 1970s and instead concentrated production in older plants which, because they were smaller, could produce a lower level of output at lower unit costs.[88]

The smaller the national economy which attempted to marshal the resources for international military and market competition, the greater the burden in terms both of disproportionate economic development and sheer waste. Hence the much remarked scale of waste in the centrally administered economies of the east.[89] Far from proving – as some writers contend[90] – how different these economies are from those of western capitalism, the level of waste testifies in fact to what east and west have in common. Each of the eastern European states is endeavouring to compete with larger, better established rivals – even the giant USSR has to try to match the arms output of an American economy which is twice its size. The scale of resources going to each investment project is determined, not by what the national economy can sustain, but by what international competition demands. Hence the way in which at the beginning of each five-year 'plan' more investment projects are started than can be completed. Hence the way that, in an attempt to finish some, others are frozen (leaving vast accumulations of wealth standing idle as unfinished plant), living standards are cut and unbearable strains are put on the balance of payments. Hence too a growing burden of waste which can be less and less afforded as the high growth rates of the 1950s give way to the near-zero growth rates of the 1980s.

Each of the factors we have looked at in the last few pages have added to the costs each national capital has to undertake in order to survive. They mean that a growing proportion of national output does not go *directly* into the means either of market competition or military competition. This is shown by the rising levels of state expenditure in all economies – and within those totals, the relative growth of non-arms spending. In the US, for instance, the share of defence in total federal expenditure declined from 64.6 per cent in 1955, to 47.6 per cent in 1960, to 40.8 per cent in 1965, to 39 per cent in 1970, and to 25.6 per cent in 1975.[91]

Yet none of these factors could, by itself, have caused the crisis. They could all be easily afforded by the system during the Great Boom. However, once the boom faltered, with a declining rate of profit, they intensified the crisis. They effectively served to reduce the national rate of profit still more. Attempts to offset them become crucial for national capitals – by cutting back 'unnecessary' expenditures and by changes in taxation policy to the detriment of workers (so effectively doubly exploiting workers: once through the sale of their labour power, the second time compelling them to hand to the state a greater part of their income – a form of exploitation typical of many pre-capitalist societies).

The new finance capital and the crisis

As individual nationally based capitals have stagnated, so they have attempted to ease the burden by moving towards a greater inter-nationalisation of production.

One expression of this is the explosive expansion of banking operations outside the control of national states. This both provides individual, nationally based capitals with the means of transcending national boundaries, but, in turn, it destroys the ability of national states to impose a degree of 'planning' upon the capitals associated with them.

The banks began to expand their international operations on an enormous scale at the end of the 1960s. Foreign currency commitments of west European banks rose from about $25 billion in 1968 to about $200 billion in 1974. These had their origin in the US balance of payments deficit. The deficit was paid for with dollars that passed into the reserves of overseas banks (including, of course, overseas branches of US banks) which were then able to use them to make loans outside the controls laid down by their own governments. The system received another tremendous boost after the 1973 oil price rise, when the banks received huge deposits from oil-producing states.

However, there was a more fundamental cause for this new banking phenomenon: as the nationally based capitals were led to attempt investments which exceeded their internal funds, they were forced to look towards the banks, which could pool the surpluses obtained by many capitals. In the US, for example, in the 1950s and early 1960s, only a little over 25 per cent of corporate spending was financed from outside the firm; by mid-1974 this had soared to 65 per cent.[92] Long term debt as a percentage of shareholdings in US corporations rose from 87 per cent in 1955 to 130 per cent in 1965 and 181 per cent in 1970.[93]

The borrowing of the US corporations was more than matched by borrowing from both the third world and eastern Europe. Between 1965 and the end of 1974 the combined debt of 74 less-developed countries rose from $39 billion to $119 billion; between 1973 and 1975 the total debt of the third world more than doubled; by 1976 these countries owed $7 billion to private banks in the US, western Europe and Japan.[94] In the 1970s eastern European borrowing similarly soared – until it exceeded $60 billion. But a price had to be paid for this dependence on the banks: a growing proportion of the surplus value of individual capitals had to be handed back to the banks in interest repayments. And this meant further dependence on the banks for access to the funds for further investment. In the USA, the net interest paid by non-financial corporations as a percentage of profits before tax soared from 5.2 per cent in 1950/59 to 11.5 per cent in 1960/69 and 33.3 per cent in 1970/78.[95]

In eastern Europe the situation was much worse, with debt servicing sometimes consuming a major proportion of the currency earned through exports:

Eastern Europe's debt problem (1980)[96]

	Net debt as percentage of GNP	Debt service as percentage of non-comecon exports
East Germany	9.2	54
Bulgaria	11.8	37
Poland	17.7	92
Romania	18.4	22
Hungary	20.2	37

This trend has very important implications for the dynamic of the system as a whole. The autarchic state capitalisms that emerged in the 1930s and at the end of the Second World War could ensure that investment took place regardless of the expected rate of profit. All that mattered was that there was some surplus value – some *mass of profit* – that the state could channel into military production or productive accumulation.

Now the *rate* of profit regains its old importance. For only if they get an adequate rate of profit can individual state capitals and individual multinational corporations pay the internationally determined rate of interest they owe to the banks. Nationally based accumulation cannot proceed unless it can match internationally determined standards of profitability.

Unless the national capital or the multinational corporation can meet these minimum standards it is operating at a loss once it has paid off its interest. And for a national economy to operate at a loss is to *contract* rather than expand. The emergence of international finance capital means that we have entered the age of the state capitalist recession.

As in the classical capitalist crisis, the tendency is for the internationally prevailing rate of interest to move in the opposite direction from the average international rate of profit. As profitability falls, the supply of funds to the banks gets tighter, yet more capitals get into difficulties which make them look to the banks for yet greater borrowing; the demand for funds rises faster than the supply, and interest rates soar, putting still further pressure on individual capitals.

The phase of capitalist history in which national capitals could ignore low profit rates by retreating into themselves is over. The old structure of the capital market – and the role played in this by financial capital – has re-emerged, at a higher, international level. Whole states are driven to abandon their half-finished investments at enormous cost, out of fear that they will not yield the level of profitability needed to pay off the bankers. The whole world becomes drawn into a single rhythm of half-hearted expansion of investment and convulsive contraction, of short, limited booms and long depressions.

Thus in the early 1970s a number of third world and east European states tried to escape from internal stagnatory pressures by recourse to international borrowing. They – and the banks – assumed they would be able to pay off their debts on the basis of sales to a world economy they expected to boom. Their own investments helped to create the boom conditions – but in doing so, contributed to the forcing up of raw material prices (especially oil) and interest rates – which led the boom to collapse. They were left with investments they could not fully complete and interest payments they could pay only by further borrowings. Brazil, Turkey, Romania, and notably Poland, boomed as never before in the early 1970s and managed to sustain relatively high rates of growth through the world recession of the mid-1970s, only to come down with a very big bump towards the end of the decade.

The bankers at least recognised the similarities between the different economies which were in hock to them. As one international banking monthly put it: 'Poland's commercial bank creditors ... are keenly aware that any agreement will set a precedent not only for the restructuring Poland itself will need over the next few years, but also for other countries'.[97]

It is as if a film of the pre-war economic crises is being rerun – but with a difference. The competing individual firms which borrowed from banks within a national economy have given way to state capitalisms and multinational firms borrowing from international banks within an international economy.

In 1929-31 the weakness of individual firms forced them to rely increasingly on the banks. The banks were temporarily boosted as a result – but were also weakened, in some cases fatally, as it became clear that firms could not repay all their debts. The crisis in industry created a crisis in banking which then deepened the crisis in industry.

In 1984, international bankers are afraid that states and firms have borrowed funds they will be unable to repay. The banks could pressurise their debtors by threatening to drive some into bankruptcy – but implementing their threats might threaten the stability of some of the banks themselves. Yet not to put the pressure on is to accept a lower level of profitability for the whole world banking system and to reduce still further the surplus available for new accumulation on a world scale. The world system is caught between the Scylla of cumulative collapse and the Charybdis of declining profitability and stagnation.

However, the pattern is not simply a return to the past. The difference is that in the 1930s the national state could provide a fixed structure within which the interplay of competing firms and banks took place. So the state could enforce a certain common discipline. Above all, it could restrict the overall level of money and credit in the economy.

The internationalisation of production and banking over the past three decades has destroyed much of the ability of the state to enforce such restriction today. The huge bank funds that flow daily from country to country make it very difficult indeed for national states to control the national supply of buying power. Restrictions on the supply of obvious forms of money (the banknotes and so on which make up what economists call M1) have little impact on the total supply including less obvious forms (M3).

In fact, governments have not attempted to enforce rigid restrictions. For success in doing so would mean the banks having to refuse credit to large industrial concerns, driving them into bankruptcy. Fear of the impact on the rest of the national economy leads governments to hold back – indeed, to urge the banks to extend still more credits. Hence the spectacle of the 'monetarist' government in Britain urging the banks to engage in lifeboat operations – as when it made them keep the Canadian-based multinational, Massey-Ferguson, in business – although the result is necessarily an expansion of credit and of the money supply.

Keynesian perspectives of state intervention to sustain the level of production and employment can no longer work because of the internationalisation of the system, but neither can the perspective of state intervention to control the money supply and reduce inflation, as put forward by supporters of Professor Friedman.

Whatever the ideology professed by the rulers of individual states – Keynesian, Stalinist or monetarist – in practice they are more and more forced to forego central control over economic activities. They are reduced merely to responding to external pressures. Each state is like a boxer on his last legs, desperately marshalling all his energies to block this punch and then that, but no longer capable of working out what to do next.

From the outside, the state and its 'planning' might seem all powerful. From the inside the picture is quite the opposite: all that can be seen is incompetence, a complete lack of overall planning, people barking out orders in an attempt to overcome the chaos that their own orders have created, departments struggling one against the other, agencies whose actions are determined by forces they believe they control but which have in reality taken control of them.

A study of Poland by critical intellectuals pointed out in 1979:

> In the real social and economic world there is no such thing as a 'central planner'. Rather there is a heterogenous collection of central institutions using a wide range of different standards to arrive at their decisions. We do know very little about how the centre operates, about how it drafts and adopts macroeconomic decisions... Not only the average citizen but many professional economists and the economic policy makers cannot answer these questions...[98]

Much the same could have been said by a study of the British treasury, the head office of a US multinational corporation or the directing centre of the Pentagon.

A new period of crisis

Since 1973 the world has been in a new period of major economic crises.

The first recession (of 1974-5) did not hit all countries with equal ferocity. A few were able to continue to expand through it either by using oil revenues (Iran, Mexico, Venezuela) or by extensive foreign borrowing (Poland, Brazil). And the others experienced some sort of economic recovery by 1978. The recovery, however, was limited and uneven. Those that had expanded through the first recession now ran into problems of their own, while those that expanded out of the recession most rapidly (especially the US) were soon plagued by inflationary and balance of payments problems which pushed them back towards recession again.

It was not long before a second worldwide contraction was under way. If this was not in general as intense as that of 1973-5, for particular countries (such as Britain and Poland) it was much worse. In this new period, levels of investment were down almost everywhere, growth rates were small and sometimes negative, unemployment doubled and then doubled again, inflation was often in double figures and rarely below 5 per cent.

The crises did not automatically resolve themselves. Ten years after the onset of the first recession, things seemed no more hopeful for the system than at the beginning.

The crisis has not yet, however, been as *deep* so far as the crisis of the 1930s. Even in Britain, where total unemployment is approaching the 1930s level, it is still a smaller proportion of the total labour force than in 1931-2. More significantly, there have not yet been the succession of industrial bankruptcies and bank collapses that characterised the years 1929-31.

There is a connection between the prolonged nature of the present phase of crises and the relative lack of depth compared to the 1930s. Whatever the ostensive ideologies of their rulers, states have been intervening to prevent industrial and financial collapse lest it do irreparable harm to the most profitable firms. And they have tended to nudge the banks into doing the same when the alternative might be the collapse of whole states: witness the amazing spectacle early in 1982 of a US government that had called for sanctions against the eastern bloc, then handing money over to US banks to prevent them foreclosing on Poland's debts. Similarly there was the rescue operation for a bankrupt Mexico in the same year, and the International Monetary Fund support given, grudgingly, to Brazil in 1983.

Yet unless the crisis forces some of the system's component units into liquidation, there can be no reducing the high organic composition of capital that created the crisis. Without this, the losses made by any single large unit of the system have to be spread out among the other units. The world rate of profit falls even more and the pressures towards stagnation get greater.

That does *not* mean that there are *no* countervailing factors at work. Every wage cut, every increase in productivity, every shifting of operations from high wage areas to low wage areas, every weakening of union organisation, serves to increase the rate of exploitation and to pump more surplus value into the possession of individual capitals. Hence the tendency towards an intensification of the struggle of capital against labour. Hence too the tendency towards the migration of labour-intensive industries to parts of the third world and the parallel tendency for there to be a certain revival of sweated labour in all parts of the world: in crisis, capital has always attempted to solve its problems by paying labour power less than its value.

However, the worldwide ratio of investment to labour power (the world organic composition of capital) is too high for an increase in the rate of exploitation to have more than a marginal impact on the rate of profit and thus alleviate the problems of the system as a whole – although of course individual capitals can still enjoy spectacular successes through such methods.

Again, rationalisation through bankruptcy has not fully disappeared. Every year a very high percentage of small, often new, firms go bankrupt. But what happens to them is peripheral to a system in which a hundred or two hundred firms in each state control more than half of total production.

Finally, the onset of the crisis has produced new pressures towards higher arms spending. As each of the superpowers has lost the economic leverage to maintain total hegemony within its own sphere of influence, it has tended to revert to militaristic posturing. The US has felt that the only way to restore its old 'leadership' of 'the free world' is to show that it is capable of military intervention whenever it wishes and that it can outface the Russians in any confrontation, however minor. On the one hand there has been the build up of the Rapid Deployment Force, the direct intervention in Grenada and the indirect intervention in Central America, on the other there has been the upsurge of strategic arms spending with Cruise missiles, Pershing, and MX. Overall, the US has felt that only by increasing the tension between its bloc and the Russians can it frighten its 'allies' into accepting its definition of things.

For the USSR, the fear of its bloc falling apart is, if anything, even greater. It has seen powerful allies switch camps – first the Chinese in the 1960s, then the Egyptians in the 1970s. It can see that the logic of economic development is exerting a pull on its European satellites away from it. And so it feels it has to compete with the US in the new arms build-up.

Yet this new arms spending can provide little relief from the global pressure towards economic crisis. Some sections of unemployed workers get new jobs and some capitals find state-guaranteed profits. But the high technological level of modern arms manufacturing means that the employment effect is small in relation to the expenditure undertaken. And most of the cost of the new arms has to be paid for by capitals that are weak when it comes to market competition. The only way for them to offset the cost is to apply further pressures to living standards and to 'non-productive' jobs. So in the US the shift upward in the arms budget in 1981 was accompanied by the introduction of social welfare cuts that will devastate most of the 'great society' programmes introduced in the 1960s. In Russia and eastern Europe the new arms spending means abandoning all the promises to raise living standards.

While arms spending in the 1940s and 1950s provided an expansion of the economy that enabled governments to tell workers 'You've never had it so good', the arms spending of the 1980s occurs under conditions where many workers begin to feel they have never had it so bad.

All the 'countervailing factors' combined prevent the rate of profit falling to catastrophically low levels and prevent the economy sinking as far down as in the 1930s. But they cannot give new life to the system. They leave it stagnating, with all countries experiencing low growth rates and a few suffering deep decline.

If figures suggest that the capital-output ratio (and therefore the organic composition) in the US has stopped rising in the past three or four years, this is not a sign of health for the system. It only indicates that investment is not proceeding at any great speed, so that the 'countervailing factors' are just enough to stop stagnation turning into a downward somersault. Stagnation can still be interspersed with short, limited booms based in the consumer goods and military hardware industries, as in the US at the time of writing (late 1983); but there does not seem to be the basis for the large-scale revival of investment, which alone could sustain a prolonged boom.

1929-33 saw the last attempt to use the crisis alone as a means of escaping from the pressures that produced crisis. But the rationalisation – the elimination of capitals – needed by the system internationally to solve its problems was too great for it to bear. Hence the severity of the slump. From then on the state has had to intervene to offset the effects of crisis. But the state has dealt with *effects*, not causes – something concealed for more than three decades by the rise of military competition. Now that the needs of military competition are continually in conflict with those of international market competition, state intervention to mitigate the crisis can only serve to prolong it indefinitely.

This does not mean that the world economy is doomed simply to decline. An overall tendency towards stagnation can still be accompanied by minor booms, with small but temporary increases in employment. Each of these, however, only aggravates the problems of the system as a whole and results in further general stagnation, and extreme devastation for particular parts of the system.

Lenin once remarked that the system could survive any crisis, providing the working class allowed itself to be forced to pay the cost in terms of suffering. That remains true. But to escape from the present phase of crisis, the scale of suffering would have to be very great indeed. The bankruptcy of two or three advanced countries, with their industries grinding to a halt and their workers literally starving, might provide the system with the opportunity to enjoy a new round of rapid accumulation. Were a 'theatre nuclear war' possible, it too might promise a new phase of expansion for those capitals that survived it.

But those who run the competing parts of the system can hardly relish either option. The bankruptcy of any major economy could well bring down the multinationals operating in it or the banks which had lent it money, thus leading to a progressive collapse of other capitals. It could also breed new revolutionary working class movements close to the heart of the system. And even US generals cannot be absolutely sure that a 'theatre war' would not develop into a global nuclear confrontation that would destroy virtually all of the US ruling class's capital.

The present phase of crisis is likely to go on and on – until it is resolved either by plunging much of the world into barbarism or by a succession of workers' revolutions.

Appendices:
Other theories of crisis

THE BASIS FOR the argument set out in this book, taking Marx's theory of crisis and extending it to explain the unprecedented boom of the 1940s to the 1970s, was developed twenty years ago by members of the International Socialists, forerunner of the present Socialist Workers Party. The argument had considerable predictive power. As early as 1960-1 we were able to predict that 'by the early 1970s' the world economy would be falling back into the pre-1939 pattern of crisis.

But our argument did not attain any significant hearing outside our own ranks. As the new crisis came to be taken for granted in the late 1960s and early 1970s — and as a whole new generation of intellectuals became interested in Marxism — our theory was peripheral to most of the discussions. A range of quite different explanations of the crisis appeared in Marxist publications.

Appendix one:
Wages as the cause of the crisis

● THE SIMPLEST EXPLANATIONS for the onset of crisis blame rising wages for cutting into profits. In Britain the best-known version of the theory comes not from Tory politicians, but was put forward by two left-wing Oxford economists, Andrew Glyn and Bob Sutcliffe, back in 1972.[1] Their explanation concentrated on British figures, but implied that the argument was of wider, international, relevance.

> British capitalism has suffered such a dramatic decline in profitability that it is now literally fighting for survival. This crisis has developed because mounting demands from the working class for a faster growth in living standards have coincided with growing competition between capitalist countries. This competition has prevented British capitalism from simply accommodating successful wage demands by pushing up prices . . . And it has intensified because the other rich capitalist countries have been subject to the same pressures from the working class as British capitalism . . .[2]

Bob Rowthorn, a Cambridge economist belonging to the British Communist Party, argued very much the same case, pointing to pressure from wages as one of the causes of the crisis in the USA: the rate of profit fell 'because the share of output going to profits fell.' Indeed for Rowthorn this 'accounts for the *entire* reduction of US profitability between 1965 and 1970.'[3]

The notion of a dramatic reversal in the balance of forces between labour and capital, leading to a squeeze on profits, also plays a role in the explanation of the crisis put forward by the Belgian Marxist economist, Ernest Mandel. He has argued that in the late 1960s internationally, the pool of unemployed workers — what Marx called 'the reserve army of labour', because they were always there in reserve, to be called into production if needed — this pool had been used up by capitalist expansion. The resulting competition among capitalists for scarce labour, he said, pushed up wages, so cutting into profits. The 'limits of the reserve army' were reached, 'and a pronounced increase in real wages started to roll back the rate of surplus value.'[4]

There are, however, decisive counter-arguments against the claim that wages have caused the crisis.

Firstly, the argument just does not fit the facts for at least two of the western economies — including the giant US economy.[5] The sources usually given to justify the argument about wages and the crisis are those of Glyn and Sutcliffe for Britain and Nordhaus for the USA.[6] Nordhaus' figures are, for instance, quoted as authoritative by

Mandel and Rowthorn. Yet they are open to considerable doubts.[7]

The radical economist Perlo has given a quite different interpretation to Nordhaus' data. Giving figures which probably exagger-
ate the level of profits,[8] he suggests that the 'share of profits' in the US
rose from 19.5 per cent in 1946 to 22.1 per cent in 1974.[9] A more recent
Brookings Papers analysis of US profits by Feldstein and Summers
also casts great doubts on the figures given by Nordhaus. This suggests
that the fall in US profits is much less than Nordhaus claimed.[10]

Percentage rate of profit for the US

	Net	Gross	Cyclically adjusted Net
1950–59	11.1	11.1	11.2
1956–65	10.9	11.3	11.9
1960–69	11.7	11.9	12.1
1970–76	7.9	9.6	10.4

It can be seen that no decline in the rate of profit, on any measure,
takes place until after 1970.

Glyn and Sutcliffe's figures for Britain claim that the share of
'wages and salaries' rose from 73.3 per cent to 78.8 per cent between
1955 and 1970, and that there was a corresponding decline in profit's
share. But the figures are subject to many of the same criticisms as
Nordhaus's. They assume that *none* of the cost of financing stock
appreciation is borne by company borrowing. And they give figures
before tax. As Glyn himself has admitted in a later article, the share of
wages and salaries does not rise, but sinks, from 55.6 per cent in 1955
to 50.2 per cent in 1970, once direct and indirect taxes are taken into
account.[11]

C J Burgess and A J Webb have shown that if you take the share of
national income in Britain going to all companies after tax, making
deductions for stock appreciation and capital consumption, and
adding on the government hand-outs to industry, you find that there
is no decline in the 1950s and 1960s.[12]

But the claim that 'a growing share going to wages' has provoked
the crisis falls down, not only on the factual evidence, but for other
reasons too. Its proponents also fail to present any adequate explanation of the mechanism which might cause the alleged upsurge of wages
at the expense of profits internationally.

An attempted explanation — given, for example, by Rowthorn
and Mandel and by the Americans Body and Crotty[13] goes something
like this. Economic expansion can take place as long as there is a
'reserve army of labour', prepared to enter employment at a relatively
low level of wages. But in the 1960s this reserve army dried up,
leading to a growth of wages (either because of upward bidding by

capitalists seeking labour or by an increase in the bargaining power of unions).

The first difficulty lies in the claim that there was a 'drying up' of the reserve army of labour. Expansion of production leads not only to the sucking of workers into production; it also means rises in productivity which drive workers out of some areas of production and into others[14] (witness the rising average level of unemployment in the US in the 1950s and 1960s; and the near doubling of unemployment in Britain through 'shake out' during the Wilson government of the late 1960s).

What is more, capitalist expansion in the 1950s and 1960s had the effect of massively *increasing* in size the worldwide reserve army: in the metropolitan countries conditions were created in which the number of married women prepared to enter the workforce rose massively; at the same time, throughout the world there was a huge migration of workers from the countryside to the towns, so that in nearly all the 'developing countries' there were vast pools of labour only too eager to get employment in the 'developed countries'. There was no sign of these pools drying up in the late 1960s. Look at the vast influx of 'illegal' Mexican labour into the US. Look at the growth of the 'foreign' population of Germany, doubling from 1.92 million in 1968 to 4.13 million in 1974, until deliberate government action was used during the crisis of 1975 to force about a million of the 'guest workers' out of the German economy and back to the 'third world'.

Rather than the 'reserve army' drying up, something quite different happened — the crisis created problems of *absorbing* the reserve army. In fact, the effect of the crisis has been to extend the reserve army: it has doubled unemployment in the OECD countries and more than doubled it in the 'developing countries'. If a 'drying up' of the reserve army was the cause of the crisis, then the crisis could never have happened, and should now be resolving itself as the reserve army grows still further.

This leads us straight into another difficulty with the 'wages share' argument — it just cannot explain why all the western economies moved into crisis at the same point in the mid-1970s. In Italy, in Britain, in Spain and in France there were important improvements in the level of working class organisation in the late 1960s and early 1970s. But there was no similar improvement in the other major economies — Japan, West Germany, and, above all, the US. Unemployment in the US grew once the Vietnam War began to wind down, and the proportion of union members in the US working class has fallen significantly since then, from 22.4 per cent of the labour force in 1965 to 20.1 per cent in 1976.[15] Furthermore, as Perlo has pointed out, for the period before the outbreak of the 1974–5 recession, 'there was a sharp decline in real wages of non-agricultural workers from late 1972 to spring 1975, while productivity on the whole increased.'[16]

Finally, the 'wages share' argument simply cannot explain the timing of the turning point from expansion to contraction. During the 1950s real wages rose, year after year, in *all* the major capitalist countries. By the mid-1950s even in the countries which had been devastated by the Second World War they were higher than the pre-war figure. Yet the rate of profit was not squeezed, investment grew, inflation remained at a relatively low level and there was near-full employment everywhere.

Even if it is assumed (despite our previous arguments) that in the late 1960s and early 1970s rising wages did cut the 'share of profits' in the output of companies and the national income, why did this happen, when it did not happen in the earlier years of the boom? The explanation can only be that the system could afford the real wage increases then, but could no longer do so. But it follows from this that it is not rising real wages that have caused the crisis, but rather the crisis which has caused real wages to cut into profits. The 'declining share of profit' becomes a product of the crisis, not its cause (even if it is a product of the crisis which feeds back into the economy to make the crisis worse).

Theories that purport to explain the crisis in terms of the 'rising share of wages' or the 'declining rate of exploitation' do no such thing. They force even their adherents to turn to other factors in an effort to overcome the contradictions in their own positions — factors such as government spending (Glyn and, in part, Rowthorn), the changing international structure (Rowthorn) or 'long waves' (Mandel).

Appendix two:
Government spending as the cause of crisis

● THE NOTION THAT excessive government spending has been the cause of the crisis is very widespread. On the right it has been presented by the Oxford economists, Bacon and Eltis.[17] On the left their conclusion has been taken up, for instance, by Aglietta, who writes: 'This analysis uses a terminology other than our own, but is governed by the same perspective', while both Mattick and Yaffe[18] had argued before Bacon and Eltis that 'stagflation' — the historically new combination of stagnation and inflation — was the result of successive Keynesian exercises in deficit budgeting designed to prevent crisis. According to Mattick, efforts by government to bring together 'labor and idle capital for the production of non-marketable goods' lead to a 'constant' growth in the 'non-profit sector' until it 'outweighs the profitable sector and therewith endangers the latter's existence'. 'Deficit financing and government induced production . . . must come to an end. The Keynesian solution will stand exposed as a pseudo-solution capable of postponing but not preventing the contradictory course of capital accumulation.'[19]

But has the 'public sector' been 'squeezing' the 'profit sector'? The evidence for such 'squeezing' is meagre indeed for the period before the onset of world crisis in the early 1970s.

Bacon and Eltis crudely gave figures for employment in the public and the 'productive' (meaning private) sectors. These showed that the former has been growing and the latter falling — and they concluded that the rise in one had *caused* the fall in the other.

But they virtually ignored the fact that the rise in public sector employment was primarily drawing in people — especially married women — who were previously not in the workforce. At the same time there was a growing pool of unemployed labour which would have welcomed work in the 'productive' sector if there had been any available. So in Britain between March 1967 and December 1975, the number of men in employment fell by more than a million; in the same period, the number of women in employment rose by more than 900,000 — and this growth was entirely in the 'service' sector.[20]

Even some bourgeois economists have pointed out that in terms of resources, Bacon and Eltis do not distinguish properly between 'public sector use of resources' and 'transfers made by the state between different components of the private sector, which has no direct impact on the output of that sector' — in other words payments made by the state to individuals and companies in the private sector.[21]

In Britain, 'In the post-war period there has been no substantial increase in the share of resources which the public sector authorities take for their own direct expenditure.'[22] Government expenditure on goods and services was 24 per cent of the GNP in the early 1950s and 27 per cent in 1973. Certainly you cannot explain the crisis which broke in Britain in 1974 by invoking 'excessive' taxation to feed the allegedly insatiable demands of government: 'the aggregate tax burden in the UK fell quite sharply between 1964 and 1973 . . .'[23] So it could not have been 'taxation' of the 'productive' sector to feed the 'unproductive' sector that caused the crisis.

This leaves open the possibility that the 'productive sector' was hit in another way, by Keynesian 'deficit financing', government spending financed by borrowing on the market which drew off the funds otherwise available for private industry. This, essentially, is the argument of Mattick and Yaffe — government borrowing postpones the crisis for a period, only to make it worse when it finally comes.

However, facts again put a huge question mark over any such explanation: real examples of deficit financing have been rare outside war conditions. As Matthews pointed out for Britain during the long boom:

> The question is whether the high level of demands that actually occurred was due to government action or whether it was due to other forces, as a result of which government action was not needed . . . The hypothesis that it was due to fiscal policy is open to a simple, basic objection. This is that throughout the post-war period, the government, so far from injecting demand into the system, has persistently had a large surplus . . .[24]

It is true that there were two periods (prior to the 1974 crisis) when the government embarked upon large *capital-spending* programmes in order to try to give a 'Keynesian' boost to the economy — the Maudling boom of 1962 which was finally ended by Labour in 1966, and the Barber boom of 1972–3 that preceded the crisis of 1974. There was also in the US an important period in which the government resorted to deficits to finance an unpopular upsurge in spending (due to the Vietnam war) — in 1965–8.

Financial balance of government sector, as a percentage of GNP/GDP[25]

	1971	1972	1973	1974	1975
US	−2	−½	—	−½	−4
Japan	−1	−1½	½	−2½	−7
W. Germany	—	—	1½	−1	−6
France	½	½	½	½	−3
Italy	−4½	−6½	−8	−5	—
UK	1½	−1½	−2½	−4½	−5

But these hardly explain the elements of crisis to which these upsurges in spending themselves were a response. So both the 1971 crisis in Britain and the 1973–4 crisis internationally followed years *not* marked by budget deficits.

Central and local government deficits, as a percentage of GNP/GDP[26]

	1974	1975	1976
Italy	−5.4	−11.1	−10
UK	−5.3	− 5.7	− 5.75
W. Germany	−1.2	− 6.3	− 5.75
Japan	0.2	− 4.3	− 4.25
US	−0.3	− 4.5	− 3
France	0.6	− 2.2	− 1.5

It can be seen from these two sets of figures that apart from Italy and to a lesser extent Britain, the deficits only became truly large once the crisis had broken, *after* 1974. But government deficits then were inevitable, unless governments were going to increase the depth of the crisis deliberately by huge cuts in their own expenditure.

As Ian Gough has noted: 'It is not the case that the great expansion of state borrowing since World War II has been financed by government borrowing; instead taxation has grown in parallel.' He also adds: 'The recent growth in public sector deficits is a conjunctural phenomenon, *following from* the present slump not precipitating it.'[27]

We have seen that you cannot claim that the state sector has been 'squeezing' the private sector — unless somehow you see the private sector as 'squeezed' by a transfer of resources between its different sectors. Nor can you claim that government borrowing has destroyed the motor spring of growth in the system. But this still leaves one argument unanswered — the claim that it is the transfer of resources, via the state, between the different parts of the private sector that has brought society to the point of crisis.[28]

The most thorough attempt to do this within a Marxist framework has been by the American economist, James O'Connor (although, as I will argue later, his categorisation is grafted on to an account of the crisis quite different from Marx's). O'Connor breaks public expenditure down into two sets of components. The first set he calls *'social capital'*. This is spending which is 'indirectly' productive for private capital, such as spending on roads or the cheap supply of electrical power to industry, which complements private capital in its drive to extract surplus value.

His second category consists of spending which is completely non-productive, but which is necessary for the social stability of the system. He calls these the 'social expenses of production'. He includes here the 'welfare system' (such as social security payments, but not national insurance benefits, which have to be earned by work), because its function is to 'keep social peace among employed workers'.[29] He also includes arms expenditure (since its aim is to protect and expand markets, not produce wealth) and payments to 'non-productive' groups such as the police and judges.

How have the different sorts of expenditure grown in relation to each other? O'Connor argues that in the US the main burden of social capital expenditure has been borne by local and state governments — which are very much influenced by local capital. The social expenses of the system, by contrast, have tended to be borne by the national capital, the federal government. 'If federal government has earned the label of the "warfare-welfare state", local and state governments deserve the name the "productivity state".'[30]

How the two sectors have grown in the US is shown by figures given recently:[31]

US government expenditure as a percentage of GNP

	Federal	Local and state
1947	12.9	5.4
1952	20.5	6.6
1956	17.6	—
1971	21.0	10.9 (1972 figure)

It would seem that the proportion of gross national product on 'non-productive' expenditure, by Federal government, has remained more or less constant since 1952. Indeed, remembering that 1947–9 was exceptional, in that arms spending fell drastically for the only time in the period since the Second World War, then 'non-productive' spending would seem to have been constant for even longer. On the other hand, 'indirectly productive' expenditure, by local and state governments, has increased steadily.

It is worth noting, however, that within 'non-productive expenditure' the proportion spent on 'warfare' has tended to decline slowly over the years (with the exception of the Vietnam War years of 1965–8), and the proportion on 'welfare' to rise.

O'Connor sees 'productive' expenditures as rising in order to sustain the growing needs of industry for a skilled workforce and for a modern 'infrastructure'. But why do the non-productive, non-military expenditures also rise?

There seem to be two reasons: firstly, demographic changes which mean that there are more old people, and therefore more people likely to be sick but not insured. Secondly, the effect of the crisis itself in producing a growing 'sub-proletariat' of permanantly unemployed — a sector that made itself felt dramatically with the ghetto uprisings of the mid-1960s.

O'Connor himself does *not* explain the crisis in terms of growing expenditure on these items. The title of his book is 'The fiscal crisis of the state', not 'The fiscal crisis of the system'. His explanation for the crisis of the system lies elsewhere — in the explanation given by Baran and Sweezy in terms of a 'growing surplus' (which is dealt with later). However, the figures from the US do show clearly that there is no simple correlation between increased state spending and the elements of crisis within the system.

In the 1920s and 1930s, government spending was at a very low level and the system was in very deep crisis. In the 1950s it was about 70 per cent higher than before the war, but the system boomed. In the 1970s it was another 20 per cent higher again, but the system no longer boomed and use of industrial capacity fell to 80 per cent in 1969–73 compared with 90 per cent in the 1950s.[32] If government spending only on 'goods and services' is measured, and transfers between parts of the private sector excluded, the increase in spending in 1969–73 over 1951–7 is only 12 per cent — and there is a decline in the proportion of GNP going to goods and services after 1974.

What may be more significant is the shift from *military* expenditure to productive (and non-productive) non-military expenditure — but that is dealt with elsewhere.

Ian Gough has applied some of O'Connor's arguments to Britain and other countries. He shows that: 'Excluding the US (where is was boosted by military spending in the 1960s) state consumption rose by 3.9 per cent in real terms in all OECD countries from 1955–69, while GNP rose 5.7 per cent. In other words, *real* state consumption expenditure has fallen as a share of GNP over the last two decades', although 'this is more than accounted for by the decline in military spending, and social transfers have continued to rise . . .'[33] This produced anything like real problems only for those countries, such as Britain, where the rate of growth of GNP was less than the average.

Gough argues that most of the growth of state expenditure was in the 'indirectly productive' area:

> The single most important conclusion that emerges is that an increasing proportion of the total are productive expenditures, producing inputs for the capitalist sector. The share of the social services, infra-structure and accumulation expenditures is growing, while that of unproductive luxury expenditure is declining. In it wrong, therefore, to regard the growth of the state as an unproductive 'burden' upon the capitalist sector; more and more it is a necessary precondition for private capital accumulation.[34]

So the biggest single area of growth of public expenditure in Britain between 1961 and 1973 was educational expenditure, which grew by 2.6 per cent of GNP. This growth was almost entirely in the sections of the educational system catering for the minority of school students who remained in the educational system after the age of 16, and was directly associated with the perception of governments that higher education had to be expanded to cope with the technological needs of British capital. Close behind the growth in educational expenditure came the growth in direct and indirect support for industry — environmental, transport (chiefly motorways) and financial grants. Welfare and social security expenditure did grow as well — but this was very much a product of the growing numbers of unemployed, a product of the crisis of the system, not a cause.

So even if you conclude that the increase in public sector spending is part of the cause of the crisis, this hardly amounts to 'the public sector squeezing the private sector'. Rather it is that the cost of sustaining the growth of capital constrains that growth itself.

However, as I have argued earlier, it is difficult to see such spending as a cause of crisis, since it happily fitted with the needs of the system in the 1940s, 1950s and 1960s. If it seems like a burden today, it must be because something else in the system has changed. That is why those, like O'Connor and Gough, who have looked closely at the matter, see the 'fiscal crisis of the state' as a product of a wider crisis. For O'Connor, this is the crisis of monopoly capital as described by Baran and Sweezy; for Gough it is a crisis arising from the 'distributional struggle' over wages. Our explanation is rather different — but we can go along with Gough and O'Connor in rejecting public expenditure as the cause.

Appendix three
'Long wave' theories of crisis

● ONE SET OF theories to gain renewed popularity in recent years are those of 'long waves'. The Russian Menshevik Kondratieff first developed such a theory in the 1920s in an effort to explain why some periods of capitalist development seem more crisis-prone than others. His ideas were taken up in the 1930s by Schumpeter, and have been 'rediscovered' by many bourgeois economists looking for an explanation for the world crisis since 1973. W Rostow wrote in praise of long wave theory in 1975; one of the best-known Keynesian economists, Paul Samuelson, has said he is now attracted in this direction; and on the left, Ernest Mandel has also been associated with the revival.

Kondratieff claimed to show, on the basis of statistical data for prices, interest rates, stocks and shares, wages, levels of foreign trade and levels of national production, that as well as short-term boom-slump cycles, there were long-term 'waves' in economic activity. For a period of 20–25 years, he said, if you averaged out boom and slump years, you would find a rising level of economic activity — with less than average interest rates, rising prices, greater than average increases in physical output and rapidly rising foreign trade. This upward movement would then peak, and would be followed by 20–25 years of downward movement, which in turn would give way to a new upward movement.

Kondratieff calculated what the trend had been over the past 100–150 years for each of his different sets of data, and drew graphs based on deviations from the trend. He claimed that these deviations showed a clear cyclical pattern.[35] The system went through 'waves': for one period expanding more rapidly than the average, then more slowly, then more rapidly, and so on.

Kondratieff does seem to have emphasised one correct point: the capitalist system has expanded more rapidly in some periods than others. A modern supporter of his ideas, Ernest Mandel, provides the following figures in justification:[36]

Annual percentage changes in industrial output

Germany		England		USA	
		1827–47	3.2		
1850–74	4.5	1848–75	4.6	1849–73	5.4
1875–92	2.5	1876–93	1.2	1874–93	4.9
1893–1913	4.3	1894–1913	2.2	1894–1913	3.9
1914–38	2.2	1914–38	2.0	1914–38	2.0
1939–67	3.9	1939–67	3.0	1939–67	5.2

But the sense in which these can be called 'waves' is very much open to doubt. Trotsky, who a year before Kondratieff had noted the existence of periods of 'upturn' and 'downturn' in the 'curve of capitalist development', was extremely critical of Kondratieff for labelling these periods 'waves'.[37] Other Russian Marxists of the time was just as critical, faulting Kondratieff on both statistical and theoretical grounds.[38]

Statistically, they argued that his method was arbitrary in the extreme. Economists such as Oparin, Granovsky, Gerzstein and V Bogdanov showed that Kondratieff's 'waves' applied only to sets of figures which were dependent on the level of prices, and not to figures for real levels of production. As Granovsky put it: 'Kondratieff only succeeded in proving that long period changes in price levels have taken place . . . Except in price movements, there is no evidence of long waves . . . they are the fruit of the imagination of Professor Kondratieff.'[39] Often during Kondratieff's 'downswings' there was, in reality, a rapid expansion of output — and during his 'upswings' there was a slowing-down in the growth of the forces of production.

But this was not all. The Russian economists also insisted that the statistical techniques he used to get his wave-like configuration for his price-based sets of figures were themselves wrong. Oparin claimed, for instance, that using different techniques he could get new curves 'that differ considerably from those of Kondratieff . . . They have completely different timing and amplitude.'[40]

The arguments used against Kondratieff's figures can be used against many subsequent attempts to develop long wave theories.

First, do the 'waves' show changes in real production, or simply in prices? Some long wave theorists hold one view, some the other. The conclusions they draw are radically different. For example Mandel, who sees waves in real production, considers the 1970s the beginning of a long 'downswing'. By contrast Rostow, who adheres to Kondratieff's own method and stresses price movements, sees 1972–3 as marking the *end* of a downward swing. 'The world economy', he writes, 'experienced a sharp turning point in foodstuffs and raw material prices — a break as sharp as those of the 1790s, the 1840s, the 1890s and the 1930s . . . I am inclined to believe the fifth Kondratieff upswing is upon us.'[41]

Secondly, the objection concerning the timing and amplitude of the different 'cycles' is just as valid. Look for instance at the figures for industrial growth reproduced above from Mandel in his attempt to justify Kondratieff's case. They lump together uneven numbers of business cycles to make each 'upturn' and 'downturn'. The first British 'downswing' lasted 20 years, the first 'upswing' 27 years, the second 'downswing' 17 years, the second 'upswing' 19 years, the third 'downswing' 24 years, and so on. In the case of Germany, starting with the first 'upswing', the period lengths are 24 years, 17 years, 20 years, 24 years. Taking one short-term slump or boom, lasting three or four years, from one 'period' and transferring it to an adjacent one could, in certain circumstances, completely change the averages for the two periods, turning 'downswing' into 'upswing' and vice-versa.

These objections together destroy the statistical case for long 'cycles' or 'waves'. This has been virtually admitted by one of the latest studies to defend the notion of long waves, that of Freeman, Clark and Soete,[42] who admit that 'the evidence is totally insufficient' to prove the existence of a '50-year cycle'. They later claim that it is possible to use Kondratieff's idea of 'long waves' without having 'to accept the idea of cycles as such and certainly not of fixed periodicity.' In fact this amounts to an admission that Trotsky and the other Russian critics of long wave theory were right, *against* Kondratieff!

The theoretical criticisms of Kondratieff and his successors have been as powerful as the statistical arguments. Kondratieff produced a theory for the cause of his long waves in February 1926 — several years after claiming to have observed them. He argued:

> Marx asserted that the material base of crises or average cycles, repeating themselves each decade, is the material wearing out, replacement and expansion of the mass of means of production in the form of machines lasting an average of 10 years. It can be suggested that the material base of

long cycles is the wearing out, replacement and expansion of fixed capital goods which require a long period of time and enormous expenditures to produce. The replacement and expansion of these goods does not proceed smoothly, but in spurts, another expression of which are the big waves of the conjuncture . . .[43]

R B Day has noted that:

The forms of investment which Kondratieff has in mind included railways, buildings and the periodic technological renovations of industry which attend the rising wave of a long cycle. A rising wave presupposes a lengthy period of saving in excess of fixed capital formation, ultimate concentration of these savings in the hands of investors and profit opportunities sufficiently attractive to induce a new wave of investment . . .[44]

Kondratieff saw the new investment wave as one bringing social and political instability and a depletion of investable funds, so that the interest rate would rise, curtailing investment and producing a new declining wave.

But in the declining wave there would accumulate, on the one hand innovations which could not be brought into production until there was a new round of massive capital accumulation, and on the other investable funds, as those on fixed incomes saw the value of their incomes rise with falling prices and therefore increased their saving.

Later 'long wave' theorists have taken up much of Kondratieff's account. Schumpeter stressed the role of 'bunches' of innovation, and this is also one of the elements stressed by Mandel. Mandel amends Kondratieff slightly, seeing the massive investment not as involving a different set of long-term capital investments to those normally undertaken in the ten-year cycle, but rather as involving a complete replacement of old capital equipment throughout industry. This massive innovation, according to Mandel, allows the system to expand for up to 25 years without encountering the Marxist crisis of the falling rate of profit.

These theoretical arguments fall apart the moment they are examined seriously.

First there is the notion that capital can be 'saved' during the 'downswings', to be invested many decades later with a new wave of innovation. The 'downswing' is a period in which short-term slumps are more severe than the average. But such slumps have, as one very important effect, the wholesale destruction and 'devaluation' of capital. What is destroyed or 'devalued' cannot be saved.

Gerzstein pointed out against Kondratieff that even if some 'income receivers' saved more in periods of depression, 'this is certainly not true of corporate businessmen'. Oparin noted that there was no sign of any real growth in the funds of savings banks during

Kondratieff's 'downswings'. And Garvey, in 1943, rammed the point home: 'Kondratieff's assumption that free loanable funds can wait as long as a quarter of a century to be re-invested, remaining unaffected by expansions and contractions of successive business cycles, is certainly one of the weakest points of his argument and one which could not withstand an empirical test.'[45]

The criticism of Kondratieff applies just as surely to his more recent followers.[46]

There is a second, and in some ways more fundamental, theoretical objection to be made by Marxists. The theory of long waves attracts people because it seems to fit the aberrant behaviour of the capitalist system during periods of deep crisis into an apparently water-tight mathematical model. Sense appears to be made out of nonsense. The decline of the system merely serves to help restore a long-term equilibrium. The long waves, like any other simple harmonic motion, oscillate around a fixed point. Any particularly deep crisis is no more than a mechanism by which the system prepares itself for another period of expansion.

Kondratieff never hid his view that his was a theory of long-term equilibrium. Like all theories of equilibrium, it assumed that however bad things seemed, there was always a hidden hand which would put things right.

Marx, by contrast, believed that capitalism was pushed towards crises from which it would find it ever more difficult to escape. With Trotsky, we can agree that there are periods when the system has expanded more rapidly than in other periods, without falling into the trap of seeing these as part of an ahistorical, self-correcting mechanism. As Sukhanov concluded in the 1920s:

> Kondratieff studies economics in the same way as an astronomer might investigate the immutable orbits of heavenly bodies. A more rational approach would be to take into account capitalism's growth, maturity, decrepitude — and even the likelihood of death.[47]

The words are an apt criticism of the methods of Schumpeter, Rostow, Mandel and the host of bourgeois economists who have been won over to long wave theories in the past decade.

Appendix four:
A crisis of hegemony?

● THE AMERICAN KEYNESIAN economist Kindelberger has described the crisis of the 1930s in the following terms:

> The world system was unstable unless some country stabilised it as Britain had up to 1913 . . . When every country turned to its national private interest, the world public interest went down the drain, and with it the private interests of all.

Between 1873 and 1913,

> British foreign lending and domestic investment were maintained in continuous counterpoint. Domestic recession stimulated foreign lending; boom at home and it went down. But boom at home expanded imports, which provided an export stimulus abroad . . . Countercyclical lending stabilised the system . . .[48]

By contrast, US overseas investment in the 1930s *accentuated* booms and slumps: 'US foreign lending was positively correlated with domestic investment, not counterposed . . .'[49]

It led to a boom in investment in Europe and elsewhere at the same time as the boom took off in the US — and caused investment to decline abroad at precisely the time it slumped at home. Unlike British overseas investment 50 years earlier, the slump in one part of the world was not compensated for by a boom elsewhere, but exacerbated.

Kindelberger then extends this argument to the 1970s, seeing this as a period when the ability of one great power, the US, to provide a structure for the rest of the world system broke down, very similarly to the 1920s and 1930s.

In the 1940s, 1950s and 1960s, the US economy was all powerful. Not only was the US the policeman of the world; it was also its financier. The dollar was the great safety net that prevented anyone else falling too hard. But the past ten years have seen a decline in the ability of the US to do this, as a result of the relative decline in its own economic predominance.[50]

Kindelberger's arguments have been taken up and refined by a number of socialist economists. For example, the American radical Arthur MacEwen argues:

> One of the fundamental aspects of the crisis of the US economy in the 1970s has been the disruption in the stability in the international capitalist economy. The 25 years following World War II were characterised by a continuous increase in integration of the world capitalist system. However, throughout those years, forces were building towards the destruction of stability . . . By the beginning of the 1970s, those forces had come

into their own, and the basis for stability — US hegemony — had been eliminated.[51]

The long expansion after 1945 rested upon the ability of the US 'to re-establish an international order which had been lacking for half a century — since the time when other nations began seriously to challenge Britain's pre-eminence.'[52]

One aspect of this new hegemony was the vast expansion of US direct investment overseas — from 11 billion dollars in 1950 to 30 billion dollars in 1960, to 70 billion dollars in 1970, to 133 billion dollars in 1976.

But the very success of the new world system based upon US hegemony began to undermine that hegemony.

> For both economic and politcal reasons, the success of the US required that it take an active role in rebuilding the war-torn areas of the capitalist system . . . Consequently, throughout the post World War II period, the other capitalist nations were able to move to a position where they could challenge the US both economically and politically. As early as the late 1950s and the early 1960s it was becoming clear that Japanese and European goods were beginning to compete effectively with US products. And other nations began to grumble about the costs of supporting a world monetary system based upon the dollar . . .

The contradictions were exacerbated by the Vietnam War. The war meant that the US domestic economy overheated — a process made worse by the policy of financing the war (because of its unpopularity) by deficit financing instead of by taxation. Internationally it led to a considerable reduction in US trade surpluses. Yet the flow of US investment abroad continued to expand, until the other economic powers believed the dollar was overvalued and that they were in effect subsidising the US economy to the tune of about two billion dollars a year. The chickens came home to roost in 1971 when Nixon devalued the dollar and brought to an end the stable international currency alignments that had been established at Bretton Woods at the end of the Second World War.

At the same time the collapse of US military hegemony — in part a function of the collapse of the economic hegemony that had backed up military power — meant that the US was no longer able to keep in line the all-important Middle East oil states when they decided to force up prices in 1973–4.

The very integration of the world economy built up on the basis of US hegemony in the previous period meant that the new instability fed back into the US domestic economy — the US was dependent on imports for 40 per cent of its oil; its exports were 10 per cent of GNP by the mid-1970s as opposed to only 5–6 per cent ten years before;

earnings from direct overseas investment made up 30 per cent of after-tax corporate profits; US-backed loans abroad had tripled in the years 1971–5.[53]

Sustained expansion after the 1974–5 recession was impossible within the existing international framework — it meant a massive surge of imports into the US, a balance of payments deficit and a further fall in the dollar, which in turn threatened to undermine the world monetary system still more. But destruction of the old integrated world system by a retreat into protectionism was too frightening to attempt. As a result the shortlived 1977–8 American boom came to an end — even though the European and Japanese economies had hardly pulled themselves out of the previous recession.

'Crises of hegemony' theories have a certain attractiveness. They certainly describe one very important aspect of what happens in periods of intensified economic instability — the break-up of the old institutional framework internationally and the decline in the stabilising power of previously predominant economies. But they do not prove that the crisis of hegemony *causes* the general crisis. Could it not, perhaps, be the other way round, with an internal economic crisis of the dominating power undermining its hegemony? Or perhaps both the internal economic crisis and the crisis of hegemony are the result of some third factor?

The questions become more emphatic when one looks more closely at the arguments of the 'crisis of hegemony' theorists, such as Kindelberger.

Take his account of British investment in the late nineteenth century. He says it sustained the stability of the world economy because savings were always invested, either at home or abroad. But simple references to Britain's dominant international position do not explain *why* they were always invested. Some factor not referred to by Kindelberger must explain why British savings were always invested somewhere in the late nineteenth century, while American funds were only ever invested abroad at times of domestic boom in the 1920s and 1930s. But then *this factor*, or its absence, is the explanation for the deepening of the crisis in the 1920s and 1930s and must be seen as provoking the crisis of hegemony.

The same might be said for the 'crisis of hegemony' in the 1970s. Certainly from the early 1960s onwards the succession of crises on the foreign exchange markets flowed from the decline of American hegemony. But did these *cause* the general economic crisis after 1973? If so, how? Certainly not through any decline in the flow of American funds abroad. The flow into the Eurodollar market was much greater in the late 1970s than, say, in the late 1950s. It was not a drying-up of savings available either in the US or internationally that caused the deepening of the crisis. The savings were there — but were not, in general, productively invested. The Eurocurrency funds flowed into speculation, financing the burgeoning debts of the 'third world' and Eastern Europe — but not, by and large, into direct investment. (This does not rule out the possibility at some point in the future of a collapse of international credit — but this would be a by-product of the wider crisis, not a cause.)

You need to explain the pattern of investment in order to explain the deepened crisis — and you can't do that *simply* by referring to the crisis of hegemony. MacEwen seems in part to recognise this. He does refer to 'the domestic economic crisis' within the US, and to the 'fundamental contradiction contained in the capitalist relations of production'. But that is to acknowledge that you have to look elsewhere than to the crisis of hegemony for the basic causes of the general crisis. In his case 'elsewhere' means to the theories of monopoly capitalism put forward by Baran and Sweezy, for which see below.

Appendix five:
A raw materials crisis?

● A SUB-VARIETY OF the 'crisis of hegemony' theory is to be found in the argument that it is an increased dependence of the advanced countries on raw material supplies located in third world countries — especially oil — that has provoked the crisis.[54] The explanation takes an extreme form, to the effect that shortages of energy sources provide an absolute limit to further economic growth. But this explanation falls down, because numerous studies have shown that there are oil reserves still in the ground that are greater than the total amount used by humanity in the whole of its history so far, and coal reserves sufficient to last another 200 years. If these have not been tapped, it is because over the past 10–15 years firms and nations have not regarded the rate of return as sufficient to justify the necessary investment: that, for instance, is the main reason that the talk of using US or Japanese technology to exploit Russia's Siberian oil reserves came to nothing in the early 1970s.

Indeed, it is not fanciful to suggest that if the *only* problem facing the world was a drying up of old oil reserves, then what you might expect would be a *boom*, as everywhere governments and firms would spend vast sums on developing alternative energy supplies. (After all, it was precisely such periodic needs to branch out into massive new investments of a special sort that Kondratieff used to explain the *upward* sections of his 'long waves'.) The international economy would then be marked by very rapid expansion, perhaps of a very unstable sort, but *not* a slide into stagnation.

A more limited explanation looks not at the absolute limits to growth caused by the energy crisis, but at the effects on the advanced western states of having to pay more to the OPEC countries for oil. This is said to cut into the funds available for expansion in the advanced countries themselves. (This is essentially Rowthorn's explanation.)

But it is an explanation with a line of reasoning missing. The funds from the western countries flow into the coffers of OPEC governments and ruling groups. Why don't they spend the funds, either on expansion of the local industrial base, on consumer goods for themselves or their subject peoples, or on investments in the advanced countries? If any of these three things happens, all that results is a redistribution of purchasing power within the world system, without any drop in overall demand, or, for that matter, in the overall level of investable funds. Some capital-owning groups (those in the advanced countries) lose out to others (the oil producers) but there should be no diminution in the possibilities of growth for the system as a whole.

We are driven back once again to ask *why* investable funds are not invested? If 'recycling' of oil surpluses does not take place, the reason must lie in some factor inside the western economies that makes OPEC governments often feel their wealth is better protected by leaving oil in the ground rather than by exchanging it for a stake in western industry.

Appendix six:
Institutional crisis theories

● ONE WAY OF attempting to fill the gap in theories of the crisis of hegemony has been to consider such crises as simply one expression of a much more widespread crisis in the institutional structure in which capitalist production takes place.

For example, an American Marxist, David Gordon, starting from certain ideas derived from Kondratieff's long waves theory, suggests that historically, capitalism has passed through a number of states of development, each based upon a different set of structures. Each stage exhausts itself beyond a certain point. The institutional structure no longer fits the needs of accumulation: for instance, all the labour available with a particular structure of the labour market is exhausted; the structure of distribution does not fit the products of some new technology; certain raw materials run out, yet institutional structures are not available to enable the use of new ones.

The changeover from one set of institutions to another cannot easily be accomplished.

Many of the institutions associated with a stage of accumulation involve mammoth infrastructural costs of organisation and construction. These primarily involve the institutions of market access — access of raw materials, intermediate goods and final consumer demand. These institutions become part of the 'built environment' fixed in concrete and steel. Once these institutions have been built up at enormous cost, the world economy becomes 'fixed into these particular infrastructural forms' while their costs are repaid.[55]

Indeed, even when these costs have been recovered, the 'fixing' continues — since 'many individual capitalists acquire strong vested interests in existing institutional structures'. It takes a massive crisis to shake up these structures and to force individual capitalists into 'abandoning their old and increasingly unprofitable ways'.[56]

According to Gordon, the breakdown of the interwar years can be seen as resulting from a breakdown in the 'prosperous combination' of before the First World War:

Reduced competition through mergers, new markets and reduced material costs through imperialist colonisation, and reduced class conflict through a combination of new production relations, progressive social welfare policies and aggressive union busting.

International competition had already intensified before the war, and the peace did not resolve the instabilities. As world trade became increasingly perilous, world commodity flows slackened . . . Their disruption threatened production . . . Once the bubble burst, prosperity could not resume until the institutional basis for a new stage of expanded reproduction had been laid . . .

World War II helped pave the way for this institutional regeneration. The US emerged from the war with enormous international economic power. The dollar and American power provided a new platform for international stability. Wartime discipline, post-war anti-Communist ideology and new collective bargaining institutions helped reintegrate workers into the accumulation process. The increased concentration of corporate power promoted more stable relations of competition . . .[57]

The post-war structure began to break down as each of its particular institutions ran into problems. Gordon lists, among others, over-investment in automation; increased borrowing by corporations from government to compensate for loss of earnings; the rebellion of third world peoples — especially in Vietnam — against US imperialism, and the costs to the US of countering this; increased trouble caused by unorganised workers; rising interest rates; shifting labour patterns, whch make the reproductive use of the school system more and more complicated; increased protests by workers at speed-up; the burgeoning success of European capitalism making American corporations face increasingly strong competition . . . and so on.

The weakness in Gordon's argument comes out when he lists the factors responsible for the breakdown of the post-war 'prosperity'. Each can be seen to be as much a result of a wider crisis as a cause of its intensification. Take the argument about 'overinvestment in automation'. There is no explanation why this should take place, nor why investment should not create a market for its own products. And above all there is no explanation why investment can go on for years without running into crisis, and then suddenly run into it in the 1970s. The nearest thing to an explanation is the Kontratieff notion of large fixed investments — but this has all the problems we found in Kondratieff's own arguments. In the same way, Gordon's account of the crisis in the labour market exhibits the same weaknesses as those theories which see increased union pressure as the cause of the crisis.

The French economist Aglietta provides another version of the 'structural crisis' theory,[58] and uses it to give quite a sophisticated explanation of the present crisis — and of that of the 1930s. His basic argument is that the mechanisation of labour in the past century has gone through three stages, each of which has provided the basis for a stage of capital accumulation:

1. *Taylorism* involved raising the productivity of labour by accelerating the speed at which tasks were done in the workplace, and cutting down the time gaps between tasks.

2. *Fordism*, which follows from Taylorism, saw the redesigning of the whole production process to ensure a continual flow of work, with the work process simplified and broken down until each worker performed only a few repetitive actions. The end-point of this development was the 'semi-automatic assembly line', leaving as little time as possible for the worker to 'recuperate' his or her energies during the working day itself.

Secondly, Fordism simultaneously absorbed the workers' consumption into the production process of capitalism as a whole, by replacing earlier forms of consumption with mass consumption through the market. For example, where previously workers prepared the vast majority of their food in their own homes, now increasing use of tinned and frozen foods turned food preparation into part of the capitalist process of production; household work became less labour-intensive due to the intervention of factory-made vacuum cleaners and such like; and the mass provision of transport brought production into yet another new area of life.

This involved 'a revolutionising of the consumption of the working class . . . Consumption was based on the individual ownership of commodities — especially motor cars and individual housing units.' It thus provided 'the recuperation needed for enhanced production inside the factory.'[59]

This raised contradictions. There is a certain insecurity built into the wages system, which is necessary for capitalism if employers are to keep wages down and maintain control of production through the ever-present threat of unemployment. Yet the system was now dependent on the workers also as consumers, and needed this new market to be organised and stable. Workers had to be able to pay for houses to live in and vehicles to get to work in, even if they feared unemployment. As Aglietta puts it, it became 'essential to limit the consequences of capitalist insecurity in the formation of the individual wage, so as not to break the continuity of the consumption process . . .'

This led to the growth of social insurance funds, state unemployment benefits, legislation to cover periods of sickness and so on: 'Fordism could regulate the evolution of private working-class consumption only by generalising the wage relation to the conditions guaranteeing the maintenance cycle of labour power: provision for the unemployed and the sick, covering of family expenses and the means of existence of retired people.'[60]

Aglietta argues that Fordism had definite effects on the overall pattern of economic development. The expansion of production in what Marx calls Department I of the economy, where the means of production are themselves produced, depended on an increase in the output of Department II, which made consumer goods, because cars, houses and so on were now a precondition for rising labour productivity at work.

But this meant that the system could be upset if Department II were allowed to contract: on the one hand, demand for the output of Department I would decline, on the other the productivity of labour in Department I would fall as living standards fell 'below the social consumption norm'.

So, for Aglietta, there is a sense in which Keynes is the prophet of Fordism. His criticism of neo-classical economics and his notion of 'effective demand' are a partial recognition of the need for production and consumption to be integrated at a certain stage of capitalist development.

3. *Neo-Fordism*, Aglietta's third stage in the mechanisation of labour, has only just begun. Fordism contained within it three 'internal obstacles' — the lack of integration between different production cycles of differing duration; the stress produced within the individual worker by continued work pressure, leading to absenteeism and industrial militancy; and the abolition of any direct link between the effort of the individual worker and his renumeration.

Neo-Fordism attempts to deal with these problems by using electronic devices such as computers to coordinate centrally productive units that are themselves small and decentralised. The managerial hierarchy is short-circuited and small groups of workers become apparently responsible only to themselves and electronic equipment for the fulfilment of centrally set norms. Labour-only subcontracting and even the workers' cooperative become the basis for labour voluntarily imposing on itself norms of exploitation decided by a distant central management.

Using this framework of three stages of mechanisation, Aglietta then sees the great periods of crisis of the past hundred years as being the transition phases between one stage and the next. They occur when one way of organising labour — and exploitation — has exhausted itself and the next not yet become established.

Hence the great crisis of the 1870s occurred when the form of organisation of labour typical of the first 'machinofacture' had reached its limits of exploitation, and lasted until Taylorism was established; the great crisis of the 1920s and 1930s occurred when the limits of exploitation within the framework of Taylorism had been reached, and lasted until Fordism had established itself; the present period of crises arises out of the exhaustion of the possibilities within Fordism and will last until the structure of accumulation is organised in a neo-Fordist mould.

The form which an 'exhaustion' of the possibilities of a structure of accumulation takes is a decline in the productivity increases that are to be gained by increased expenditure (whether direct, or indirect 'non-productive' expenditure by governments). But what *causes* this decline?

Here Aglietta falls back on an argument whose weakness we have already examined: he sees a long-term rise in the level of class struggle, taking place as the structure of accumulation becomes widespread, which cuts into the possibilities for increasing the rate of exploitation:

> The crisis of Fordism is first of all the crisis of the mode of labour organisation. It is expressed above all in the intensification of the class struggle at the point of production. By challenging conditions of work bound up with the fragmentation of tasks and intensification of effort,

these struggles showed the limits to the increase in the rate of surplus value that were inherent in the relations of production organised in this type of labour process. This was the root of the crisis . . .

It can be seen in the halt in the fall of real wage costs that occurred simultaneously with the outbreak of sporadic conflicts and endemic contradictions challenging work disciplines of the kind that Fordism had established.[61]

From this initial source, the crisis spreads throughout the economy. The growth of Department I of the economy is retarded because it no longer produces new techniques capable of increasing productivity and so counteracting the tendency for the organic composition of capital to rise. There is a decline in investment, growing unemployment and increased job insecurity. At the same time, the failure of productivity to grow in industries producing consumer goods leads management to attack living standards. This attack has to be accompanied by an attack upon 'so-called collective consumption' (what is often called the 'social wage') — since productivity in the sectors producing 'collective consumption' goods and services rises much more slowly than in the other sectors of the economy.

Either these services are produced by capitalists with under-developed methods, and their costs grow astronomically, as social demand for them rises [, or] these services are produced by public bodies. They then absorb labour which is unproductive from the point of view of surplus value . . . Far from being complementary to labour that does produce surplus value, this unproductive labour is from the capitalist standpoint antagonistic to it when it absorbs a share of social value that grows more quickly than the sum total of surplus value.

A point is reached where the 'Fordist' conditions which allowed an expansion of the capitalist system begin instead to throw it into crisis.

As long as major transformations in the production of standardised commodities and a corresponding upsurge in the mode of consumption were predominant, the collective costs of the reproduction of wage labour could be held steady and the rising rate of surplus value could still be imposed. But these forces themselves generate a more and more rapid increase in the collective costs, at the same time as they exhaust the potentialities contained in the mechanisation of wage labour. It is not surprising, therefore, that the crisis of Fordist work organisation should at the same time have been the occasion for a general drive of the capitalist class to curtail social expenditures . . .[62]

Aglietta clearly makes a number of powerful points. But there are weaknesses in his explanation of the onset of deepened crisis, very similar to those of a number of the earlier theorists. He does not really explain why, at a certain point in time, the expansive elements in

Fordism should suddenly cease to operate. Take, for instance, the possibilities of raising labour productivity. Aglietta seems to imply that a point is reached where the worker can (or will) not work any harder. But labour productivity is increased not only by the worker working harder — indeed, it has to be proven that workers today work that much harder than workers a hundred years ago. What increases labour productivity is a rise in the technical level of production. And Aglietta provides neither proof that the technical level of production stopped rising in the mid-1960s, nor any explanation as to why it should have done.

Even if 'Fordist' forms of raising labour productivity have been exhausted in the old industrial centres of Western Europe and North America, what about parts of the globe where 'Fordism' has barely been introduced? Should not the system gain a new lease of life, on Aglietta's argument, by shifting growing sectors of production to parts of the globe where 'Fordism' can still displace previous forms of organisation of the production process? This is the conclusion of some thinkers who share Aglietta's terminology. Why does Aglietta himself argue otherwise? Why does he insist that *global* productivity can no longer be raised on a 'Fordist' basis?

It only needs to be added that key points in Aglietta's argument depend upon dubious generalisations about the growth of 'unproductive' government expenditure, like those of Bacon and Eltis, and an international increase in the level of class struggle, taken from 'wage push' theorists, which, as we have seen earlier, can by no means be taken for granted.

The gaps in Aglietta's argument could be filled in *if* it was first shown that investment had to fall before the beginning of his periods of crisis. Then much else of what he has to say would follow. But you cannot explain a decline in investment on Aglietta's own premises. He cannot really say why, in the heyday of the first forward rush of Fordism, in 1929, the bottom should suddenly have dropped out of capitalist expansion, or why a new wave of 'Fordist' expansion should be grinding to a halt today. So other explanations have to be looked for. Taken by itself, his account is as unconvincing as those which merely talk of 'waves of innovation' or 'long waves' or wage push or rising public expenditure.

Appendix seven:
Theories of monopoly and stagnation

● THE AMERICAN MARXISTS Baran and Sweezy,[63] on the one hand, and the neo-Keynesian Steindl[64] on the other have developed theories that ascribe the onset of general crisis to the monopolisation of production. These were originally intended to explain, not the crisis of the 1970s, but the great depression of the 1930s. But they have been used to explain the new lurch into world crisis since 1973.

Both Baran and Sweezy and Steindl see a tendency towards stagnation as a necessary result of the effect of monopolisation on profit margins.

For Steindl, the growth of monopolistic trends from the 1890s onwards led to an increase in the level of profit margins, combined with a deliberate policy of developing excess capacity in order to protect profits. This in turn led to a lower rate of accumulation, so that in the decade before 1899 the rate of growth of the US economy was 5 per cent, in the 1920s it was 3 per cent, in the 1930s nil.[65] 'An increased fear of excess capacity, due to the transition to monopoly, will always reduce the limiting rate of growth [by which he means the maximum rate of growth that is possible] . . . I believe this has in fact been the main explanation of the decline in the rate of growth which has been going on in the US from the end of the last century . . .'[66]

But reducing investment and cutting the rate of growth does not restore full capacity utilisation and protect profit margins. Instead, it reduces effective demand and leads to still greater excess capacity: 'A given degree of capacity utilisation can be restored adequately only by the method of eliminating capacity by price-cutting, but never by the method of reducing investment, because this leads only to an even greater excess capacity . . .'[67]

The result is a general crisis, unless other factors mask it:

> Stagnation did not come overnight, preceding it there had been a long process of secular change which passed almost unnoticed . . . Hardly anyone during the 'New Era' was aware of the fact that the annual rate of growth of business capital was only half what it had been thirty years earlier.[68]

For Steindl the 'masking' factor since the Second World War has been a much higher level of government expenditure than previously. 'The post-war economy has been transformed by the unprecedented role which government public policy and politics have played.'[69] The decline in cold war tension on the one hand, and the preoccupation of governments with inflation and public debt on the other, reduced government willingness to spend. But a fall in government spending in no way leads to a rise in the willingness of industry to invest. So even the new lower level of government spending can, according to Steindl, be financed only by budget deficits.

Baran and Sweezy's argument is not fundamentally different, although they express it in Marxist rather than Keynesian language. They argue that under monopoly conditions, the determination of prices no longer depends on the free play of market forces. The trend is for corporations to increase their profits, and for the total 'surplus' of society, what remains after workers' consumption and depreciation have been accounted for, to grow. The monopolies are disinclined to transfer this surplus to shareholders for private consumption, and so, 'not only the surplus, but also the investment-seeking part of the surplus tends to rise as a proportion of total income.'[70]

But it is not possible for investment to rise fast enough to absorb this proportion of the surplus that is not privately consumed.

> If total income grows at an accelerating rate, then a larger and larger share has to be devoted to investment and conversely, if a larger and larger share is devoted to investment, total income must grow at an accelerating rate. What this implies, however, is nonsensical from an economic standpoint. It means that a larger and larger volume of producer goods would have to be turned out for the sole purpose of producing a still larger and larger volume of producer goods in the future . . .
>
> One is left with the inescapable conclusion that the actual investment of an amount of surplus which rises relative to income must mean that the economy's capacity to produce rises faster than its income . . . Sooner or later excess capacity grows so large that it discourages further investment. When investment declines, so do income and employment and hence the surplus itself.
>
> In other words, this investment pattern is self-limiting and ends in an economic downturn — the beginning of the recession or depression.[71]

Again they argue

> These mechanisms tend to generate a steadily rising supply of investment-seeking surplus, but . . . in the nature of the case they cannot generate a corresponding rise in the magnitude of investment outlets. Hence if [these] investment outlets were the only ones available, monopoly capitalism would bog down in a permanent state of depression.
>
> Fluctuations of the kind associated with the expansion and contraction of inventories would occur, but they would take place within a relatively narrow range, the upper limit of which would be far below the economy's potential.[72]

This, for them, is the explanation of the 1930s. But they go on to argue that exceptional forms of investment were able, for a time, to counter these pressures towards stagnation in the 1940s, 1950s and

1960s. Such, they argue, was the case when technological innovation necessitated massive new investment — as did the spread of the railways in the last century, and the spread of the automobile in the 1920s and the 1940s and 1950s. They also see expenditure on the sales effort itself, through advertising and promotion of goods as disposing of some of the 'surplus'. So too does foreign investment.

They conclude, however, that the most important recent form of 'surplus absorption' has in fact been the activity of government, especially its military activity. They show the huge shifts in the pattern of expenditure before 1929 and after the Second World War.

US government spending 1929–57 as a percentage of GNP[73]

	1929	1957
Non-defence purchases	7.5	9.2
Transfer payments	1.6	5.9
Defence purchases	0.7	10.3
Total	9.8	25.4

In other words:

> Some six or seven million workers, more than 9 per cent of the workforce, are now dependent for their jobs on the arms budget. If military spending were reduced once again to pre-Second World War proportions the nation's economy would return to a state of profound depression, characterised by unemployment rates of 15 per cent and up, such as prevailed during the 1930s.[74]

Baran and Sweezy show, in passing, that attempts to end the crisis of the 1930s on bases other than military expenditure, did not succeed.

> Measured in current dollars, government spending increased from 1929 to 1939 more than 70 per cent. At the same time, GNP declines . . . 12.7 per cent, and unemployment rose from 3.2 per cent to 17.2 per cent . . . Regarded as a salvage operation for the US economy as a whole, the New Deal was a clear failure . . .
> War spending accomplished what welfare spending had failed to accomplish. From 17.2 per cent of the labour force, unemployment declined to a minimum of 1.2 per cent in 1944.[75]

Baran and Sweezy's account of the fluctuations of the world economy in the past 80 years has the merit that it seems, at first sight, to fit reality. In this respect it has a great advantage over most of the theorists we have looked at so far — and, for that matter, over various writers (from Yaffe to Bleaney) who simply dismiss Baran and Sweezy's theories out of hand as 'underconsumptionist'. It is true that their theory does depart from Marx's account of capitalist crisis in a 'Keynesian' or 'underconsumptionist' direction, as I will attempt to show later. But they do capture *empirically* some of the major shifts in the dynamic of capitalism as most of their critics do not.

Baran and Sweezy conclude from their analysis that the trend has been towards the stagnation of the world economy ever since the first development of monopoly capital towards the end of the last century.

> If the depressive effects of growing monopoly had operated unchecked, the United States economy would have entered a period of stagnation long before the end of the 19th century, and it is unlikely that capitalism would have survived into the second half of the 20th century.[76]

But, they argue, this was avoided in the US of the 1880s and 1890s by continuing huge expenditure on railways. 'Census data suggest that from 1850 to 1900 investment in railways exceeded investment in all manufacturing industries combined' until 'the crisis of 1907 precipitated a sharp drop in railway investment' which 'remained permanently at a lower level.'[77]

This, they argue, has an immediate effect on the general dynamism of the economy. After 1908, the tendency is for depressions to last longer and for booms to be shorter than previously. Unemployment rose so that even in the 'boom' years of 1909–10 and 1912–13 it was no higher than in the 'slump' years of 1900 and 1904.

The First World War lifted the economy out of this stagnation, and the restructuring of industry associated with the first wave of 'automobilisation' continued to keep stagnation at bay throughout the 1920s. But this first wave soon exhausted itself, and from 1923 onwards, excess capacity accumulated rapidly until in 1920 it hit production and the great slump of the 1930s began.

This, as we have seen, was ended for Baran and Sweezy by the Second World War. After the war stagnation was again kept at bay as in the 1920s — this time partly by a second wave of automobilisation, but more importantly by a level of arms spending much higher than at any previous peacetime period.

> With the aftermath [post war] boom triggering a great upheaval in the living patterns of tens of millions of people, and with arms spending growing nearly five fold, it is probably safe to say that never since the height of the railway epoch has the American economy been subject in peacetime to such powerful stimuli . . .

Yet it was already running out by the mid-1950s.

> What is remarkable is that despite the strength and the persistence of these stimuli, the familiar symptoms of inadequate surplus absorption — unemployment and under-utilisation of capacity — began to appear at an early stage, and, apart from cyclical fluctuations, have been gradually growing more severe . . .[78]

Despite its descriptive power, there are overwhelming objections of both an empirical and a theoretical kind to be made to Baran and

Sweezy's account.

First of all, it is by no means certain that the 'surplus' has increased in the long-term way suggested by Baran and Sweezy. Their collaborator, Phillips, purports to give factual evidence for its growth. But this depends upon the assumption that *all* government spending is part of the surplus. If some of it is not (for instance, if some is indirectly part of wages or is directly productive as nationalised industry investment) then the figures can show a *fall*, not a rise.[79]

Baran and Sweezy try to counter such objections in advance by insisting they are talking about 'potential surplus' — the surplus which would exist if industry worked at full capacity. But clearly this counter argument cannot apply to periods like 1942-5 or the early 1950s when industry actually *did* work very close to full capacity.

Secondly, the *timing* of the transition from periods of growth to periods of stagnation seems very arbitrary. Why, for instance, should automobilisation have led to massive new investments in the early 1920s and not in the late 1920s?

Baran and Sweezy provide no real explanation — unless it is the old Keynesian explanation that government did not then understand the needs of the system, and that the war taught them otherwise. The same gap in explanation characterises their account of the move from boom to stagnation over the past 25 years. They seem to suggest it resulted from accidents.[80]

If coincidental factors have produced stagnation, it would seem that other coincidental factors (or changes in government policy) could reverse the trend again. Indeed, it has been suggested by O'Connor that the move from the 'Warfare State' to the 'Warfare-Welfare State' could open up just such a new period of capitalist expansion.

Steindl's account of the 1950s and 1960s discussed above can be faulted on many of the same grounds. The 'theory' of 'maturity and stagnation' becomes so overlaid with 'accidental' countervailing influences as to provide no guide at all to understanding what is likely to happen in future.

Thirdly, the whole basis of Baran and Sweezy's (and Steindl's) argument, the notion of 'monopoly profits' as the cause of the 'rising surplus', is open to factual criticism — as the Argentinian Marxist Alejandro Dabat has shown. He gives figures that indicate that US monopoly concerns do *not* have higher than average profits:

> The spheres of business in which the average rate of profit is more than a third above the general corporate average are not, in general, those with a high monopolistic concentration, except for the tobacco industry, the brewing industry and petrol distribution and sales.

At the same time, the spheres which obtain a corporate rate of profit a third less than the average are highly concentrated spheres.

The most important industries of the North American economy, almost all totally controlled by a very few monopoly enterprises (automobiles, aerospace, the electrical industry, the food industry, telephone and electrical utilities, petroleum extraction and coal mining) are found in an intermediate position, close to the average rate of profit.[81]

These factual criticisms of Baran and Sweezy are reinforced by criticisms of a theoretical nature.

Fourthly, on the basis of Marx's theory of profits, there are clear limits to the growth of the 'surplus' accruing to the monopolies. As Dabat has argued, once monopolisation has proceeded beyond a certain point, it is very difficult for monopoly profits to maintain themselves above the average. For monopoly profits do not come out of thin air — but are a result of the ability of some firms, through monopoly prices, to force smaller firms to give them an unduly large share of the total surplus value.

But as the proportion of industry that is monopolised grows, and as the non-monopoly sector correspondingly shrinks, the creation of surplus value comes to take place predominantly in the monopoly sphere itself. That means there is less and less non-monopoly surplus value for the monopolies to gain control of through their pricing policy. A point will eventually be reached at which factors other than monopolisation will determine where any super-profits go — especially the extent to which different firms are in the most dynamic, rapidly growing sectors of the economy. But such is the scale of their fixed investment in established industries that many monopolies find it difficult to switch to the newer, more dynamic industries. Non-monopoly firms are as likely to be found there as monopoly firms.[82]

In this way Dabat destroys Baran and Sweezy's theoretical edifice. In doing so he also destroys certain conclusions drawn by their followers, for instance O'Connor, who argues that the workers in monopolies are privileged because the monopolies' ability to protect their profits leads them to grant wage increases more or less automatically.

Fifthly, underlying Baran and Sweezy's and Steindl's argument is the assumption that declining *price* competition between monopolies also means a decline in the pressure to use the surplus at their disposal for accumulation. Instead, they can try to protect their profits by not investing and by maintaining surplus capacity. Yet there is much evidence that declining price competition is accompanied by an increase in other forms of competition: pressures for the innovation of products, pressures for the expansion of the scale of production so as to reduce costs and raise profits at existing prices, pressures on the state to expand its investment in arms industries so as to provide the military wherewithal to back up the monopolies in their international struggle for markets. At the same time the greater internationalisation of production has often made the various national markets become the meeting point for competition between the monopolies of different nations.

Taking the international aerospace, car, or chemicals industry over the past decade — a decade which has seen a growing trend towards stagnation — it is difficult to claim that there has been a reduction in competitive pressures for component firms to invest, even though they are near-monopolies within national markets. If they have not invested all the 'surplus', it has not been because there was reduced (international) competitive pressure on them — some other factor has made them frightened to expend the huge sums needed to finance their response to such pressures.[83]

A final theoretical point against Baran and Sweezy. They make the mistake of all 'under-consumptionists' of assuming that capitalism has to have a rational goal. What else can be meant by their argument that capitalism cannot simply produce means of production in order to produce further means of production?

It certainly can, providing it finds it profitable to do so. Since, for Baran and Sweezy, the 'surplus' goes on rising indefinitely then production of means of production should be able to go on rising indefinitely. The fact that no humans beings benefit from this in terms of improved consumption does not prove that capitalism *must* break down. It only proves that capitalism is a dehumanised system, that, as Marx put it in the **Communist Manifesto**, 'in bourgeois society, living labour is but a means to increase accumulated labour.'

The mistake made by Baran and Sweezy is not new. It is the same made by Rosa Luxemburg[84] to justify her view that capitalism must break down eventually. But it is surprising that Sweezy makes this mistake, since he explicitly denounces the notion, in one of his earlier works, that 'all economic behaviour' under capitalism, 'is directed towards the satisfaction of human need.'[85]

In making this final criticism of Baran and Sweezy we are also, however, indicating the route towards the discovery of the rational core of their mistaken analyses. *If* it could be found that over time the dynamic of capitalist growth, the creation of profit, was somehow slowed down, then regardless of whether 'surplus' grew or contracted, you would expect the conditions for its investment to become more and more unfavourable. Then you would get precisely the stagnation described by Baran and Sweezy.

Thus our criticism here, as with other theories of the crisis, leads back to the main arguments of the book.

Notes

Introduction

1.   **The Guardian**, 26 September 1983.
2.   For a detailed examination of these theories, and where they fall down, see the Appendices: 'Other Theories of the Crisis'.
3.   Nigel Harris, **Of Bread and Guns**, Penguin Books (Harmondsworth 1983).
4.   For those who wish to refer to the originals, they may be found in **ISJ** series 2, issue 9 (summer 1980), issue 11 (winter 1981), issue 13 (summer 1981) and issue 16 (spring 1982).

Chapter 1: Marx's theory of crisis and its critics

1.   Karl Marx, **Grundrisse** (London 1973) pages 623 and 637.
2.   Karl Marx, **Capital: One**, page 645. All quotations from **Capital** are from the Moscow edition.
3.   Although it did not necessarily follow that the *employed* section of the working classes would grow poorer. See Rosdolsky's account of Marx's views on this question, in **The Making of Marx's Capital** (London 1977) pages 300–303.
4.   **Grundrisse**, page 749. There is a certain difference of tone between the **Grundrisse** and **Capital**. **Grundrisse** was an unpublished work, written at a feverish pace in the middle of a crisis which Marx thought might lead to the overthrow of the system, whereas the three volumes of **Capital** were an (unfinished) rewriting, reordering and more careful presentation of material and arguments. See Rosdolsky, **The Making of Marx's Capital**.
5.   **Capital: One**, page 6.
6.   See for example the article by Thomas Weiss, **Cambridge Journal of Economics**, December 1979.

7.   For instance those who accept the theories of monopoly associated with Baran and Sweezy; the Sraffian, neo-Ricardian current of Harrison, Steedman, Hodgson, Glyn and others; also critics of the Sraffians such as Bob Rowthorn.

8.   Ben Fine and Lawrence Harris, **Rereading Capital** (London 1979) page 64.

9.   **Capital: Three**, pages 236–7.

10.   **Capital: Three**, page 237.

11.   **Capital: Three**, page 245.

12.   **Capital: Three**, page 248.

13.   **Capital: Three**, page 208.

14.   **Capital: One**, page 622.

15.   The organic composition was depicted algebraically by Marx by the formula c/v, where c = constant capital and v = variable capital. Fine and Harris argue that there is a further, distinct but related concept in Marx — that of the 'value composition of capital': the ratio of the *current* value of the means and material of production consumed to the current value of labour power consumed. The point is that the current value of the capital consumed is not necessarily the same as the value of the original investment — indeed, a point we will deal with later, the value of consumed capital will tend to be *less* than the value of invested capital, as increased capital reduces the socially necessary labour needed to produce each unit of capital. See Fine and Harris, pages 58–60.

16.   **Capital: One**, page 622.

17.   This is a consequence of the labour theory of value. I do not intend here to go into the debate over the validity of this theory. Readers are referred to the replies to the marginalists by Hilferding (reprinted in the English edition of Böhm-Bawerk, **Karl Marx and the Close of his System**) and Bukharin, **The Economic Theory of the Leisure Classes**, and to the replies to the Sraffians by Fine and Harris, and Pete Green, **International Socialism**, series 2, issues 3 and 4.

18.   Assuming, that is, that the rate of exploitation does not change. We will look later at what happens if it does.

19.   'Alternative perspectives in Marxist theories of accumulation and crisis' in Jesse Schwartz (editor), **The Subtle Anatomy of Capitalism** (San Diego 1977) pages 207–8. Compare also Phillippe van Parijs, 'The Falling Rate of Profit Theory of the Crisis, a rational reconstruction by way of an obituary' in **Review of Radical Political Economy** 12:1 (spring 1980) pages 3–4. I regard Parijs as being an accessory to a case of flagrant premature burial.

20.   **Capital: Three**, page 222.

21.   As for example Ernest Mandel does in his **Late Capitalism** (London 1975), where on page 11 he asserts that the renewal of fixed capital after crises is 'at a higher level of technology' and therefore 'with an increasing organic composition'.

22.   **Capital: One**, page 624.

23.   **Grundrisse**, pages 750–1.

24.   Michael Kidron, **Western Capitalism since the War** (London 1968) page 46.

25.   **Capital: Three**, page 231.

26.   The argument is usually expressed in terms of the need to 'go beyond Marx' and to take account (as he did not) of the need to transform the value of the inputs of the production process into prices as well as the output. This solution to the 'transformation problem' is said to be due to the Polish economist of the turn of the century, von Bortkiewicz. So Glyn, for example, claims that von Bortkiewicz's 'simultaneous solution for the prices of production and the rate of profit demonstrates that any technique introduced by capitalists in order to cut costs will in fact increase the rate of profit if real wages are unchanged.' (**Bulletin of CSE** Autumn 1973.)

27.   This point was made by Robin Murray in a reply to an attempt by Glyn to use a 'corn model' to disprove the falling rate of profit. (**CSE Bulletin** 1973.)

28.   Fine and Harris, page 59. I say 'they claim', because it is not self-evident that

Marx makes the distinction as clearly as they do (see **Capital: One** page 612). However, this is not to detract from the utility of the distinction that they make. Unfortunately, they themselves do not seem to draw all the advantages they could from the distinction; they later seem to backtrack by saying that 'the debate between Glyn and Murray over whether the organic composition should be evaluated at current or historic value is essentially irrelevant.' (page 61.)

29.   The rate of profit using the original investment cost as the base for calculation would be $r = s/c + v$.

The effect of the devaluation of constant capital on this rate is two-fold. Firstly it cuts into the mass of profits by a sum, k, equal to this devaluation. Secondly it reduces the quantity of capital between which these profits must be shared.

To get the 'corrected' rate of profit we would therefore have to reduce both the numerator and the denominator in the above formula by the same sum, k.

If $c + v$ is greater than s, the effect will be to *reduce* the rate of profit. If it is the other way about it will *increase* the rate of profit. The latter can therefore only occur when s is greater than $c + v$, ie. where the rate of profit exceeds 100%! This, of course, could not generally be the case.

30.   Of course, there is also the limiting case in which constant capital depreciation is just covered, with no surplus value being produced. There is also the more concrete case — which we will look at later — where a little surplus is produced, and used to cover the consumption of the capitalist class and its hangers on, but is not available for investment.

31.   Here it is worth commenting on one disproof of the mathematical arguments of Okishio and Himmelweit — Anwar Shaikh, 'Political Economy and Capitalism: Notes on Dobbs' Theory of Crisis', **Cambridge Journal of Economics** Vol. 2, No. 2, June 1978. Shaikh argues that the disproofs ignore the existence of fixed capital. In this he is quite right. But his own mathematical disproof of Okishio and Himmelweit contains an assumption that makes it of very limited value. He takes the example of where the introduction of a new technique involves moving from a capital with a turnover of one cycle of production to that involving several cycles (ie. from 1 to n). The rate of profit on fixed capital must fall under these circumstances but this does not mean that the rate of profit must fall when there is a larger fixed capital *with the same turnover time*.

In such circumstances, if you continue — as Shaikh does — to accept the assumption of Okishio and Himmelweit that devaluation of fixed capital reduces the capital on which the rate of profit is calculated, then the rate of profit will rise. Shaikh's mistake is in not going far enough in challenging their assumptions.

32.   **Capital: Three**, pages 227 and following.

33.   **Capital: Three**, page 234. For an account of all of Marx's arguments on this score, see Rosdolsky, pages 398 and following.

34.   **Theory of Capitalist Development** (London 1946) pages 101–2.

35.   See for instance, Okishio, 'A Formal Proof of Marx's Two Theorems', **Kobe University Review**, No. 18, 1972. Compare also Ian Steedman, **Marx After Sraffa** (London 1977).

36.   I Steedman, **Marx After Sraffa** page 64; compare also pages 128–9.

37.   **Bulletin of the Conference of Socialist Economists** (Autumn 1973) page 103.

38.   **Marxist Economics for Socialists** (London 1978) page 103.

39.   'Technical change and the rate of profit' in **Kobe University Economic Review** (1961) pages 85 and following.

40.   **Bulletin of CSE** (Autumn 1974).

41.   'If one hour's labour is embodied in sixpence, a value of six shillings will be produced in a working day of 12 hours. Suppose with the prevailing productiveness of labour, 12 articles are produced in those 12 hours, let the value of the means of production used up in each article be sixpence. Under these circumstances each article

costs one shilling: sixpence for the value of the means of production and sixpence for the value newly added in working with these means. Now let some capitalist contrive to double the productiveness of labour . . . The value of the means of production remaining the same the value of each article will fall to ninepence . . . Despite the doubled productiveness of labour, the day's labour creates as before a new value of six shillings and no more, which, however, is now spread over twice as many articles . . . The individual value of these articles is now below their social value: in other words, they have cost less labour time than the great bulk of the same article produced under the average social conditions . . . The real value of the commodity is not its individual value, but its social value, that is to say, the real value is measured not by the labour time the article in each individual case costs the producer, but labour time socially required for production. If, therefore, the capitalist who applies the new method sells his commodity at its social value of one shilling, he sells it above its individual value, and thus realises an extra surplus value of threepence each . . .' (**Capital: One** pages 316–17).

42. Stage Three of this example enables us to see the apparent plausibility of the argument of Glyn, Harrison, Okishio and Himmelweit. If the whole world-wide production of a certain sort of goods came from a single firm, with no substitutes available, then it would certainly not introduce new techniques if the result of doing so was to raise the organic composition of capital and reduce the rate of profit. The only thing giving it an incentive to raise the organic composition of capital would be a rise in labour costs which itself would cut the rate of profit anyway.

The whole argument of Steedman, Glyn, Harrison, Himmelweit, Okishio rests on this, unstated assumption. For their argument is about what happens in 'industries', not firms. So Steedman writes of the 'selection of production techniques, industry by industry'. In their mathematical arguments, using matrix algebra, Okishio and Himmelweit refer to the effects of technical change in the 'nth industry'.

Under capitalism, the units of production are not 'industries', but firms competing with each other in the same industries and straddling industries. And, as Marx shows, the individual capitalist firm can do things which lead to deleterious effects for the cost structure and rate of profit of the industry as a whole. The 'disproof' of Marx by these writers consists in arguing that the rate of profit cannot fall . . . in a society which is not organised along capitalist lines. For there is no room in their matrices for the most basic unit of capitalism, the individual firm.

It is this too which enables some people who hold this view of the rate of profit also to hold the view that the labour theory of value is redundant. Their view of an economy organised into industries, not firms, can be fitted into a neo-Ricardian, Sraffian model of the economy, which sees as superfluous Marx's insistence that interrelations between firms are based upon the law of value — the continual reduction of different, concrete labours to abstract labour. For elaboration of this point, see Pete Green, 'The Necessity of Value', in **International Socialism** 2:3 and 2:4.

43. The point is well argued in Fine and Harris, page 84 and pages 60–61.

44. **Capital: Three**, page 244.

45. **Capital: Three**, page 244.

46. This is the implication of the argument put forward by 'Long Wave', 'structural crises' and 'crises of hegemony' theorists dealt with in the appendices to this book. It also seems to me to be the implication of the position developed by Fine and Harris, despite their general closeness to many of my arguments so far.

47. This is a very sketchy summary of a complex process. To fill out some of the details see Nigel Harris, 'World Crisis and the System', **IS** (old series) 100, and 'The Asian Boom Economies', **IS** 2:3; see also Chris Harman, 'Poland and the Crisis of State Capitalism', **IS** (old series) 93–94. Also Nigel Harris, **Of Bread and Guns** (Penguin 1983).

48.   This insight into the aging of the system is due to Mike Kidron; see for example 'The Wall Street Seizure', **IS** (old series) 44.

49.   Section on Foreign Trade in **Capital: Three,** chapter 14, pages 232–3.

50.   See Lenin, **Imperialism, the Highest Stage of Capitalism.** Barratt Brown (**Essays in Imperialism,** page 35) and Kiernan (**Marxism and Imperialism,** page 29) object that this overseas investment led to interest returning to Britain greater than the outflow of funds, and that therefore this outflow could not have provided a way to siphon off investment-seeking surplus value. The objection does not hold. Had the overseas investment not initially taken place, there would have been a much higher pool of funds seeking invstment in Britain and therefore a higher level of investment with a higher organic composition. This extra investment would have generated its income in Britain just as the investment that went abroad did. This would have sought further investment in Britain in conditions of a higher organic composition than actually prevailed after the outflow of much previous investment-seeking surplus value. Overseas investment eased the problem of accumulation in Britain, despite the fact that it eventually led to an inflow of funds greater than the outflow.

51.   It was the great merit of Rosa Luxemburg's **The Accumulation of Capital** to grasp this and the historically transitory role that imperialism could play in stabilising the capitalist system. However, she did not see this role in terms of its effect on the rate of profit. For a critique of her position, see N Bukharin in R Luxemburg and N Bukharin, **Imperialism and the Accumulation of Capital** (London 1972), and Tony Cliff, **Rosa Luxemburg** (London 1980).

52.   Lenin, **Imperialism, the highest state of capitalism**, and Nicolai Bukharin, **Imperialism** (London 1972).

53.   Lenin and Bukharin do not seem to have noticed the effect of war expenditures on Marx's law.

54.   Shane Mage, **The 'Law of the Falling Rate of Profit', its place in the Marxian theoretical system and its relevance for the US Economy** (PhD thesis, Columbia University 1963) page 228.

55.   **Grundrisse,** pages 750–51.

56.   See 'Rejoinder to Left Reformism', **IS** (old series) 7 (winter 1961–62).

57.   **IS** (old series) 27, page 10.

58.   Kidron, **Capitalism and Theory** (London 1974) page 16.

59.   **Capitalism and Theory,** pages 16–17. At first Kidron argued that the 'leakage' had to be of capital-intensive goods, and suggested that a leakage of labour-intensive goods would have the opposite effect. But, as he later recognised, either form of leakage would reduce the volume of surplus value available for further investment, and so offset the rising organic composition of capital and the falling rate of profit.

60.   Ernest Mandel, **The Inconsistencies of State Capitalism** (London 1969) pages 4 and 6.

61.   **Late Capitalism** (London 1975) page 288.

62.   **Late Capitalism**, page 289. The article he refers to is 'The Inconsistencies of Ernest Mandel', in **IS** (old series) 41.

63.   Kidron himself confuses the issue a little. He defines labour which creates goods which are then unproductively consumed as itself 'unproductive'. I do not think this definition is helpful. (See my review of **Capital and Theory** in **IS** (old series) 76.)

    He has not been alone in recognising the peculiar effect of a large 'third department' on the trends in the organic composition of capital. M Cogoy ('Teoria del Valore e Capitalismo Contemporaneo', in Alberto Martinelli (editor), **Stato e accumulazione de capitale**) notes that where you have a two-sector economy, what is productive for each capital is, via reproduction, reproductive for capital-as-a-whole. But when you have a three-sector economy, this no longer applies. Part of the surplus value becomes *revenue* for department three, which gives nothing back in return.

'The accumulation of total capital is no longer equal to the sum of the surplus value produced by each of the individual capitals, but is the sum of the total surplus value *minus* the total value of production of the third sector. The capital in the third sector is capitalistically unproductive, insofar as it does not contribute to the accumulation of capital' (page 112).

Cogoy does not make the mistake Kidron makes, in seeing *only* the constant capital in the third sector as a leak. 'Total accumulation is not only diminished by the accumulation of sector III, but by all of sector III.' (page 112.)

However, there is a weakness in his position compared to Kidron's (or at least the earlier Kidron) — he does not complete his analysis over the effect of these 'revenues' on the rate of profit and tends to see them rather as diminishing the rate of profit. This is a point we will return to in a few pages.

64.   This was the argument against any resort to von Bortkiewicz used by David Yaffe's followers when they were in the International Socialists. See for example Dan Siquerra, 'Marx, Bortkiewicz and IS' in **IS Internal Bulletin**, April 1972.

65.   Von Bortkiewicz's formulae ended up suggesting that the total profit in the system was not equal to total surplus value or that total prices did not equal total value. Von Bortkiewicz and those who have followed him have gone on to claim that this proves the general uselessness of the labour theory of value and the conclusions drawn from it in relation to the trend in the rate of profit.

66.   Above all, the use of simultaneous equations can make people forget that production does not take place 'simultaneously', but over time.

67.   Anwar Shaikh, in Jesse Schwartz (editor), **The Subtle Anatomy of Capitalism**, pages 106 and following; Miguel Angel Garcia in 'Karl Marx and the formation of the average rate of profit', **International Socialism** 2:5. In both cases the divergences of total price from total value and total surplus value from total profit exist.

The reason for these divergences is no deep mystery. The formation of average prices takes place when profit rates are equalised between different capitals having different organic compositions. The prices of products produced by high organic composition rises above their value, and of those produced by low organic composition below their values. If workers' consumption goods are produced by high organic compositions, their price will rise above their values, while goods going to the capitalists (as luxury goods or means of production) will fall.

When this happens, the distribution of the social product between the classes is changed a little, altering the total profit. If account is not taken of this in equations total price seems to vary from total value and Marx to be 'refuted'.

But the variation of total profit from total surplus value is not random. One depends on the other, and, in theory one could be calculated from the other. As Anwar Shaikh has put the argument (in 'Marx's theory of value and the transformation problem', in J Schwartz, **The Subtle Anatomy of Capitalism**, page 125):

'Beginning with prices proportional to values, a sector's total price must fall (or rise) relative to its money cost price according to whether its organic composition is lower (or higher) than the social average if its particular money rate of profit is to conform to the general rate . . .

'It does not follow that the general *money* rate of profit will continue to equal the general *value* rate of profit, once prices deviate from a strict proportionality with values . . . The aggregate price of commodities is the total price of the commodities which form the social product. On the other hand, the aggregate cost price is the total price of the commodities — the means of production and the labour power — which form the inputs into the aggregate process of production . . . The aggregate cost price is, in effect, the total price of the means of production and the means of subsistence.'

In that case any change in relative prices will change the total money profit, since it depends on the total costs of products in money terms which have deviated from the total costs of production in value terms. Shaikh insists however, that the deviation does not affect the general validity of Marx's argument about the labour theory of value and the dynamics of capitalism.

It is only necessary 'to carefully distinguish between value which stems from production, and money price which is the form taken by value in circulation. With this distinction in hand, it is possible to see that money magnitudes are always different, both qualitatively and quantitatively from value magnitudes' (page 125).

For, 'Like the deviations of prices of production from direct prices, the money and value profit rate deviation is systematic and determinate . . . It can be shown that the money rate of profit will vary with the value rate . . .' (page 134). From Marx's analysis of capitalism one can grasp the trend of the value rate of profit, which in turn will directly influence the trend of the money rate of profit.

This was why Marx himself insisted that 'The fact that prices diverge from values cannot, however, exert any influence on the movement of social capital. On the whole there is the same exchange of products, although the individual capitalists are involved in value relations no longer proportionate to their respective advances and to the quantities of surplus value produced singly by each one of them.' (**Capital: Two**, page 393.)

However, Shaikh adds, that 'From the point of view of individual capitals the situation is quite different . . . Different forms of value have different effects on individual capitals, and these in turn have different implications for the dynamic process of accumulation and reproduction. It is through the actual movement of money prices that the system is regulated; as such the analysis of prices of production and their relation to values is of the utmost importance to concrete analysis. The first step (which in most discussions of the "transformation problem" is the *only* step) along this path is the derivation of prices of production from direct prices.' (Shaikh, page 127.)

The same argument as Shaikh's is put forward by a 1974 article of Okishio — ('Value and production price', **Kobe University Review**, 1974, page 1 and following). He shows, using an extension of Marx's schema, 'It is immediately clear that the second proposition of Marx, that the total surplus value of all sectors is equal to the total profit, does not generally hold, when we take into consideration the transformation of cost price into production price'. He gives a numerical example where the total surplus value is 120, but the total profit is 114. This, he says, is because with the equalisation of the rate of profit, the cost price in terms of production prices rises above the cost price in terms of values.

This in turn is because 'In the example, sector II is the wage good sector, and sector I is the production good sector. As we assume the organic composition of capital in sector II is lower, and that in sector I higher than the average organic composition of capital, the production price in sector II is lower than its value and the production price in sector I is higher than its value. Thus in each sector the evolution of the part C in terms of production price is higher and that of the part V is lower than its value.

'As in our example, C is greater than V as a whole, the total of the cost price as a whole increases when the cost price is evaluated in terms of production price.'

But 'If the amount of the surplus product measured in terms of value is reestimated in terms of production price . . . This is equal to the total profit already calculated in terms of production price . . . The amounts 120 and 114 only differ because the same surplus product is differently estimated, the former in terms of value and the latter in terms of production price. Therefore it remains completely unchanged that the surplus labour of workers is the unique source of profit.' (page 6.)

Miguel Garcia's account of the transformation of values into prices which is very similar to Shaikh's (although arrived at independently) manages to evade the problem of 'deviations' of total profit from total surplus value in two ways.

First, he assumes that in the process of the transformation, the rate of exploitation (or rather the measure of it, the rate of surplus value) changes. This is a realistic assumption, in that the transformation of values into prices does not affect the use values which workers consume as their real wages. It does however affect the price of these goods, and therefore the proportion of the total social wealth that has to be expended on labour power.

The difference between Garcia's calculations and that of Shaikh and Okishio is in reality only one of presentation. Garcia's method does bring out more clearly, however, the fact that it is the basic value relations that determine the rate of profit.

Garcia's second point is that in practice there is unlikely to be any great difference in the organic composition of capital between the sector producing means of production and that producing wage goods. The means of production do include some items produced with a very high organic composition of capital — steel works, for instance — but they also include raw materials and semi-manufactured goods — produced by labour intensive processes. And all sorts of products can serve indiscriminately as means of production or wage goods (electricity, petrol, foodstuffs — which are means of production when fed to animals, or processed in factories, wage goods when bought directly by workers — buildings, vehicles, etc.).

However in one important respect Garcia overstates his case. He fails to draw the conclusion from his own method for the rate of profit in circumstances where the organic composition of the luxury goods sector is higher than average. This is a point which we will return to later.

68.   This peculiar effect of a high organic composition of capital in department III was one thing von Bortkiewicz did grasp. However, his method of simultaneous equations made him see the fall and rise in the average rate of profit as taking place at the same time, cancelling each other out, rather than seeing the fall as preceding the rise in time. But this does not excuse a succession of Marxist economists who have simply dismissed out of hand his discovery about the impact of department III.

69.   **Capital: One**, page 544.

70.   **Capital: Three**, page 293.

71.   **Capital: Three**, page 296.

72.   Which is why those who advise capitalism at the national level have been able to work out 'rates of return' on certain state expenditures. See for example the Robbins Report on Higher Education.

73.   Mike Kidron, **Western Capitalism since the War** (London 1968) page 40.

74.   N Bukharin, 'Address to the Fourth Congress of the Comintern', in **Bulletin of the Fourth Congress**, vol. 1, Moscow, 24 November 1922, page 7.

75.   When I speak of 'new' dimensions of competition, I do not mean to imply that they did not exist before. In its early 'mercantile' period capitalism was closely dependent upon the activities of the state. But Marx, following the classical political economists, saw this as a declining phenomenon as capitalism became a self sustaining system. The point is that once capitalism entered the 'imperialist' stage, resort to the state became once again an increasing phenomenon in a way unforeseen by Marx.

76.   **Capital: Three**, pages 292–4.

77.   As is argued, for instance, by Mandel, **Late Capitalism** (London 1978) pages 292–93.

78.   By Mike Kidron, in **Western Capitalism since the War** (London 1968) and **Capitalism and Theory** (London 1974), and by myself in a rejoinder to Mike Kidron, 'Better a Valid Insight than a Wrong Theory', **IS** (old series) 100.

79.   This was certainly true in both Germany and Britain in 1943–4. It was also true in Russia during the Stalin period. For an elaboration of the argument as applied to Russia, see Tony Cliff, **State Capitalism in Russia** (London 1974).

Chapter 2: The crisis last time

1. Quoted in D M Gordon, 'Up and Down the Long Roller Coaster', in **US Capitalism in Crisis**, URPE (New York 1978) page 23.
2. Lewis Corey, **The Decline of American Capitalism** (London 1935) page 27.
3. Eric Hobsbawm, **Industry and Empire** (London 1969) page 129.
4. Hobsbawm, pages 130–1.
5. Corey, page 30.
6. Here and later a number of different sources are used for empirical measurements of the organic composition of capital, the related capital-output ratio and the rate of profit. The two major studies for the US economy are Joseph Gillman, **The Falling Rate of Profit** (London 1956) and Shane Mage, **The 'Law of the Falling Rate of Profit', its place in the Marxian theoretical system and its relevance for the US economy** (PhD thesis, Columbia University 1963, released through University Microfilms, Ann Arbor, Michigan.)

These two sources adopt different conceptual interpretations of some points of Marx's theory and they measure different hings. Gillman deals with manufacturing alone and in the main body of his work deals with profit levels before tax. Mage covers what he calls 'the commodity producing industries in the capitalist sector — agricultural services, forestry and fishing, manufacturing, transportation, communications, construction, public utilities and services . . .', and all profits are measured *after* tax. But there are similarities in the picture they give up to 1919.

Other calculations have come to similar conclusions as regard the capital-output ratio for manufacturing industry. Kalecki, for instance, in **The Theory of Economic Dynamics** (London 1954) page 70, shows a rise of 31 per cent in the ratio of fixed capital to output in US manufacturing between 1899 and 1914, and Kuznets (**Capital in the American Economy** (Princeton 1961) page 199) shows an increase of 100 per cent in the ratio of fixed capital stock to net product between 1880 and 1922 for manufacturing. Rowthorn (**NLR** 98, page 65) has argued that Kuznets' data show that this is more than compensated for by a fall in the ratio in public utilities — but it is doubtful how sound this argument can be, given the inflated figures of capitalisation with which rail companies were often launched (see, for instance, Corey, page 28), and the extent to which they were hit — and devalued — more than the average in the crises of 1884 and 1892.

7. Gillman, page 36.
8. M Flamand and J Singer-Kerel, **Modern Economic Crises** (London 1970).
9. Hobsbawm, page 131.
10. Flamand and Singer-Kerel, page 38.
11. Figures given in H Feis, **Europe, the World's Banker 1879–1914** (Yale 1931) quoted in Kidron, 'Imperialism, the highest stage but one', in **IS** (first series) 9, page 18.
12. Figures from Colin Clarke, **Oxford Economic Papers** (November 1978) page 401. For his own reasons Clarke increases the value of equipment in his equations by 50 per cent, but this should not affect the trends.
13. Clarke, page 401.
14. Fritz Sternberg, **Capitalism and Socialism on Trial** (London 1951) page 178.
15. Clarke.
16. Gillman.
17. Mage.
18. Corey.
19. Both quoted in Fritz Sternberg, **The Coming Crisis** (London 1947).

20. Figures in Sternberg, **The Coming Crisis**, page 23.

21. Baran and Sweezy, **Monopoly Capital** (London 1973) chapter 8; Gillman, chapter 9; Sternberg (both titles).

22. Corey, pages 181–3.

23. Karl Marx, **Capital: Three** (Moscow 1962) pages 472–3.

24. Gillman, page 58. Mage, page 208. Even Corey, who sees the low rate of profit as a crucial component of the crisis (and who therefore is closer to Marx than most theorists of the 1930s crisis) provides figures that do not really prove a fall in the rate of profit between 1923 and the beginning of 1929 (see Corey, page 125).

25. Steindl, **Maturity and Stagnation in the American Economy** (London 1953) pages 155 and following.

26. On the basis of the results given by Kuznets, page 126.

27. Kuznets, page 228.

28. Corey, page 157.

29. Corey, page 170.

30. Corey, page 170.

31. Corey, page 163.

32. Corey, page 97.

33. Corey, page 172. Compare also Gillman, pages 129–30.

34. Figures given in Baran and Sweezy, page 232.

35. Corey, page 163.

36. This is one of the reasons why those who see 'wage push' and 'overaccumulation' as the core of the Marxist theory of crisis (for instance Glyn and Harrison, **The British Economic Disaster** (London 1980)) must be wrong: the theory fails at its biggest test.

37. Figures in current dollars given in A D H Kaplan, **The Liquidation of War Production** (New York 1944) pages 90–91. On the basis of *constant* dollars Robert Keller calculates the the peak of investment was 1926, with 1928 not far behind (**Review of Radical Political Economy**, vol. 7, no. 4 (winter 1975)). But this does not affect the argument about the disproportions arising from a high level of investment when overcapacity already exists.

38. Of course, other people may be involved in lending and borrowing, but this does not alter the essential argument.

39. Marx, **Capital: Three**, chapter 30. For a coherent statement of Marx's position, see Kahoto Itoh, **Value and Crisis** (London 1981) page 109.

40. For this version of events see, for example, Flamand and Singer-Kerel, page 61.

41. Kindelberger, **The World in Depression 1929–39** (London 1973) page 117.

42. Kindelberger, page 117.

43. Last series of figures from Corey, page 184.

44. Kindelberger, page 117.

45. Alvin H Hansen, **Economic Stagnation** (New York 1971) page 81.

46. Kindelberger, page 117.

47. Sternberg, **Capitalism and Socialism**, page 28.

48. See, for instance, Lenin, 'The Tax in Kind', **Collected Works** vol. 32, pages 334 and following.

49. This tends to be the term used in Bukharin's **Imperialism and the World Economy** of 1915 (London 1972).

50. Lenin, **Collected Works**, and Bukharin, **Economics of the Transformation Period** (New York 1971).

51. Details from Corey and Sternberg.

52. Kindelberger, page 233.

53. Kindelberger, page 232.

54. Kindelberger, page 272.

55. Figures quoted in Baran and Sweezy, page 237.

56. Daniel Guerin, **Fascism and Big Business** (New York 1972), page 236.

57. Figures given in Sternberg, **Capitalism and Socialism**, page 353.

58. Arthur Schweitzer, **Big Business in the Third Reich**, page 336.

59. Schweitzer, page 335.

60. Schweitzer, page 329.

61. Schweitzer, page 342.

62. Schweitzer, page 306.

63. Schweitzer, page 443.

64. Schweitzer, pages 442–3.

65. Sternberg, **Capitalism and Socialism**, page 232.

66. Sternberg, page 365.

67. See, for example, Chris Harman, 'How the revolution was lost', in **IS** (first series) 30; also Alan Gibbons, **Russia: How the Revolution was Lost** (London 1980).

68. Figures given by Alex Nove, **An Economic History of the** USSR (London 1969) page 191 and page 225.

69. Figures given in Sternberg, page 373.

70. For proofs of this contention, see Tony Cliff, **Russia: A Marxist Analysis** (London 1963) pages 33–44.

71. Cliff, page 42. For different figures for the period 1928–33, see E H Carr and R W Davies, **Foundations of the Planned Economy**, vol. 1 (London 1969) page 342.

72. V Voitinisky, **The Social Consequences of the Great Depression** (Geneva 1956) page 66.

73. Bukharin, **Economics of the Transformation Period**, page 45.

74. As total war proceeds arms expenditure can also eat into existing values; factories are run down to pay for weapons and so on. When this happens, the fate of the combatants is settled not just by the rate of profit, but by the total amount of value that each side can find to convert into guns.

75. Sternberg, pages 494–5.

76. A D H Kaplan, page 91.

77. Kaplan, page 3.

78. Kaplan, page 3.

79. Kenneth Galbraith, **American Capitalism**, page 65.

Chapter 3: State capitalism, the arms economy, and the crisis today

1. H Marcuse, **One Dimensional Man**.

2. C Wright Mills 'Letter to the New Left', **New Left Review** 1960 and **The Causes of World War Three**, New York 1960.

3. P Baran and P Sweezy, **Monopoly Capital**, Harmondsworth 1973.

4. See his article, 'The Economics of Neo-capitalism', **Socialist Register** 1964.

5. W T Oakes, 'Towards a Permanent War Economy', **Politics**, (New York) February 1944, compare also 'Reconstruction to what?', **Politics** November 1944 and various book reviews in **Politics** 1944-5.

6. Some of Oakes' formulations have been criticised for being 'non Marxist' and 'ahistorical' (for example by Mandel in **Late Capitalism**). The critics do not seem to have read all of the 1944 article in which these formulations first appeared. He is

accused of being 'ahistorical' and 'underconsumptionist' because he says that in any 'class society . . . the root of all economic difficulties lies in the fact that the ruling class appropriates a portion of the labour expended by the working class or classes in the form of unpaid labour. The expropriation of this unpaid labour presents its own problems; generally, however, they do not become critical until a point is reached where it is necessary to pile up accumulations of labour. When these accumulations beget new accumulations . . . the stability of society is threatened . . . To allow these growing . . . accumulations means to undermine the very foundations of society . . .' Oakes uses the pyramids of Egypt as an example of destroying 'surplus labour' in the same way as the war preparations of aging capitalism.

Now Oakes' formulation is certainly obscure. It does tend to give the impression that there is nothing specifically *capitalist* about the capitalist crisis. However, to interpret Oakes in this sense is to provide an interpretation which is out of character with his formulations elsewhere in the article, where he deals at length with the question of the specifically capitalist cause of crisis – the falling rate of profit. A more charitable interpretation of this passage is to say that he is arguing, as Marx did, that any class society performs a *progressive* function up to a certain point by developing the forces of production (what, under capitalism, is called accumulation). But any further development beyond that point produces new relations of production that threaten the ruling class. Therefore the ruling class has to find a way of 'freezing' the development of the forces of production – to 'destroy surplus labour'.

There are, undoubtedly, faults with Oakes' way of formulating the matter, but the faults are neither those of 'underconsumptionism' nor of being 'ahistorical'.

There is, however, a more serious error in Oakes' analysis. It assumes tht the war economy must mean a fall in workers' living standards. Yet this certainly did not happen for most of the great boom – here his mistake is not to carry far enough his insight into how arms production can allow accumulation in the civilian sector.

7.   The articles were reprinted as a collection edited by H Draper, **The Permanent Arms Economy**, Berkeley, 1970.

8.   Tony Cliff, 'Perspectives on the Permanent Arms Economy', **Socialist Review** May 1957, reprinted in **A Socialist Review**, London 1965.

9.   See 'Reform or Revolution: Rejoinder to Left Reformism', **International Socialism** (old series) 7, winter 1961-2, and **Western Capitalism Since the War**, London 1968.

10.   Vance advances his earlier analysis (under the name Oakes) by noting that there is a level of arms spending – about 10 per cent of total output – 'that is sufficient, in the short term at any rate, to maintain the average rate of profit at a higher level than existed in 1929 or even 1940', but that if arms spending rises much higher than this it produces powerful inflationary pressures, demanding physical controls on distribution and production.

Cliff takes the argument a little further still (although he *presents* the argument – for simple exposition in a popular publication – in 'underconsumptionist' rather than 'rate of profit' terms). He points to the factors that can be expected to push arms expenditure too high or too low, and by spelling out how an increasing level of arms spending is needed to maintain full employment – although such a rising level would create other problems for the system.

Kidron provides the first *rounded* analysis, fully integrating these different points, stressing that it is the increased competition for *markets* that over time forces the US to reduce the proportion of its output going on arms just as full employment demands an increasing proportion of arms spending, and underlining the implications of this contradiction for the rate of profit. The only fault in Kidron's analysis in 1961 was that it mistakenly saw the increased market competition as coming from the USSR rather than Japan and West Germany.

11. Figures given in T N Vance, 'The Permanent War Economy', **New International** Jan-Feb 1951, reprinted in **The Permanent Arms Economy**.

12. Vance, page 32.

13. Gillman, **The Falling Rate of Profit**, London 1956, page 54.

14. Shane Mage, **The 'Law of the falling tendency of the rate of profit', its place in the Marxian theoretical system and its relevance to the** US **economy**, PhD thesis, Columbia University 1963, distributed by University Microfilms, Ann Arbor, Michigan, pages 174-5.

15. For a discussion on this, see chapter 2, note 6.

16. Vance and Mage.

17. Figures given in Mage and Mandel, 'Late Capitalism, London 1975, page 276.

18. For example by Mandel, page 213.

19. William Nordhaus, 'The falling share of profits', **Brookings Papers on Economic Activity**, 1974:1, page 180.

20. **Brookings Papers**, 1977:1, page 216. For a survey of figures which paint a similar picture, see H I Liebling, US **Corporate Profitability and Capital Formation**, New York 1980, pages 57-60.

21. Various calculations given in Glyn and Sutcliffe, **British capitalism, workers and the profits squeeze**, Harmondsworth 1972, page 248.

22. Glyn and Sutcliffe.

23. Alvater and others, 'On the analysis of imperialism in the metropolitan countries', **Bulletin of the Conference of Socialist Economists**, Spring 1974, page 13.

24. To put it as simply as possible: if average rates of profits are earned (or fixed) in an arms sector with a high capital-labour ratio, then some of the surplus value created in the other (wage good and capital good producing) sectors will be transferred to it. This will reduce the prices the capitalists in these sectors get for their output, and this in turn will *initially* reduce profit rates. But wage goods and capital goods are not merely things sold by these sectors; they are also *inputs into them*. If they fall in price, the costs of production fall – tending to restore profitability. What is taken away with one hand is restored by the other. For a fuller discussion of this point and its significance for Marx's theory of capitalist crisis see chapter 1.

25. For comparisons of the pre- and post-war cycles, see R A Gordon, **Business Fluctuations**, New York 1961, page 272.

26. M Kidron, page 11.

27. Vance, **The Permanent Arms Economy**.

28. R Matthews, 'Why has Britain had full employment since the war?', **Economic Journal**, September 1968.

29. **Testing Monetarism**, London 1981, page 76.

30. Examples of this failure include D Yaffe, 'State Expenditure and the Marxian theory of crisis', IS **Internal Bulletin**, 1972, and E Mandel, **Marxist Economic Theory**, London 1968.

31. See C Harman, 'Poland and the Crisis of State Capitalism', IS (old series) 93 and 94, for a longer discussion on this. For empirical details see Goldman and Korba, **Economic Growth in Czechoslovakia**, Prague 1969, page 41; Branko Horvat, 'Business Cycles in Yugoslavia', **East European Economics**, vol X no. 3-4.

32. For details of this process, see C Harman, **Class Struggles in Eastern Europe**, London 1983, chapter 2.

33. For accounts of Russian attempts to exploit China see Y Gluckstein, **Mao's China**, London 1957, pages 64-75; C Harman, 'Prospects for the Seventies, The Stalinist States', IS (old series) 42, page 17.

34. Indeed, at the time of the discussion on the division of the world in 1944-5, the US had at first resisted any formal division into spheres of influence, believing that in the absence of such a division the whole world would fall under its hegemony – the question

is discussed fully in G Kolko, **The Politics of War**.

35.   F Sternberg, **Capitalism and Socialism on Trial**, London 1950, page 508.

36.   Figures given in O G Wichel, **Survey of Current Business**, August 1980, page 18.

37.   For an early exposition of the implications of this for the theory of imperialism, see M Kidron, 'Imperialism, the Highest State But One', IS (old series) 9, Summer 1962; for a later exposition, see N Harris, 'Imperialism Today' in **World Crisis**, (ed. Harris and Palmer), London 1971.

38.   **New York Times**, July 5th 1951, quoted in Vance, page 37.

39.   See, for instance, Mike Kidron, 'Two insights do not make a theory', IS (old series) 100.

40.   Alvater and others, page 10.

41.   Alvater and others, page 20.

42.   G C Allen, **A short Economic History of Japan**, London 1971, pages 174-75.

43.   Allen, page 179.

44.   Kirame and Sekiguchi, in Patrick and Rosowsky, (ed) **Asia's New Giant**, pages 418-9.

45.   Alvater.

46.   Shonoharu, **Structural Changes in Japan's Economic Development**, Tokyo 1970, page 2.

47.   Shonoharu.

48.   K Hartani, **The Japanese Economic System**, Lexington 1976, page 135.

48.   K Hartani, **The Japanese Economic System**, Lexington 1976, page 135.

49.   Hartani.

50.   See Allen, page 191.

51.   Shonaharu, page 22.

52.   Hartani, page 92.

53.   Quoted in Trezise and Suzulei, in Patrick and Rosowsky, page 793.

54.   Figures are for non-residential business capital from Patrick and Rosowsky, page 112.

55.   Figures from Patrick and Rosowsky, pages 11-12 and 55.

56.   OECD figures.

57.   OECD figures.

58.   US Department of Commerce figures given in Joseph Steindl, 'Stagnation Theory and Policy', **Cambridge Journal of Economics**, vol 3, March 1979.

59.   See the discussion in the appendix.

60.   For figures, see C Harman, 'Poland and the Crisis of State Capitalism'.

61.   Kidron, page 62.

62.   Patrick and Rosowsky, page 8.

63.   Alvater.

64.   This is why capital/output figures for Japan can be misleading. The output is measured according to international yardsticks of price, and therefore is higher than it would be if it were a self-contained economy, with the price of its output determined by the internal productivity of labour.

65.   For an elaboration of this argument see chapter 1.

66.   Figures from N M Bailey, 'Productivity and the Services of Labor and Capital', **Brooking Papers**, 1981:1, page 22.

67.   The argument is N M Bailey's (although, of course, he does not present it in Marxist terms) on how concrete labour in the US translates itself into value in terms of abstract labour that is fixed at an international level.

68.   Measurement of capital/labour ratios are bedevilled by two things:

(1) Most published figures include armaments production in the global statistics. But armaments production has a quite different effect on the rate of profit to that output destined for productive consumption – wage and capital goods. If the armaments sector

is one with a higher than average capital/labour ratio, it can distort the real picture for the civilian economy.

(2) In an economy that was initially virtually self-contained, the value of existing capital will have to be marked down once the economy is opened up to the competition of economies with more efficient techniques – and this happened to the US in the 1970s. So the capital/output ratio could appear to grow more slowly than before, whereas in reality it was being measured in a different way, according to world rather than purely local standards. This could explain the apparent slowdown in the growth rate of the US capital/labour ratio from 1974 onwards.

69. See the figures in Bailey, for the ratio of the stock of equipment plus structures to total labour hours. See also figures from P K Clarke, 'Issues in the Analysis of Capital Formation and Labour Productivity', **Brookings Papers** 1979:2.

70. Colin Clarke, **Oxford Economic Papers**, Nov 1978, page 40.

71. **Bank of England Quarterly Bulletin**, 1978, page 517.

72. **Financial Times**, 3 March 1977.

73. Although only up to a certain point. See the discussion on these questions in chapter 1.

74. Figures given in Castells, **The Economic Crisis and American Society**, page 157.

75. See Ruth Milkman, 'Women's work and economic crisis: some lessons of the great depression', **Review of Radical Political Economy**, vol 8 no 1, Spring 1976.

76. This is not contradicted by the impressive evidence of deskilling – the reduction in the level of skill needed for particular jobs as the result of new technology – provided by Bravermann, **Labour and Monopoly Capital**. For the other side of deskilling in individual jobs has been an increase in the average level of education required so that people can be trained quickly to do new, not very highly skilled, jobs.

77. For Britain, see, for instance, **Social Trends** 1970, which showed that the vast bulk of increasing educational expenditure was concentrated in these areas, while primary education expenditures grew hardly at all.

78. J O'Connor, **The Fiscal Crisis of the State**

79. So in the formula for the rate of profit $(s/(c+v))$ the denominator tends to get bigger (whether the expenditures are included in c or v does not matter here). These expenditures could not, in themselves, increase s. This could only happen if the increase in productivity they brought about reduced the overall cost of labour power, thus causing an increase in the rate of exploitation. But as we saw in chapter one, that could only counteract the decline in the rate of profit to a limited extent.

80. Figures from Aglietta, page 222.

81. S Aaronovitch and M Sawyer, 'The concentration of British manufacturing', **Lloyds Bank Review**, 1975, page 117.

82. M Campbell, **Capitalism in the UK**, London 1981.

83. Howard Sherman, 'Class conflict and macropolicy', **Review of Radical Political Economy**, Summer 1976, page 56.

84. J Patrick Wright, **On a Clear Day You Can See General Motors**, page 4.

85. Wright, pages 7-8.

86. Sidney Lens, **The Military Industrial Complex**, Philadelphia 1970, page 6.

87. Promine, quoted in Lens, page 6.

88. R J Gordon makes this point on the basis of studies of the US power generating industry, see his comments on Bailey, **Brooking Papers**, page 54.

89. For accounts of the scale of this see Tony Cliff: **Russia a Marxist Analysis**, London 1963, part II; Hillel Ticktin, **Critique** no 1 1973; C Harman, **Bureaucracy and Revolution**, pages 258-60.

90. Particularly Ticktin, but also many 'reform Communists' in Eastern Europe too.

91. Aglietta, page 240.

92.   Figures given in Castells, page 117.

93.   Figures given in **Monthly Review**, February 1975.

94.   Figures given in J Hill, 'Financial Instability, Debt and the Third World', US **Capitalism in crisis**, New York 1978, pages 138-9.

95.   Liebling, page 78.

96.   Shirrel.

97.   Sarah Martin, 'The secrets of the Polish memorandum', **Euromoney**, April 1981.

98.   **Poland, The state of the republic**, by the Experiences and Future Discussion Group of Warsaw, ed Michael Wade, London 1981.

APPENDICES: Other theories of crisis

1.   Glyn and Sutcliffe, **British capitalism, workers and the Profits Squeeze** (Harmondsworth 1972).

2.   Glyn and Sutcliffe, page 10.

3.   **New Left Review** 98, page 67.

4.   Ernest Mandel, **Late Capitalism** (London 1975) page 179.

5.   See report of National Institute for Social and Economic Research 1978 no. 4.

6.   See his articles in **Brookings Papers on Economic Activity** 1977.

7.   The figures given are for 'industrial and commercial corporations in the US' *before* tax and after deducting stock appreciation and capital consumption.

But (a) the after tax figure would be likely to show a quite different trend, since 'the level of taxation on US profits has fallen continually throughout the post-war period, and was 48.5 per cent in 1961 and only 26.9 per cent in 1970' (figures given by Victor Perlo in the **Review of Radical Economics**, Fall 1976. I use Perlo's critique of the Nordhaus figures here, although I think he can be faulted on certain points).

(b) Corporations have an incentive to overstate their capital consumption costs, since these are tax deductible. 'During the first five years after World War II corporate profits after taxes were about three times as large as corporate capital consumption allowances. But during the 1970s corporate capital consumption allowances were considerably larger than profits after tax. This did not reflect itself in the real rate of wear and tear on equipment and structures.' (Perlo)

(c) The figures exclude interest and rents, which are transferred from industrial capital to financial capital.

(d) The figures exclude from profits all company write-offs for stock appreciation, although in a period of rapid inflation a good proportion of the rising cost of financing stocks will be paid for by borrowing at interest rates which may well be negative in real terms (ie less than the rate of inflation). The result is 'double accounting' that *under-estimates* the real level of profits (this, incidentally, is the criticism made by the **Cambridge Economic Policy Review** 1978, page 65, of the Sandilands procedure for inflation accounting in Britain).

8.   He includes *all* the cost of stock appreciation and capital consumption in profits.

9.   Perlo.

10.   Source: **Brookings Papers** 1977 no. 1, page 216. The figures are for total returns (profits plus interest payments), before tax, to non-financial capital, after deducting

stock appreciation, and based on net capital stock.

11.   Conference of Socialist Economists, **Bulletin**, February 1975, page 8.

12.   **Lloyds Bank Review** 1974 no. 112, page 11. It is true, however, that recent issues of the **Bank of England Quarterly Bulletin** have provided figures showing that the share of profits added (for manufacture, service and distribution), after deducting stock appreciation and capital consumption, has been falling for many years. 'They show a significant downward trend in profitability throughout the 1960s and a sharp decline since 1973' (**Bank of England Bulletin** 1978, page 517). But these figures must be subject to the same charge of 'double accounting' made by the **Cambridge Economic Policy Review** as the American figures. In any case, the **Bank of England Quarterly** itself points out that this alleged fall in the 'share of profits' in company value added is insufficient in itself to account for the scale of the fall in the rate of profit in recent years. Something else besides the allegedly 'rising share' of wages must be responsible for that (page 517).

13.   **Review of Radical Political Economy**, Spring 1975.

14.   This point is elaborated in an article by Weeks in **Science and Society**, Fall 1979.

15.   US Department of Commerce, **1978 Statistical Abstract of the United States**, page 429.

16.   Perlo, page 62. This is hardly consistent with the view that the 'increased strength' of the workers provided the mechanism for the 'squeeze on profits'. Furthermore, in a review of research into US labour productivity, C Bourdon of the Harvard Business School 'sets out the evidence to show that the power of organised labour has actually diminished during the past decade' (**Financial Times**, 21 November 1979).

17.   They presented their view first of all in a series of sensational articles in the **Sunday Times** which was later expanded into a book: R Bacon and W Eltis, **Britain's Economic Problem: Too few producers**, London 1976.

18.   P Mattick, **Marx and Keynes**, London 1971; D Yaffe and R Schmiede, 'State expenditure and the Marxist theory of crisis' (IS internal publications, London 1972).

19.   Mattick, pages 161–3.

20.   Sources: **British Labour Statistics Year Book** and **Economic Trends**.

21.   F T Blackaby in F T Blackaby (editor), **British Economic Policy 1960–74**, page 649.

22.   Blackaby, page 649.

23.   Blackaby, page 650.

24.   R Matthews in **The Economic Journal**, September 1968.

25.   Source: D Glynn in **Lloyds Bank Review**, October 1976, page 23.

26.   Source: **The Economist**, 31 July 1976.

27.   **New Left Review** 92, pages 57 and 83.

28.   This, effectively, is the argument produced by Glyn in 1975 to justify his claim that it is a 'declining share' of profit that has produced crisis. He argued that the share after tax of profit has declined, even though the share after tax of wages has also declined — because of a rise in the 'social wage' of workers.

He assumes that the 'workers' share' of public expenditure amounts to '92 per cent of current expenditure on housing, health, education and other social services; half expenditure on fire services, a quarter of expenditure on roads; plus current grants to persons (net of tax) and consumption of social service means of production . . .'

Using these proportions he finds that 'far from there being a fall in the share of the net social product going to labour, there has been a rise from 69.3 per cent in 1955 to 73.7 per cent in 1972.'

Even on his own terms, Glyn's figures are open to objection. As I have argued elsewhere (**Socialist Review** no. 10, London 1979) a much larger proportion of the services he lists benefit the ruling class and the petty bourgeoisie (old and new) than he claims. On a rough calculation, revised figures could not produce a total increase in the 'share' of workers in the National Income of more than 2 per cent over 20 years — quite insufficient to explain the scale of the crisis.

29.   J O'Connor, **The Fiscal Crisis of the State**, New York 1973, page 6.

30.   O'Connor, page 99.

31.   J Cypher, **Review of Radical Political Economy**, Fall 1974.

32.   Source: Steindl, **Cambridge Journal of Economics**, March 1979.

33.   **New Left Review** 92, page 64.

34.   **New Left Review** 92, page 80.

35.   The deviations were averaged, running 19-year deviations from the trend. For one version of Kondratieff's theory, see the translation of his 'Long waves in economic life' reprinted in **Lloyds Bank Review**, July 1978.

36.   Mandel, pages 141–2.

37.   See for instance L Trotsky, **The First Five Years of the Communist International**, New York 1945, page 174, and the article by R B Day in **New Left Review** 99. In his essay 'The Curve of Capitalist Development' (**Fourth International**, May 1941), he argued that 'It is already possible to refute in advance Professor Kondratieff's attempt to invest epochs labelled by him "major cycles" with the self same rigid lawful rhythm that is observable in minor cycles. The character and duration (of large sections of the capitalist curve of development) is determined not by the cyclical interplay of capitalist forces, but by those external conditions through whose channel capitalist development flows.'

Trotsky sees these 'external conditions' as 'the absorption by capitalism of new countries and continents, the discovery of new natural resources, and, in addition, significant factors of a "superstructural" order, such as wars and revolutions . . .'

The point at issue between Kondratieff on the one hand and Trotsky on the other was *not* whether there were periods in which the system expanded more rapidly than others. It was whether the periodisation could be explained in terms of waves, of patterns which not only had occurred empirically, but which were bound to recur, with each downturn preparing the way for a new upturn.

38.   There is an excellent account of these criticisms in George Garvey, **Review of Economic Statistics** vol. XXV no. 4 (November 1943). This article is a devastating rejoinder to all theories of long waves.

39.   Quoted in Garvey.

40.   Quoted in Garvey, page 210.

41.   W Rostow, 'Trend periods revisited' in **Journal of Economic History** 1975, page 749.

42.   Freeman, Clark and Soete, **Unemployment and Technical Innovation** (London 1982) page 22.

43.   Quoted in R B Day, **New Left Review** 99, page 77.

44.   Day, page 77.

45.   Garvey.

46.   For a fuller critique of Mandel's version of the theory, see my review of **Late Capitalism** in **International Socialism** (new series) 1.

47.   Quoted in Day, pages 78–9.

48.   Kindelberger, **The World in Depression 1929–39** (London 1973) page 292.

49.   Kindelberger, page 293.

50.   Kindelberger, pages 307–8.

51.   Arthur MacEwan, 'US Capitalism in Crisis' in URPE 1977, page 46.

52.   MacEwan, page 46.

53.   MacEwan, page 51.

54.   An example is Rowthorn.

55.   D Gordon, US **Capitalism in Crisis**, page 31.

56.   Gordon, page 30.

57. Gordon, page 29.
58. P Aglietta, **Theory of Capitalist Regulation** (London 1979).
59. Aglietta, page 154.
60. Aglietta, page 165.
61. Aglietta, page 162.
62. Aglietta, page 167.
63. Baran and Sweezy, **Monopoly Capital**.
64. J Steindl, **Maturity and Stagnation in American Capitalism** (London 1953).
65. Steindl, page 155 and following.
66. Steindl, page 255.
67. Steindl, page 135.
68. Steindl, page 166.
69. Steindl, **Cambridge Journal of Economics**, March 1973, page 8.
70. Baran and Sweezy, page 89.
71. Baran and Sweezy, page 70.
72. Baran and Sweezy, page 95.
73. Baran and Sweezy, page 155.
74. Baran and Sweezy, pages 155–6.
75. Baran and Sweezy, page 162.
76. Baran and Sweezy, page 216.
77. Baran and Sweezy, pages 218 and 223.
78. Baran and Sweezy, page 240.
79. This is the point made by Bleaney in his **Underconsumptionist Theories** (London 1977) page 230.
80. See Baran and Sweezy, page 243.
81. A Dabat, **Debate**, May/June 1979, page 17 (my translation).
82. Dabat.
83. It is because Baran and Sweezy claim such external pressures are of diminished importance in firms' handling of the product of exploiting labour that they call it a 'surplus' — we follow Marx in calling it surplus value because it is not a self-contained entity, but something continually related, by national and international competitive forces, to the surplus value in the hands of other firms.
84. See R Luxemburg, **The Accumulation of Capital**, and her **Anti-Critique**.
85. P Sweezy, **Theory of Capitalist Development** (London 1946), page 82.

Glossary

Abstract labour: See Concrete labour.

Autarchy: Attempt to cut an economy off from trade links with the rest of the world.

Capitals: Term often used to describe competing units of capitalist system (whether individual owners, firms or states).

Centralisation of capital: Tendency for capital to pass into fewer and fewer hands, so that whole capitalist system is under direct control of a few competing capitals.

Chicago school: Followers of Milton Friedman and monetarism.

Concentration of capital: Growth in size of the individual competing capitals that make up the capitalist system.

Concrete labour: Refers to the specific material characteristics of any act of labour — what distinguishes, for example, the labour of a carpenter from that of a bus driver. **Abstract labour**, on the other hand, refers to the social characteristics that all types of labour have in common under the production of commodities for the market.

Constant capital: Marx's term for a capitalist's investment in plant, machinery, raw material and components (in other words the means and materials of production), denoted by C.

Deficit financing: The method by which a government pays for the excess of expenditure over receipts from taxation by borrowing or printing money.

Department One: Section of economy which is involved in turning out means and material for further production.

Department Two: Section of economy which is concerned with turning out goods which will be consumed by workers (sometimes called 'wage goods').

Department Three: Section of economy which turns out goods which will not be used as means and materials of production, and which will not be consumed by workers either — in other words the section that turns out 'luxury goods' for consumption by the ruling class, armaments and so on.

Depreciation of capital: Reduction in the value of plant, machinery and so on during their period of operation. This can be due to wear and tear, or to the 'devaluation' of capital (see below).

Devaluation of capital: Reduction in the value of plant, equipment and so on as technical advance makes it cheaper to produce.

Euromoney (Eurodollars): Vast pool of finance which grew up in late 1960s and 1970s, beyond the control of national governments. Based upon the ability of the banks in one country to borrow from a second country and then lend to a third.

Expenses of production: Spending which capitals have to undertake to stay in business, but which does not materially expand the output of commodities (for instance, spending on marketing goods, advertising, protecting plant and machinery).

Exploitation, rate of: Ratio of surplus value to wages (strictly speaking only the wages of workers who materially produce commodities should be counted). It can be expressed another way, as the ratio of the time the worker spends producing surplus value for the capitalist, compared to the time he or she spends on producing goods equivalent to his or her living standard. Denoted as S/V.

Keynesianism: Economic doctrine based upon ideas of the British economist of the inter-war years, J M Keynes. Holds that governments can prevent recessions and slumps by spending which is greater than their income from taxation (so-called 'deficit financing').

Labour theory of value: View developed by Marx (on basis of ideas of previous thinkers such as Smith and Ricardo) that there is an objective measurement of the value of goods, which is ultimately responsible for determining their prices. This is the 'socially necessary' labour needed to produce them — in other words the average throughout the system as a whole, using an average level of technique, skill and effort. For Marx's own accounts of the theory, see **Wage Labour and Capital, The Critique of Political Economy** and chapter one of **Capital**, volume one.

Monetarism: Doctrine which holds crises cannot be solved by governments increasing their spending to more than their tax income. Increasing the supply of money, this holds, will simply lead to higher prices. Under the name the quantity theory of money, this was the orthodoxy in bourgeois economics before the rise of Keynesianism in the 1930s, and became fashionable again in the mid-1970s.

Neo-classical economics: Dominant school in bourgeois economics since the end of the nineteenth century. Believes value is a measure of the 'marginal' satisfaction people get from goods, and justifies profit as a result of the 'marginal productivity of capital'.

Non-productive consumption: The use of goods in ways which serve neither to produce new plant, machinery, raw materials and so on ('means of production') nor to provide for the consumption needs of workers. The use of goods for the consumption of the ruling class, for advertising and marketing, or for arms, all fall into this category.

Non-productive expenditures: Expenditures undertaken by capitalists or the state over and above what is necessary for the material production of commodities (includes spending on consumption of the ruling class, on its personal servants, on the 'expenses of production' and so on).

Organic composition of capital: Ratio of the value of investment in plant, machinery, raw materials and so on ('means of production') to the value of expenditure on employing productive labour. Using Marxist terminology, this is the ratio of constant capital to variable capital, or C/V. See also Technical composition of capital.

Productive expenditures: Spending which is necessary if commodities are to be produced and surplus value created (spending on the means and materials of production on the one hand, and on workers' wages on the other).

Profits, mass of: Total profits of a particular capitalist. Measured in pounds, dollars and other currency.

Profit, rate of: Ratio of total profit to investment. Measured as a percentage. Denoted as $S/(C+V)$.

Profit share: Proportion of total output of a firm or country that goes in profits, as opposed to wages.

Socially-necessary labour: Amount of labour needed to produce a certain good, using average level of techniques prevailing throughout economy and working at average intensity of effort.

Sraffa, Piero: Cambridge economist who refuted basic contentions of orthodox bourgeois economics, the 'neo-classical' marginalist school. But he also rejected the labour theory of value, and instead tried to develop a theory of value of his own, based on ideas in the pre-Marxist economist Ricardo. His followers reject the Marxist theory of the falling rate of profit, and usually see crisis as arising when wages cut into profits.

Surplus value: Marx's term for the total profit made by capital from the exploitation of workers (the profit of the individual capitalist plus what he pays out to other capitalists in the form of rent and interest payments, plus what he spends on 'non-productive activities'). Denoted by S.

Taylorism: Technique of so-called 'scientific management', based upon time-and-motion studies of every act of labour. Spread through industry in the early 20th century.

Technical composition of capital: Physical ratio of plant, machinery, raw materials and so on ('means and materials of production') to total labour employed. When this ratio is measured in value terms rather than physical terms, it becomes the 'organic composition of capital'.

Transformation problem: Problem which arises when the attempt is made to move from Marx's account of capitalism in terms of value to the prices at which goods are actually bought and sold. Many economists have claimed it is impossible to solve the problem, and that therefore Marxist economics must be abandoned.

Under-consumptionism: Theory which blames capitalist crisis not on the law of the falling rate of profit, but on the alleged inability of capitalism to provide a market for all goods produced within it. The first versions of the theory were put forward by early 19th century economists such as Sismondi, but it has been developed since both by Marxists (from Rosa Luxemburg to Baran and Sweezy) and by Keynesians.

Variable capital: What the capitalist invests on employing wage labour. Denoted by V.

Index

Accumulation (general law of) 14, (rate of) 57, (and military competition) 73
Ageing of capitalism 33, (and unproductive expenditures) 43, (and dimensions of competition) 45, (and 'countervailing factors') 50, (and inflation) 109–110, (and permanent stagnation) 120–121
Aglietta 126, 143–147
Agriculture (and industrial growth) 130
Argentina 91
Arms expenditure (and profit rates) 46–49, 79–80, 82–83, 84, (levels of) 78–79, 94, 98, 99, 113, 150, (growth of) 93, 119, (as 'social expenses of production') 129, (and employment levels) 150
Autarchy (in 1930s) 67, 70–71, (in Eastern Europe) 83–84, 91, (in Latin America) 91

Boom (Marx on) 14, 59–60, (speculative, of late 1920s) 58, (of 1940s–1970s) 75–77, 80, 82, 138, 151
Bacon and Eltis 126, 127, 147
Balance of payments crises 98
Banking system (in 1929–32) 60–62, (fears of collapse in 1980s) 34, 116, (and economic crises) 60–62, 116
Baran, Paul 56, 57, 77, 130, 148–154
Barber boom (of 1972–73) 128
Bleaney 150
Blue Streak 112
Body and Croty 124

Bogdanov, V 133
Bortkiewicz, von 40, 41, 81, 156, 160, 162
Brazil 9, 34, 91, 114, 118
Bretton Woods 138
Brittan, Samuel 12 (quoted 101)
Britain (in 1870s–1890s) 51, (in 1930s) 62, 69–70, (in World War Two) 73–74, (post-war) 75, 98, 101, 108, 125, 128–129, (arms expenditure) 94, 98, (in crisis) 118, (employment trends in) 127, (government expenditure in) 131
Brown, Michael Barratt (criticism of Lenin on imperialism) 159
Bruning 63
Budget deficits (of US in 1980s) 10
Bukharin, Nicolai 72, (on imperialism) 37, 78, (on non-market forms of competition) 45, (on state capitalism) 63, 84
Burgess, C J 124
Business cycle 10

Callaghan, James 11, 12
Cambridge Economic Policy Review 10
Capital formation, rate of 57, 96, 148
Capital–labour ratio (problems of measuring) 168–169
Capital–output ratio 163, (in 19th century) 53, (in first decade of 20th century) 54, (after World War One) 54
Carnegie, Andrew (quoted) 51

Central America 119
Centralisation of capital tendency
  (tendency towards) 33, (on world
  scale) 33, (in 20th century) 108–109
Chicago school of economists 11
Chile 12
China 75, 91
Classical capitalism 51–52, 88
Cliff, Tony 13, 78, 166
Coal (supplies world-wide) 140
Cogoy, M 159–160
Cold War (origins of) 85–86
'Collectivisation' 103
Comintern, Fourth Congress of 45
Communist Manifesto (quoted) 154
Competition (forms of) 35, 43,
  (military) 71–72, 73, 83, 88, (and state
  capitalism) 84
Concentration of capital (tendency
  towards) 33, (in 1870s and 1880s) 52,
  53, (in US 1950 and 1967) 33, (and
  laws of motion of system) 34,
  109–110, (in US and Britain) 108–109
Concorde 112
Consumption, mass 143–144
Corey, Lewis (pseudonym of Fraina,
  Lewis) 57–58
'Countervailing factors' (to fall in rate of
  profit) 16, 19, 27, 34, 35, 50, (in
  1980s) 119
Credit (and cyclical crisis) 59–60
Cripps, Francis 10
Crisis (and rate of profit) 32, (periods
  of) 50, (of 1870s–1890s) 51–52, (of
  1929) 19, (cyclical, Marx on) 59–60,
  (of 1970s and 1930s compared) 118,
  (permanent) 120–121 (*see also* slumps,
  recessions)
Cruise missiles 119
Cuba crisis 90
'Cuts' 113
Czechoslovakia 9, 90

Dabat, Alejandro 152–153
Day, R B (quoted) 135
Debt (growth of in 1960s and 1970s)
  114–115
Decentralisation of production 145
Deficit financing (in 1930s) 66, (in
  1940s–1970s) 82, 127, 128–129
Demographic changes (and
  government expenditure) 130
Department III 40–41, (and rate of
  profit) 42–43
Depreciation of capital 24, (and falling
  rate of profit) 30–32
Desai, Megan (quoted) 82
Destruction of capital (in 1930s and
  early 1940s) 37

Detente (reasons for) 90
Devaluation of capital 24, (and rate of
  profit) 30–32

Eastern bloc 9
Eastern Europe 9, 91, (debts of) 114,
  115
Education (growth of) 105,
  (expenditures) 131
Employment, in public and private
  sector 127
Energy supplies (and the crisis)
  140–141
Engels, Friedrich 15
Euromoney 91, 139–140
Expenses of production 44, 58
Exploitation, rate of 27–28, 32

Feldstein and Summers 80, 124
'Final crisis' (Marx and Engels on) 15
Fine, Ben, and Harris, Lawrence 24
Financial institutions (role in capitalist
  system) 59–60
'Fiscal crisis of the state' 129–132
'Fordism' 143, 147
France (1945–1970) 75, 125
'Free labour' (and Great Boom)
  106–107
Freeman, Clark and Soete 134
Friedman, Milton 11, 117
'Fundamentalists' 77

Galbraith, Kenneth (quoted) 74
Garvey, George 136
Garcia, Miguel Angel 41, (on trans-
  formation problem) 160, 161–162
Gästarbeiter 125
General Motors 111
Gerzstein 133, 135
Gillman, Joseph 56, 57, 79
Glyn, Andrew (criticism of law of
  falling rate of profit) 28, (on wages as
  cause of crisis) 123, 124, (criticism of
  his figures) 171
Germany, economy (in 1870s and
  1880s) 51, 53, (in 1920s) 55, (in
  1929–1932) 61, (under Nazi rule)
  65–68
Germany, West 49, 75, 89, 94, 125,
  (role of state in economy) 94
Ghetto uprisings 106
Goering 66
Gordon, David 142
Gough, Ian 129, 131, 132
Government expenditure (and the
  crisis) 126–132, (US) 150
Granovsky 133
'Great Depression' (of 1870s–1890s)
  51–52, 55

'Great society' 106
Grenada, invasion of 119
Gross national products (relative, of major countries) 97
Grundrisse (tone of) 155

Hansen, Alvin H (quoted) 55
Harris, Nigel 13
Harrison, John (criticism of the law of falling rate of profit) 28
Health (growth of expenditures on) 105
Hegemony, the crisis of 137–140
Hilferding, R 156
Himmelweit, Susan (criticism of law of falling rate of profit) 28, 158
Hitler, Adolf 64, 65
Hoare, Quintin (quoted) 105–106
Hobsbawm, Eric (quoted) 51, 52
Hobson 35
Hoover, President 63
Hungary 9

Immigration (illegal) 125 (*see also* migration)
Imperialism (and rate of profit) 35–36, (and war) 37, (and World War One) 54, (in 1880s and 1890s) 52–53, (German in 1930s) 67–68, (Japanese in 1930s) 68, (Russian) 69, 86, (and World War Two) 71, (and state capitalism) 85, 89, (US) 86–89, (and Cold War) 87–88, 89–90
India 75, 91
Industrial production (of US in 1920s) 56, (fall after 1929) 55, (of Japan in 1930s) 68
Institutional crisis theories 141–147
Interest rates (causes of fluctuations in) 60, (in 1980s) 10, 114, (and rate of profit) 115
International banks 113–114, (support for bankrupt companies) 118
International Monetary Fund 9, 118
International Socialists 122
Internationalisation (of capital) 36–37, (of production) 91, 113, 116
Italy 125
Investment (in US) 151

Japan 49, (in 1930s) 68, (1940–1970) 75, 94–95, 95–97, 125, (state capitalism in) 95–99
Johnson, President 98, 106

Keynes, J M 144
Keynesianism 10, 76, 77, 82, 117, 127, 128
Keynesians 11, 132

Kidron, Michael 13, 21, 38, 40, 78, 159–160, 166
Kiernan, V (criticism of Lenin on imperialism) 159
Kindelberger 60, 137, 139
Kondratieff 132–136, 141, 143
Korean War 86, 88, 98

Labour-only subcontracting 145
Labour Party Conference (of 1976) 11
Labour force (in the great boom) 103
Latin America 75
Lenin, Vladimir 121, (on imperialism) 35, 37, 78, (on state capitalism) 63
'Long waves' 132–136, 141
Luxemburg, Rosa 83, 154, 159

'M1' 117
'M3' 12, 117
Macdonald, Ramsey 63
MacEwan, Arthur 137–138, 140
Mage, Shane 37, 56, 79, 80
Mandel, Ernest 39–40, 77, 123, 132–133, 134, 135, 136, 156, 166
Marcuse, Herbert 76
Marx, Karl (theory of crisis) 12, 14–19, (on depreciation of constant capital) 23, 24, (on increased rate of exploitation) 27–28, (on depreciation of capital and crises) 30–32, (on unproductive consumption) 38, (on move from boom to slump) 59
Massey Ferguson 117
Matthews, R 128
Mattick, Paul 127, 128
Maudling boom (of 1962–1964) 128
Meiji restoration 68
Merchants' capital (and the rate of profit) 46
Mexico 9, 34, 118
Middle East War (of 1973) 90
Migration (in Great Boom) 103, 104
Military expenditure (*see* arms expenditure)
Mills, C Wright 76
MITI 95–96
Monetarism 11, 77, (limits of) 117
Money supply 12, 116–117
Monopolies (first growth of) 52, (and stagnation theories) 148–154
Multinationals 91–93
Murray, Robin 156
MX missiles 119

National Recovery Act 64
Negative reproduction 72
'Neo-fordism' 145
New Cold War 119
New Deal 64–65, 66–67, 150

'New Era' (of 1920s) 148
New International 78
Newly industrialising countries 9
Nixon, President 98, (devalues dollar) 138
Non-productive consumption (in 1920s) 57–58, (in the 1930s) 65, (see also unproductive consumption)
Nordhaus 80, 123, 124, (criticism of his profit figures) 170

Oaks, W T (see Vance, T N)
O'Connor (quoted) 105, 129–132, 152, 153
Oil (and the crisis) 140
Oil-producing states 9, 138
Okishio (criticism of law of falling rate of profit) 28, 157, 158, (and transformation problem) 161
Old age pensions 105
Oparin 133, 135
OPEC 140
Organic composition of capital (definition of) 18, (trend of) 19, (failure to rise) 32, (and unproductive consumption) 38–40, (in 1880s and 1890s) 52–53, (effects of World War One on) 54, (effects of arms economy on) 79–81, 84, (1950s–1970s) 99–100, 101, (in crisis of 1970s–1980s) 118–119, 120, (different ways of estimating) 163
Over-investment 113
Over-production (and falling rate of profit) 57 (see also under-consumptionism)
Overseas investment (Britain pre-World War One) 35, (and rate of profit) 36, (European and American in 1920s) 54–55, (in Great Boom) 87, 138

Papen, von 63
Penn Central 109
Perlo, Victor 124, 125–126
Permanent Arms Economy 77–84, 88–89, (and decolonisation) 89–90, (contradictions within) 89, 90–99
Pinochet, General 12
Planning 69, 91, 117
Poland 34, (crisis of 1980s) 108, 114, 117, 118
Prices (and crisis) 109
Productive and non-productive expenditures (Marx's views of) 44, (in inter-war years) 58, (under ageing capitalism) 44–45, 129–131
Productivity 100, 144–145
Profit, mass of 19

Profit, rate of (see rate of profit)
'Profits share' 123, 124, 126
'Productivity state' 129
Protectionism 70

Rapid deployment force 119
Rate of profit, equalisation of 31
— law of tendency to decline 16–19, (arguments against) 20, (and technical progress) 20–23, (and cheapening of means of production) 23, (and increased rate of exploitation) 27, (and spread of new technology) 28–30, (and devaluation of capital) 30–32, (and crises) 28–30, (and overseas investment) 36, (and unproductive consumption) 38–42, (in monopoly and non-monopoly industries) 152–153
— measures of (1880–1929) 56–57
— and overproduction 56
— and total war 72–73, 79–80
— and arms economy 80–81, 83
— in US economy (1950–1976) 123, 124
— in British economy (1955–1970) 124
— different ways of estimating 163
Raw materials (and the crisis) 140–141
Reagan, President 12
Recession (of 1973–1975) 9, 77, 118, 139, (of 1979–1982) 9, 118, (under state capitalism) 115–116
Recycling (of funds) 141
Reproduction of labour force 63, (intervention of state in) 103–108
'Revisionists' 77
Reserve army of labour 123, 125
Rolls-Royce 109
Roosevelt, President 64
Rostow, W 132, 133, 136
Rowthorne, Bob 123, 124, 126, 141
Rumania 9, 116
Russia 9, (state capitalism in) 68–69, (effect of 1930s slump on) 69, (1940–1970) 75, 91, (arms expenditure of) 94, (rate of growth) 98–99, (quarrels with China and Egypt) 119

Samuelson, Paul 132
Schleicher 63
Schumpeter 132, 135, 136
Shaikh, Anwar 40, (reply to Okishio and others) 157, (on transformation problem) 160–161
Sherman, Howard (quoted) 109–110
Slump (Marx on) 14, (of 1929–1934) 55, 56–62, 150, (of 1937) 65
'Social capital' 129
'Social expenses of production' 129–130

Social security 105, 129, 131
Social wage 107
Socialist Workers Party (Britain) 122
Sombart, Werner (quoted) 55
Spain 125
Stagnation (theories of) 148–154
State (intervention in labour market) 103
State capitalism 33, (Lenin and Bukharin on) 63, (worldwide growth of) 62–64, 69, 70, (and Nazi Germany) 65–68, (in Russia) 68–69, 83, (in World War Two) 72–74, (after World War Two) 78, (and military competition) 83, (and crisis) 84, (and arms economy) 84, (and inter-nationalisation of capital) 92–93, 112, 113–115, 116–117, (and imperialism) 85, (non-military) 93–97, (in Japan) 95–96
State expenditure 34, 63, (in US) 130–131, (in Britain) 131, (in all OEC countries) 131, (and rate of profit) 46–49 (*see also* government expenditure)
Steindl, J 148–149, 152, 153–154
Sternberg, Fritz 56
Strachey, John 76
Sukharov (quoted) 136
'Surplus' 149–150, 152 (contrasted with surplus value) 173
Sutcliffe, Bob 123, 124
Sweezy, Paul 56–57, 77, 130, (theory of monopoly and stagnation) 148–154, (criticises law of falling rate of profit) 28
Samuelson, Paul 10
Saudi Arabia 9

Taxation (trends in) 127, (policy) 113
Taylorism 143
Technical composition of capital (definition of) 18, 23
Thatcher, Margaret 12, 107
Thatcherism 63
Theatre nuclear war 121
Tory government (1970–1974) 109
Transformation problem 40–43, 156, 160–162
Trotsky, Leon (refutes 'long waves') 133, 134, 172
Trusts 52

Under-consumption (according to Marx) 56, (theories) 56

Underconsumptionism 150, 154
Unemployment (pre-World War One) 151, (in 1929) 61, (in 1932–1933) 62, (in 1937) 65, (in Nazi Germany) 66, (in World War Two) 74, (in Great Boom) 102, (in 1970s and 1980s) 118, 125, (and New Cold War) 120
United States, economy (in 1870s and 1880s) 51, (pre-World War One) 151, (in 1920s) 55–57, 148, (in 1930s) 64–67, 74, 148, 150, (1940–1970) 75, (in 1983) 10, 12, (slow post-war rate of economic growth) 49, (boom of 1983–1984) 120
— overseas investment 87, 138
— foreign trade 100, 138–139
— class struggle in 125
— arms expenditure 94, 98, 113, 131
— government expenditure 130–131
Unproductive consumption 38–40
Unproductive expenditures 43

Value composition of capital (definition of) 24, 156
Vance, T N 13, 77–78, 79–80, 165–166
Venezuela 9
Vietnam War 90, 130

Wages (and crisis of 1970s) 123–126
Wages, real (in US in 1920s) 56, (in 1950s–1970s) 126
Wall Street Crash (of 1929) 60–61
War (and Marx's 'law' of the rate of profit) 37, 39, (all-out) 48, 71–74
Waste 100–113, (and monopolisation) 110–111, (and new technology) 111–112, (in US and Britain) 111–112, (in Eastern states) 112–113
Webb, A J 124
'Welfare state' 105–106
Women (entry into paid labour force) 103, 104
World trade (in 1880s and 1930s) 55, 70, (shares in, in 1970s) 97
World War One (and imperialism) 54, (and state capitalism) 63, (effects on dynamic of system) 54–55
World War Two (origins of) 71, (and state capitalism) 71–74
Wright, Eric Olin 20

Yaffe, David 127, 128
Yalta conference 85

Other books published by

BOOKMARKS

The Revolutionary Ideas of Karl Marx
by Alex Callinicos
Marx is one of only a handful of people in history who have
fundamentally changed the way we look at the world. This book is an
introduction to his life and ideas — on the structure of capitalist
society, on historical change, on economic crisis, on revolution.
£3.95 / US$7.85

What is the real Marxist tradition?
by John Molyneux
'All I know,' said Marx, 'is that I am not a Marxist.' What in the 1870s
was a neat dialectical joke has since been transformed into a major
political problem. The hundred years since Marx's death have seen
the emergence of innumerable divergent and conflicting 'Marxisms'.
This short book sets out to untangle the knot, to establish criteria for
accepting claims to the title of Marxism, and to examine the conflicting
claims of Social Democracy, Stalinism, and the movements of Third
World liberation.
£1.95 / US$3.75

The Comintern
by Duncan Hallas
Internationalism is the bedrock of socialism. The Communist
International, which arose out of the Russian workers' revolution of
October 1917, was an essential part of that revolution — essential if it
was to survive, essential if there was to be movement towards socialism
elsewhere in the world. Conversely, the events that ten years later
turned the Comintern — as it had come to be known — into a tool of
Russian foreign policy, reflected the strangling of workers' power
inside Russia by the new ruling bureaucracy under Stalin.
£3.75 / US$6.50

The Lost Revolution: Germany 1918-23
by Chris Harman
Revolutions that are defeated are soon forgotten. Yet the mass
working-class upheavals that swept Germany after the First World
War shaped the world we live in as radically as any event in this
century — for the defeat of this revolution was a key link in the rise to
power of both Hitler and Stalin.
£5.95 / US$11.00

Bailing out the System
Reformist socialism in Western Europe 1944-85
by Ian Birchall
In 1945 an astute Tory politician told the House of Commons: 'If you
do not give the people reform, they are going to give you revolution.'
In the years since then, reformism has again and again saved the
capitalist system from disaster, defusing working-class struggle
whenever it threatened to bring radical change.
£5.95 / US$12.00

Marxism and Trade Union Struggle: The General Strike of 1926
by Tony Cliff and Donny Gluckstein
The 1926 general strike put the political ideas of the day to the
ultimate test of practice. This book uses a detailed account of the
events leading up to the strike and the strike itself to examine key
questions relevant to the trade union and socialist struggle today.
£6.25 / US$12.50

The Western Soviets
Workers' councils versus Parliament 1915-1920
by Donny Gluckstein
The workers' council movements of Italy, Germany, Britain and
Russia proposed an alternative mass democracy to the parliamentary
channels that had failed them, allowing the slaughter of the First
World War — and are failing now, in a world of mass unemployment
and economic crisis. This book examines that alternative, needed now
more than ever.
£5.95 / US$11.00

BOOKMARKS LONDON: 265 Seven Sisters Road, Finsbury Park,
London N4 2DE, England.
BOOKMARKS CHICAGO: PO Box 16085, Chicago, IL 60616,
USA.
BOOKMARKS MELBOURNE: GPO Box 1473N, Melbourne 3001,
Australia.

Bookmarks is a socialist bookshop in North London, where you'll find two floors of books on socialism, internationalism, trade unions, working-class history, economics, women's issues, socialist novels and much more. We're just around the corner from Finsbury Park tube station. If you live too far away to call in, we run a large socialist mail order service too, sending books all over the world. Just drop us a line for our latest booklists.

BOOKMARKS, 265 Seven Sisters Road, London N4 2DE, England.